Sexuality

Your Sons and Daughters with Intellectual Disabilities

by

Karin Melberg Schwier

and

Dave Hingsburger, M.Ed.

Jessica Kingsley *Publishers*
London

First published in the United States of America in 2000 by
Paul H. Brookes Publishing Co.
Post Office Box 10624
Baltimore, Maryland 21285-0624
USA

www.brookespublishing.com

First published in the United Kingdom in 2000 by
Jessica Kingsley Publishers
116 Pentonville Road
London N1 9JB
ENGLAND

www.jkp.com

Typeset by Pro-Image Corp., Techna-Type Division, York, Pennsylvania.
Manufactured in the United States of America by
Versa Press, East Peoria, Illinois.

The individuals featured in the vignettes in this book have kindly granted permission for
their actual names, stories, and photographs to be used. Pseudonyms have been used for
other individuals and some institutions.

Cover photograph of Jim Schwier, Richard Schwier, and Karin Melberg Schwier taken by
Todd Zazelenchuk. All other photographs taken by Karin Melberg Schwier.

Library of Congress Cataloging-in-Publication Data
Schwier, Karin Melberg.
    Sexuality : your sons and daughters with intellectual disabilities / by Karin Melberg
  Schwier and Dave Hingsburger.
       p.   cm.
     ISBN 1-55766-428-5
     1. Sex instruction for the mentally handicapped.   2. Sex instruction for mentally
  handicapped children.   3. Social skills—Study and teaching.   4. Self-esteem—Study
  and teaching.   5. Parents of handicapped children.   I. Hingsburger, David, 1952–   II.
  Title.

  HQ54.3 .S38 2000
  613.9'5'0874—dc21   99-046726

British Library Cataloguing in Publication data are available from the British Library.

Contents

About the Authors

Karin Melberg Schwier, Copestone Writing, 908 University Drive, Saskatoon, Saskatchewan S7N 0K1, CANADA, is an author and illustrator whose most noted works are about people with intellectual disabilities. She has received awards for her writing from the Canadian Association for Community Living (CACL), the Council for Exceptional Children, and the National Down Syndrome Congress, among others. Some of her most recent publications include the illustrated children's book *Idea Man* (Diverse City Press, 1997), winner of the Saskatchewan Writer's Guild children's literature award; *Couples with Intellectual Disabilities Talk About Living and Loving* (Woodbine House, 1994), winner of the CACL award in its first year of release and, in 1995, winner of the Joan Kershaw Publications Award from the Canadian Council for Exceptional Children; *Keith Edward's Different Day*, an illustrated children's story about individual differences (Impact Publishers, 1992; The Roeher Institute, 1988); and *Speakeasy: People with Mental Handicaps Talk About Their Lives in Institutions and in the Community* (PRO-ED, 1990). She produces a provincial magazine, *Dialect*, for the Saskatchewan Association for Community Living, an advocacy organization for people with intellectual disabilities. She is a member of the national editorial board of *entourage*, a magazine published by the CACL. She is working on her first novel, in which the main character has an intellectual disability. She lives in Saskatoon, Saskatchewan, Canada, with her husband, Richard, a professor of education. They have two sons and a daughter: Jim, 25, Erin, 23, and Ben, 19.

Dave Hingsburger, M.Ed., Diverse City Press, BM 272, 33 des Floralies, Eastman, Québec J0E 1P0, CANADA, is a well-known author and lecturer and a sexuality counselor for people with developmental disabilities. He has provided direct care to people with intellectual disabilities throughout his career. From working in a group home to providing individual counseling or group training, he continues to have personal contact with people who have disabilities. Dave also provides consultation and training for parents, agencies, schools, and churches regarding support for people who have intellectual disabilities. For 6 years, he was the sex clinic coordinator at York Behaviour Management Services in Richmond Hill, Ontario, Canada. Since 1991, he has maintained his involvement at the clinic as a consultant and is in private practice. He has been a sessional lecturer in the departments of psychology and education at Bishop's University in Québec. In 1996, he received the Award for Advocacy from the American Association on Mental Retardation Special Interest Group on Social and Sexual Concerns. His published works are extensive, including *Finger Tips* (2000), *Do? Be? Do?* (1998), *Behaviour Self!* (1996), *Hand Made Love* (1995), and *Just Say Know!* (1995), all from Diverse City Press. Dave also is a member of the national advisory council of the Sexual Information and Education Council of Canada and is a contributing/reviewing editor for the *Mental Health Aspects of Developmental Disabilities* and for the American Association on Mental Retardation journal *Mental Retardation*. As a volunteer, Dave is a self-advocacy mentor for people with disabilities and is a regular writer for *Mouth* magazine. He lives in Eastman, Québec, Canada, where he and Joe Jobes are coordinators of Diverse City Press.

Foreword

After reading the manuscript for this outstanding text, I have so many reactions to it. One is that I feel inadequate to write a foreword for a book that needs no foreword, only a proclamation that for all concerned about preparing our children who have challenges for the sometimes cruel world, this book is a *MUST*.

My second reaction is that I am so proud to be counted among the many parents who are included in this book. Once my husband and I faced the reality of the task that lay ahead of us, we proceeded with acceptance, determination, and, most of all, love. The parents and authors who have shared their experiences and expertise in this book have done so with intelligence and a deep-rooted desire to assist everyone in making life as typical and enjoyable as possible for our children. The success of our endeavors is so evident in the fact that we hear so many young adults proclaiming that they are happy with who they are and that they wouldn't exchange their life for any other. We know this is a result of constant support and guidance on the part of parents to channel their children's growth and achievements. It is only through achievement that any adult can value him- or herself. All parents of all children should be extremely aware of their offspring's abilities and should be certain to help them obtain the proper education and guidance so they can realize their dreams.

My third reaction is that over and over again family has proven to be the mainstay of the successful rearing of a child with a disability. In our own case, Chris was our fourth child, and as I have so often said, he had five parents. Our three older children, Ellen, Anne, and J.R., took to Chris without hesitation, loved him, played with him, and strengthened him both physically and mentally; always insisting, as Frank and I did too, on proper and appropriate behavior. It is so very important for our children to grow up with the knowledge of how to conduct themselves in the proper manner with all of the people who are part of their everyday lives. The important thing, though, is giving our children a good start, and this is accomplished by loving families who truly care for their sons, daughters, and siblings. That is the very foundation of self-worth—knowing you are part of a family who loves you, enjoys you, and is proud of your accomplishments.

When in an environment of this nature, the respect we accord each other assists us all and prepares us for the future. Everyone needs to be treated with respect and understanding, and in that way, we learn to attend to all our needs, including sexuality, in a proper and private way.

My compliments to the parents who have dedicated so much of their time to making this book possible and to the authors and publisher for their awareness of the importance of presenting a book that is so essential in this world of many-faceted people.

—Marian Burke
Mother of Chris Burke, actor and star of the television show, *Life Goes On*

Acknowledgments

Thanks to the many who helped and supported us during the creation of this book, especially all of the families and individuals with disabilities who were willing to share personal and sometimes intimate details of their lives.

To all of the "Lisas" at Brookes Publishing (Lisa Benson, Lisa Rapisarda, and Lisa Yurwit) and to book production editor Mika Sam: It was an absolute pleasure working with each of you. You smoothed all of the rough edges and made a big project so much easier to wrap up. Karin gives special thanks to resource librarian Lalita Martfeld at the Saskatchewan Association for Community Living, who tirelessly put information within reach, and to Richard Schwier, for never-ending encouragement. Dave is grateful to York Behaviour Management Services Sexuality Clinic in Richmond Hill, Ontario, Canada, which has served people with disabilities and their families for more than 2 decades. His experience of working at the clinic with so many families has enriched this text with examples and warmth.

For Angelica Campos-Abrego and Andrea Cardenas of Panama,
two little girls whose hearts, even with holes in them,
were strong enough to erase international borders,
dissolve the barriers of language,
and make strangers friends.

And for Samantha Misanchuk,
who continues to teach us about love and devotion.

—KMS

To Sandra Jensen,
a young woman with a disability
whose hearts, old and new,
taught the world about love and change.

—DH

Sexuality

George, Michael, and Peggy Creamer
Harrison, Ohio

Chapter 1

Your Journey

"She was just beautiful."

When Rebecca Garner was born 3 weeks premature, the doctor's suspicion of an extra chromosome was the least of her parents' concerns. The odds were against the baby. One third to one half of infants born with Down syndrome have heart problems (National Down Syndrome Congress, 1993); Rebecca's walnut-sized heart had three large holes and valve defects. During her birth, doctors carefully unwound the umbilical cord from her neck. Her parents sought a second opinion, and the baby had open heart surgery when she was just 5½ weeks old.

Today, at 15 months, an energetic Rebecca plays happily on the floor with Spooky, the family dog, opening her mouth wide for a wet canine kiss. Despite all of the bad news around Rebecca's dramatic entrance into the world, her mother's first impression was that her new baby girl was beautiful.

Beauty often isn't the first thing celebrated when a baby is born with an intellectual disability. The worried looks, the scurrying nurses speaking in hushed tones, the uncommunicative doctors, and the tests "just to be sure" are elements of an almost universal scene played out for new parents around the world. Sometimes there are complications, like Rebecca's heart problems, but even when the birth is routine and the baby is healthy, gloom often descends. It has been so for decades, but now times are changing.

This book is not just for parents of newborns or young children. If your child with an intellectual disability is already an adult, please don't be concerned that you might have missed teaching or didn't know how to teach about sexuality and relationships when your son or daughter was young. Your child grew up— and you learned to be a parent—in a different time, and you may have done things differently. Don't be disheartened if your 47-year-old son has difficulty with the concept of privacy. You can still teach. And, most important, he can still learn. If your son or daughter no longer lives in your home, you can help the people with whom he or she lives to teach. The point is that each of us learns healthy self-concept and sexuality through a logical series of steps, one thing growing naturally from something learned before. This book will still be helpful to you if you understand that you simply start at the beginning, whether your child is 4 months old or 40 years old.

Every infant, child, teenager, and adult who has an intellectual disability, like anyone else, is a sexual being. For all of us, sexuality is the integration of feelings, needs, and desires into a unique personality that expresses maleness or femaleness (Ludwig & Hingsburger, 1993). *Sex* can simply mean gender, whether you're male or female. *Sex* can also mean the physical act of sexual intercourse. *Sexuality,* on the other hand, really refers to the whole person—your thoughts, feelings, attitudes, and behavior toward yourself and others (Maksym, 1990a, 1990b). Learning how, when, where, and with whom to interact and express our sexuality as a male or female is very important to our well being and to how well we will be welcomed and accepted by our community.

Healthy sexuality, a sense of self, and confidence are part of what makes us all well adjusted and strong. You may be a single parent, older, younger, gay, a noncustodial parent, or a stepparent. The only consistent thing about parents of sons and daughters with a disability is that each parent is different. But philosophies may be shared, parenting strategies may be similar, and all parents have worries and hopes about their child.

Not long ago, a woman contacted the Saskatchewan Association for Community Living, an advocacy group for people with intellectual disabilities. Her son and daughter-in-law had just had a new baby, and the doctor had told them, rather crisply, that the child "was Down syndrome." The doctor did not say that the child *had* Down syndrome but that he *was* Down syndrome. The grandmother asked Karin (co-author of this book), in an unsteady voice, if there were some pamphlets she could read and pass along to the new parents who were, she said, quite devastated. Before getting her address, Karin congratulated her on her new grandson and asked his name. There was a brief silence, and then the woman began to cry. It was the first congratulations she had heard, even though the baby was already a week old.

Since then, we've heard of families who send out birth announcements that feature messages like this: "Hi! My name is Meaghan Jean and I arrived on July 21 at 5 lbs., 8 ounces. Mom and Dad are tired, but very happy that I'm finally here and healthy. I also have an intellectual disability, so I will depend on my brothers Mark and Gregory to help me learn. I hope to meet you soon!"

No matter what you are told, no matter what era you grew up in or when your child was born, no matter what you have always believed about people with intellectual disabilities, your son or daughter will bring you joy, humor, frustration, pain, pride, and hope, just like any child.

If your newborn has an intellectual disability, you are going to have to learn what you can do. You'll occasionally feel overwhelmed. Reading this book will be more positive for you right now than the experience of many parents in the past, some of whom were given a 400-page medical textbook from the 1950s. Don't even blow the dust off the covers of those! You probably want to read, so we encourage you to refer to the resource list featured at the end of this book for the most current and best literature. If you're already an experienced parent of a son or daughter with an intellectual disability, keep your mind open to new ideas, attitudes, and options.

You've probably already noticed that we are using the term *intellectual disability*. We are talking about people with cognitive disabilities. One of us is the parent of a young man with Down syndrome, which is one of the most common causes of intellectual disability, so some of the perspectives and references in this book come from that experience. Although there are different terms and individuals have preferences for which ones to use, the important thing to remember is that we are talking about *people*.

In 1974, Karin's husband Richard was told that his newborn first child was "a mongoloid." The first image that went through his mind was the old blue schoolbus that rumbled through his neighborhood during his childhood. Children with disabilities climbed onto or were carried to that bus as it headed to a segregated school in Indianapolis. As the words sunk in, he remembered the children's faces pressed against the windows of the old blue bus, staring out at a neighborhood of which they were not part in the 1950s. In the hospital, Richard, scared to death, held his days-old son. He could not know how this child would change his life, but he decided then that Jim would not become one of those faces peering out at a community that was not his own.

It was a determination reinforced by Richard's grandmother, Theodocia Liming, in her eighties at the time, whom Richard had always viewed with reverence as tough, strict, and a little scary. She is remembered for the time she sat at the piano during a Christmas gathering and sternly played for the family the musical selection she wanted for her own funeral. No one ignored Grandma, so everyone sang along, "Thou art the potter, I am the clay."

"Take that baby home and love him," she said to Richard in the spring of 1974. "God gave you this baby just like any other, so you just love him and raise him. He won't be that different than any other child. You just go home and get on with it." Grandma had always been quite unapologetic about life since her husband had been killed, leaving her to raise six children on her own. Her frank words set the stage for what Jim's parents expected of him. Time and time again, in all things, expectations make all the difference.

Our friend Jean Edwards told a remarkable story about her friend, David Dawson, a young man with Down syndrome. This story speaks to the power of a gentle spirit and the compassion that springs from self-worth:

> Before we left on this trip [to the National Down Syndrome Congress conference]...one of David's customers from work gave him the phone number of his brother who lives in Boston and told David to call him when we arrived. I was hesitant about this offer and wondered if the man realized that David would follow up. Well, right away, David got the brother on the phone. No, his brother hadn't called him but, yes, if David was a friend of his brother, he wanted to take him to dinner. David explained that he was travelling with a couple of ladies [Jean and Mary, a friend of David's] and asked if they could join the dinner party. Before I knew it, we had a dinner date with the brother of a man I had never met and I was trembling in my shoes wondering if this man could accept two young adults with Down syndrome and one slightly strange college professor!
>
> At 7:00 P.M., we met at the front of the hotel. We greeted one another and Sam (the brother) took a long look at David and Mary. He was quiet a few minutes and then said: "God bless my dear brother. God bless my dear brother. Oh, I wish my wife could be here to meet you. God bless my brother."
>
> As we drove away in his car (David and Mary in the backseat), Sam looked at David and Mary over and over in the rearview mirror. He kept repeating how happy he was to meet us and how sad he was that his wife couldn't join us. He asked David questions about his brother back in Portland and about his job. Slowly, through specific questions, he pieced together the lives of David and Mary. He took us to one of Boston's finest restaurants and sat with the most joyous smile on his face as he watched David order Top Sirloin Pizzaila, eggplant ratatouille, potatoes with onions and a glass of red wine. This ala carte menu was the real test of the menu reading skill of David and Mary.
>
> Mary followed suit without hesitation. "I'll have the same." But David countered with: "Mary, I think it has a lot of garlic in it. I think you would like the Chicken Cordon Bleu better." Mary smiled and appreciated the help. The ala carte menu was beyond her present skills. "She'll have the carrots with dill and seasoned rice with that," David said.
>
> Once again, Sam said, "I wish my wife could be here."
>
> After dinner, Sam asked if we would be willing to drive out to his home. His wife was home and he really wanted us to meet her. David told him it was late and we probably shouldn't, but Sam kept insisting. So, soon we were at his home, being greeted by a very shocked wife who looked as though she had not slept in many days. She looked weak, sad and depressed. But as we got through the formalities of meeting, greeting and the taking of coats, wife Carol started coming alive. She was delighted to meet David and Mary and while she was slow at warming up, she was warming up!

Then we heard a little baby cry in the next room. Carol ran off and returned with a beautiful little five-week old baby boy. David was delighted with the baby and asked to hold him. Then he and Mary sat talking babytalk as Sam and Carol sat across from them, staring. The room was quiet except for David and Mary's playing with the baby.

Suddenly, David and Mary also fell quiet and looked at each other...then the baby...then back at each other.

David broke the silence. He looked up at Sam and Carol and said, "This baby is like us." He looked back at Mary.

Carol started to cry. David handed the baby to Mary, got up, went and put his arm around Carol and Sam said, "He'll be okay. He's just different."

I don't know what David knows about Down syndrome. Once I told him he had an extra chromosome. But he does know about feelings, and comforting and reassurance. That night in Boston, David and Mary brought hope and encouragement to two struggling parents who were wrestling with all sorts of questions, anger, and inner conflicts. And I had to agree with Sam as he repeated again, "God bless my brother!" (Edwards & Dawson, 1983, pp. 47–48)

We said earlier that it's important to remember that we're talking about *people*. There will be times throughout your son or daughter's life when the disability seems paramount, and there will be times when it will, indeed, be the focus. But while the disability is part of your child, it is not your child. At one conference, a mother whose child was born with a cleft lip and palate spoke of the fear she faced on the eve of showing her newborn off for the first time at a family gathering. It was before the baby's corrective surgery, and the infant looked rather startling. The mother steeled herself for the looks of horror and repulsion she imagined would appear on the faces of people unaccustomed to disabilities.

The next day, she carried the baby in and began to peel off the blankets. Climbing up on the couch, her 5-year-old nephew asked if he could hold his new cousin. Heart pounding, she put the sleeping baby carefully in his arms. He peered down into the infant's face and asked seriously, "Why does her mouth look like that?" As simply as possible, the mother explained that the little girl's lip had grown a bit differently than his own. The boy considered this for a moment, and she held her breath. Then he bent down, kissed the baby on the mouth, and announced, "I love my new baby cousin!" His next question was why was his auntie crying.

In the following chapter, "Your Guides," you will meet a variety of parents who will give you advice and ideas and share their own personal stories throughout this book. This array includes parents of all ages, situations, and philosophical viewpoints. Not all of these families are the traditional Mom, Dad, two kids, and a dog. What all these people do represent, however, are the questions, concerns, and observations shared by many—if not most—people who are parents of people with intellectual disabilities. Their suggestions, ideas, hopes, and fears are sprinkled throughout the rest of the book to guide, encourage, and sustain you.

As authors in the field of intellectual disability, we believe that some of the most powerful stories come from parents and especially from people with disabilities. Robert Bogdan and Steven J. Taylor (1994) said in their book *The Social Meaning of Mental Retardation: Two Life Stories* that to disregard or devalue the perspective of a person with a disability as naive, unsophisticated, or immature simply justifies a dangerous tendency to do things to people in a very arrogant

Rebecca,
Jacqueline, Courtney,
and Dawn Thompson
Vernon, British Columbia

fashion without listening to what they have to say. An equally important contribution to this book, then, are the voices of people who have intellectual disabilities. In the "Your Guides" chapter, too, you will meet several people with disabilities who will be featured throughout the book, telling you—in their own words—what is important to them in life. You'll learn what kinds of people they dream of becoming and how their own sense of self and sexuality is fundamental to that growth. You'll see how they perceive themselves in this world. If your child is very young, these people may provide you with a glimpse of the future. If your son or daughter is older, he or she may find a comrade or a role model or at least someone who is expressing some of the same feelings and dreams. In the passages called "Dave's Story" and "Karin's Story," we authors share vignettes from our lives that you may find useful and thought provoking.

The voices of people with disabilities should call out to every teacher, doctor, nurse, next-door neighbor, and community member to disregard any sentence that begins with "They're *all* like..."or "They're *all* so..." And, as parents, if we ever find ourselves saying things like this, we should bite down on our own tongues—hard. While we struggle through the complexities of societal and technological change, the dreams of people with intellectual disabilities remind us to be better people to ourselves and to each other. While you are busy teaching your child how to be a proud, confident human being, the lessons you are learning about yourself just might surprise you.

There's no one particular path to take in a given situation. Your child is unique (this may be the understatement of the century). But so are each of your other children, and so is your family. It's impossible for us to provide a list of one-shot answers that will work for all families, everywhere, all the time, and we wouldn't presume to anyway! What we can do, though, is share with you a few basic questions that many parents ask and some suggestions we've come up with. You'll find these Q and A sections at the ends of Chapters 3 through 8. We also encourage you to buy or borrow some of the resources we list at the end of the book so that you can help your child learn in a way that is appropriate to her age and your family's circumstances, values, and beliefs.

Portions of this book may be disturbing to you. Realize that much of the information about safety for our sons and daughters is really about what is necessary for all children, not only those who have an intellectual disability. The fact remains that people with disabilities are more vulnerable to exploitation and abuse. As parents, one of our most important jobs is to teach our sons and daughters how to be strong, how to reduce the risk of victimization, how to be confident decision makers, and how to avoid becoming the victims of labels and stereotypes.

And, isn't a sense of confidence what we hope for and work toward in each of our children? We hope our children not only will learn from us but also will absorb good things from the people they meet in the community. We all remember a teacher or a camp counselor we wanted to be "just like" when we grew up. What often attracts us to others is how comfortable they are with themselves.

Sometimes gaining self-esteem is an elusive thing for people with disabilities. For example, at one of her aquafitness classes, Karin noticed a wide-eyed, attractive young woman with blushes of red in her cheeks. She was very young, perhaps still in her teens, and very obese. Yet, here she was, struggling against the current as she stretched and marched through the class with the help of someone Karin assumed was her support worker. As Karin watched, she was pleased to see other aquafitters spontaneously offering encouragement to the young woman as she fought to overcome her nervousness in the water. With each comment, the young woman beamed. At the end of the class, the instructor directed everyone to "hug the most important person in the pool." The young woman immediately reached out to hug not herself as the rest did but her assistant. Her mistake inspired a good-natured chuckle from those around her, and she blushed deeply. When she realized she was supposed to hug herself, she reddened even more, giggled, and hid her face in her hands. Self-confidence is sometimes elusive, but it is worth the pursuit. As a parent, you can help guide the journey.

The words used to describe people with an extra chromosome and other disabilities have changed over the years. Our sons, daughters, family members, and friends have been called a great many things, sometimes with good intentions, sometimes without. Some people complain that the answer to "What's the right terminology to use?" isn't always clear and that it seems to keep shifting. What is important is society's recognition that labels can be limiting and dehumanizing. The fact is that someone's intellectual disability is only one aspect of that person. It usually doesn't count for much when we look at who he is to his family, his friends, and the community.

A disability is usually unexpected, and it causes a shift in what parents expect. But listen carefully: Your child is not a "Down syndrome child." Your adult daughter is not a "cri-du-chat" or a "fragile X." Your son or daughter is a *person with* a disability...a teenager with red hair...a child with Grandmother's nose, with Aunt Gwen's laugh, with a unique personality, or with dimples like Cousin Eric. Your daughter is a young woman with her father's eyes. Your son is the first one to write a thank-you note or remember your birthday. Your child hates olives. All of these pieces make up the person your son or daughter is, and more pieces will make up the person he or she becomes. Throughout life he or she will continue to grow and learn.

Your son or daughter comes with a disability but no operator's manual. Don't let the disability be the only aspect that steers your parenting. All infants are born into the role of scientist and explorer. The more they learn and discover, the greater their capacity to do more learning and discovering. This process is lifelong for them and for you.

As a parent, you may find yourself being more deliberate, more obvious, and more thoughtful in how you help your son or daughter learn and grow. Be calm and consistent. Be firm. Cherish your sense of humor. If you don't have one, get one; it makes life more fun. The kind of person you hope your child will become is not determined by disability but by her family, friends, teachers, you, and herself. Your child needs to learn from you that she is loved, valued, witty, gorgeous, strong, and an irreplaceable part of your family. Those people who make the annoying "I'm the proud parent of a Hillsboro honor student!" bumper stickers haven't gotten around to making ones that say "I'm the proud parent of a 21-year-old who just learned to tie his shoes!" or "I'm the proud parent of a teenager who remembered to use the bathroom with the door closed." Maybe someday they will make stickers like this. In the meantime, let your child eavesdrop on you when you are saying wonderful things about her to other people, and tell her these things. Let your child know her concept of "me" rhymes with "good."

Sometimes when Karin and her husband look at Jim, they think they haven't done enough, taught him well enough, or offered him enough opportunities—this probably happens to all parents. Jim's such a great guy in spite of them! They should be doing this or that. They should have done more; we should be doing more. Doesn't everyone who's got kids have these doubts? Karin looks at all three of her stepchildren and hopes that they will be kind and thoughtful adults, confident in themselves and their strengths as they plow ahead through life into a changing world. As we parents try to guide our *all* of our children, the important thing is to be aware and appreciate the fact they are growing and developing and are inherently sexual beings. We first need to understand what that means. Then, as we encourage and support and teach, we need to try, try again, then try another way to encourage them to be whole, satisfied, interest*ing,* and interest*ed* people.

Winifred Kempton of Haverford, Pennsylvania, has been called one of America's foremost sexuality educators and is truly a pioneer when it comes to helping people with intellectual disabilities understand their sexuality. She agreed that it's not always easy to teach your child—in fact, *any* of your children—about social-sexual issues. But parents of a child with an intellectual disability have a few more barriers in their path. Kempton said,

> From the time of the birth of a disabled child, it would be wonderful if the parents consider him as a social-sexual being with the same pleasant attitude as they do the child's other selves (intellectual, athletic, musical); if they could look forward to developing *all* aspects of their child's [life] as indications of [his] interests and abilities unfold. However, many parents have been sidetracked from this positive attitude of their child being a social person. First, because of early predictions that *your child will never be able to...* from professionals and non-professionals and, second, parents are prone to have extra anxiety towards their social-being child because it includes sexuality. But remember the days of sterilization at puberty? Gross ignorance is gone, and the sexual revolution is enabling [parents] to lift the ban on their child joining many social circles. If parents have not had the opportunity to do so at an early age, it is not too late to begin, no matter how old the person. (personal communication, 1996)

Kempton is the author of some of the most widely used sex education programs. The key to success, she said, is that parents provide information, set appropriate behavioral limits, and have the patience to help sons and daughters develop that knowledge. "We must insist that parents understand clearly that their children, with or without disabilities, *all* receive the training that will deem them socially acceptable by an open-minded public" (personal communication, 1996).

In the following chapters, we will share information, stories, ideas, tips, and strategies. We're not just talking about babies and young children and new parents in this book, but about people with disabilities and parents all ages. Remember, cultures and families differ. As we've said, there's no operator's manual. Sexuality, sex, and social skills education doesn't happen at some magical age when you give your child a nervous lecture about the birds and the bees. Our friend Leslie Walker-Hirsch, co-creator of the *Circles* (Champagne & Walker-Hirsch, 1986–1993) social-sexual training program, likened it to being an interior decorator: Good social/sexuality education starts with

The basic paint, a color on the walls, and a carpet on the floor, the self-esteem and security of being a valued family member. The concept lays down the parameters of relationships. The next thing I'd do is select and bring in the furniture, the concrete information. Then I'd add the curtains, the details, the artwork, the subtleties of social skills, interactions, relationships, behavior. (personal communication, 1996)

This is a lifetime journey for all of us.

Bob Manwaring, Katherine Manwaring, and Darryl Davey
Winnipeg, Manitoba

Chapter 2

Your Guides

Don and Ronalyn Bradshaw, Saskatoon, Saskatchewan

Riley, age 10, is the Bradshaws' only child. Don is an airworthiness inspector and is a part owner of an all-terrain recreational vehicle company. Ronalyn has had a number of part-time jobs, including jewelry salesperson, children's face painter, and clown, and has been the primary caregiver for their son. Riley does not walk without braces and a walker and usually gets around in his wheelchair. The couple has faced long battles with the education system. Don and Ronalyn push against what they feel are traditional attitudes and rules that seem to respect the service system before recognizing friendships and social interactions. They are bolstered by a large, supportive family and feel that their battles are worth it when they see the interactions between Riley and his classmates.

David and Cathy Conrad, Cincinnati, Ohio

Married for 3 years, David and Cathy are helped by support workers and family, particularly David's mom, Eda. "She went with us on our honeymoon!" said the couple. Cathy, 34, stays at home; David, 38, clerks and stocks shelves at Carpentry Plus in a suburb of Cincinnati. Despite finding it difficult to learn money management and to cope with a next-door neighbor who calls them "retards," the couple love being together in their own home. When the couple met, David lived in a group home; Cathy lived in a more independent apartment that was arranged by an advocacy group. Despite an agency policy on privacy, staff at David's group home balked when the couple wanted time alone together. "We got in trouble," says Cathy. "Now we have our house, and we take care of each other. He is my guardian. I am his guardian."

Peggy and George Creamer, Harrison, Ohio

Peggy and George met when George was a handsome but painfully shy Kentucky soldier just home from World War II in Europe. Planning for a tour of duty in Japan, he came home for a 2-week rest and "looked across the street and there she was. Man, she was something else." Married for nearly 50 years, the Creamers have raised four children. Their youngest, Michael, born in 1966 with an intellectual disability, still lives at home. He works a few hours a week at a center for older adults. Mom and son are Cincinnati Reds baseball fans and members of the Rosie Reds booster club. An avid traveler, Peggy has taken Michael everywhere and insisted that he learn from and absorb the world around him. During a tour of the White House, soft-spoken and polite Michael asked a Secret Service agent if he might talk to President Bill Clinton to "give him a piece of my mind."

Chelsea Duffey, Mount Dora, Florida

As an only child, 7-year-old Chelsea often invites friends for sleepovers and pool parties, something her parents encourage to keep her involved with other children. Chelsea takes care of her dog, Wizard B. Oz, and her birds. She is a talkative, strong-minded child who doesn't hesitate to show off her swimming skills in the backyard pool.

Denise and Thomas Duffey, Mount Dora, Florida

The Duffey family lives in Mount Dora, a small central Florida town, an antique collector's paradise. Denise and Thomas ran a company called Lake Technology Products, which designed and manufactured electronic highway information signs ("Yes, that was [our sign] that Steve Martin was talking to in *L.A. Story!*" said Denise and Thomas). Convinced that their daughter Chelsea's developmental delay could be significantly helped by growth hormone and thyroid supplements, the couple became involved with the Institute for Basic Research in New York. Though controversial, the Duffeys credit their daughter's growth to the treatments. Chelsea attends first grade at her local elementary school. The family is starting a private Montessori school, which Chelsea will attend. Since the family was interviewed, 7-year-old Ashley was adopted and joined the family. "The girls are sisters," says Thomas. "I don't think Ashley really knows that Chelsea has Down syndrome or that she's different from any other kid. It's working out great. Chelsea actually picked Ashley for her sister." The Duffeys sold Lake Technology Products and started another engineering company, Traffic Management Associates, which also handles the design and integration of highway traffic systems.

Gayle Foy, Indianapolis, Indiana

"We just loved babies," says Gayle, parent of 10 children. "We tell people I was pregnant for 15 years." When the youngest, Chris, was born with Down syndrome in 1974, an local support agency kept asking her when they could offer her early intervention. Her response, "I've got nine other kids! How much more intervention can this baby take?" When Chris was 18 months old, the family took a 3-week family camping trip across the country to Disneyland—all in one van. All of the Foy siblings remain close, though several have moved away with families of their own. Expectations for Chris have always been high, from taking over the family's hand-me-down paper route to learning to live independently one day. A rock-solid work ethic and an ability to get along with people and be someone whom people enjoy knowing are the keys to Chris's success. Formerly an actress and now a parent educator, Gayle says families can never stop learning, changing, and asking for more.

Brian and Shelly Garner, Moose Jaw, Saskatchewan

Baby Rebecca's entrance into the world was dramatic. Three weeks premature, she was born with the umbilical cord around her neck, and her walnut-sized heart had a hole in it. At $5\frac{1}{2}$ weeks old, before she weighed even 7 pounds, Rebecca had open heart surgery. Today, she demands attention from her older sisters, Sheena, 18, Jana, 16, and Desiree, 6; from her parents; and from the family dog, Spooky. Since Rebecca's birth, Shelly and another mother have rejuvenated a local support group to make sure other parents find the information and help they need. The Garners celebrated the birth of a fifth child, Logan, in 1996.

Peggy Hutchison and John Lord, Kitchener, Ontario

Peggy is an associate professor at Brock University's Department of Recreation and Leisure Studies with a cross-appointment in the Department of Education. John is a social research consultant, author, and co-founder of the Centre for Research and Education in Human Services. The couple have four teenagers; since their first date, they talked about having children of their own and adopting those who needed a family. In 1982, Peggy saw a baby picture in a newspaper ad that the Ontario government had run to place children with disabilities in homes through adoption. That evening, Peggy announced, "I've just seen our third child." Peggy and John have presented their thoughts on community life for people with disabilities through books, articles, conferences, and human services consulting.

Karen Lord, Kitchener, Ontario

Karen is 16 years old and lives with her parents, her older sister Krista, her younger sister Sarah, and the family dog Angus. Karen is an active teenager teetering on the verge of womanhood, sometimes unsure whether she'd rather be treated as a girl or a woman. She takes karate and art lessons, attends Pathfinders (similar to Senior Girl Scouts) and her church youth group, sings in the choir at school, is a member of the swim team, and turns out to show her support for other school sports. She is part of a family that doesn't sit still for long, and she swims at her grandfather's cottage, enjoys cross country skiing, and is an enthusiastic game player in the living room at home.

Brad Magnus, Salt Spring Island, British Columbia

Brad, 23, has become internationally known for his interpretive dance. He has performed for community events and for national and international conferences. He lives on a farm with his parents and works shoulder to shoulder with his brothers Nolan, Duncan, and Chris. Living on an island that is connected to Vancouver Island by a ferry system, Brad has learned to make his way to and from activities and dance lessons in Victoria. Brad also took some courses at a community college in southern British Columbia. He carefully tends his own horse named Lana and dreams of one day becoming a dance teacher.

John and Ethel Magnus, Salt Spring Island, British Columbia

The couple has four sons, now all young men, who work the family's horse ranch and custom haying operation near the Gulf Island community of Ganges. John, formerly a lawyer in Calgary, and Ethel moved to the eclectic island off Canada's west coast to provide an accepting sense of community not only for Brad but also for all of their sons. While Brad's brothers are away from the island at college, Brad takes on many more of the farm chores. When they return, the family expands to a boisterous size. The family further expanded recently to include Jennifer, Ethel's daughter, who was born in 1961 and had been given up for adoption. Ethel spearheaded the writing of the family's story, which became the book *A Family Love Story* (see the "Recommended Resources" at the end of this book for more information on this book). Brad's dancing and the family's matter-of-fact views on raising children have led to worldwide invitations to speak and perform.

Bob Manwaring and Darryl Davey, Winnipeg, Manitoba

In 1970, Bob and Joyce Manwaring had been married for about 20 years and had three daughters; the youngest, Katherine, was born with Down syndrome in 1981. Despite a nice home and a life that was "going well," Bob carried a "deep sense that things just weren't quite right." Eventually, the couple brought the children together to make a painful divorce as smooth as possible. Today Joyce, a social worker, is a single parent in Winnipeg. Bob, who works with an advocacy group for people with disabilities in that city, has made a new life with a new partner, Darryl Davey, a florist. The parents and daughters have sorted out the new family dynamics. Katherine, 14, spends every other weekend with Bob and Darryl, who live minutes away.

Katherine Manwaring, Winnipeg, Manitoba

Fourteen-year-old Katherine lives with her mom Joyce and stays with her dad and his partner Darryl every other weekend. She seems to view her parents' divorce and her father's gay partnership with a matter-of-fact air, enjoying the expanded family that second marriages often bring. Katherine is a Girl Guide, takes jazz dancing lessons, and has a penchant for musicals and horror movies.

Greg and Elizabeth Popowich, Yorkton, Saskatchewan

Greg is a writer/producer, and Elizabeth is an on-air personality with a local television station. The couple was married 4 years before deciding to have children. When their first son Nicholas was just 20 months old, he was named one of Johnson & Johnson's Adorable Babies in Canada. National judges chose Baby Nic as a $10,000 education scholarship winner. Nic was followed by Lucas in 1992. Nic, now 5 years old, is a graduate of an early childhood intervention program and preschool and goes to kindergarten with an assistant.

Nannie Sanchez, Albuquerque, New Mexico

Twenty-one-year-old Nannie has been considered as a first in many things in her life. As the first college student with an intellectual disability, she's finishing her fourth year at the Career Preparation Academy in business occupations. She's the first person with an intellectual disability to work in the administrative offices at the Albuquerque International Airport. A careful and eloquent speaker, Nannie has quietly but forcefully earned standing ovations at major conferences, seminars, hearings, and the legislative session for the government of New Mexico. Given up at birth by a 16-year-old mother who was told that her baby would never walk, talk, or feed "itself," Nannie was adopted by Rosemarie Sanchez, a woman Nannie calls her "mother and mentor," whose job at the time was to place babies for adoption. Unable to find a home for the baby, Rosemarie feared Nannie would be sent to an institution in Los Lunas. Rosemarie, already a single parent, decided to adopt the infant herself. In fact, in 1965, Rosemarie's second son, Dean, had been born with Down syndrome and other disabilities. Professionals advised her to stop feeding him, and she refused, returning to New Mexico with her two sons. Despite his mother's fight, Dean died when he was 6 months old. When she discussed her plans to adopt a new baby, her first son, who was then 19 years old, said, "Mom, you're crazy."

Enrolled at 6 weeks of age in an Esperanza infant stimulation class and encouraged from infancy to think for herself, Nannie has always been reflective about her career. When she was in ninth grade, she announced that she wanted to attend college. It took the threat of a lawsuit and a complaint with the Office of Civil Rights, but she was eventually admitted to a college. Her dreams are clear: "I want to keep working at the airport because I like it there, and they treat me like equal...and I would like to be famous. That would be cool."

Francis Schaan, Saskatoon, Saskatchewan

Francis, 35, works at McDonald's and marked his 15th anniversary with the company in 1995. The youngest of seven children, Francis lives in a group home with eight men and often talks about getting his own place, maybe with his friend Roy, who works at a sheltered workshop. With support from friends, he meets a reading tutor once a week and has swimming lessons on Saturday. Francis is a walking collection of facts and figures on the World Wrestling Federation and rarely misses a match on television or a live show in the city. He is never afraid to use the telephone to stay connected with everyone from his social worker to casual friends and is a master at organizing his own support network. His father Tony, 81, and his mother Magdalena, 78, live in a nearby complex for older adults so that Francis can "keep an eye on them" as he puts it.

Catherine Schaefer, Winnipeg, Manitoba

In the summer of 1996, Catherine's family and friends came together for her 35th birthday party and a celebration to mark 10 years of interdependent living in her own house. She lives on the main floor in a stately old home in Winnipeg with a "helper" and friends without disabilities who live in the two upstairs apartments. True to the doctor's prognosis in 1961, Catherine has never spoken or walked, and her mother Nicola still often wonders just what her daughter makes of the world around her. Nicola's book about her daughter, *Does She Know She's There?* was published by Fitzhenry & Whiteside in 1978. The book sold more than 60,000 copies worldwide and was eventually printed in five languages. A new update to chronicle Catherine's life in her own home was published in 1982, and another update came out in 1999. Her co-op housing and friendship network was described in Robert Perske's (1988) *Circles of Friends*. The strength of Catherine's presence—and that of her family—has changed the assumptions of many people around the world.

Florence Schulten, Ocala, Florida

Nearly 90 years old, Florence Schulten still stands straight and proud. She rides horses and attends church regularly with her "kids" who are, in fact, adults who have lived with her since she started a school in the 1940s. It was a time when society didn't believe education dollars should be "wasted" on children with disabilities. Tired from the battle and going broke, Florence and her husband, a physical therapist, nearly gave up on their school. When her daughter Loretta was born with an intellectual disability, despite pressure to institutionalize the baby, Florence took her daughter's birth as a sign that the school should remain open. People with intellectual disabilities could and would learn, said Florence, and Loretta became an accomplished horsewoman, perhaps inheriting a passion for horses from her mother and her grandfather, the Captain of the King's Guard in Denmark. She "brought light to every heart she touched," says Florence. More 50 years after her daughter's birth, it is no less painful for Florence to remember Loretta's death in 1978 at the age of 31. Florence still raises Paso Fino horses on her ranch outside Ocala.

Jim Schwier, Saskatoon, Saskatchewan, and Visalia, California

At 22 years old, Jim calls two countries home. Now that school is over, his time is spent equally with both sets of parents. He volunteers at a local butcher shop, the YMCA, and at a community technical college in the commercial kitchen and student cafeteria. He says, "I keep skinny" with racquetball and aquafitness classes at the Y. Family is important; Jim's an avid letter writer to relatives and family, and a speakerphone helps him stay in touch. Several ear operations as an infant left him with a significant hearing loss, so hearing aids, ongoing speech therapy, and daily "speech homework" help with his communication skills. He's a Trekkie and a fan of Elvis and the Beatles, and he practices the drums on a snare drum in "both bedrooms" in Canada and California. Each year, he plans in advance his trips between his two homes around his jobs, volunteer work, speech support, literacy class, and social commitments.

Richard Schwier and Karin Melberg Schwier, Saskatoon, Saskatchewan

Richard is a professor of education at the University of Saskatchewan; Karin is a writer and communications coordinator with the Saskatchewan Association for Community Living, an advocacy organization for people with intellectual disabilities. After Richard's separation from his first wife in 1983, he learned first to be a single parent and then a parent at a distance when his three children moved to California to live with their mother. When Richard and his first wife separated, Ben was 3, Erin was 7, and Jim, who has an intellectual disability, was 10. Richard says that summers and school holidays together, weekly telephone calls, letters, audiotapes, and videotapes have played an important part in "keeping us together as a family, even though there were 1,500 miles between us most of the year." In 1986, Richard married Karin Melberg, and the dynamics changed again.

Donna Serblowski, Bruno, Saskatchewan

Donna, the last of 10 children, was born in 1967 to Arthur and Wallis Serblowski, Polish immigrants who with their families escaped dictatorships in 1905 and 1937, respectively. The couple believed in the strength of family and hard work on their farm on the Canadian prairie. "We never knew anything was wrong," says Wallis of her youngest. "Our doctor said 'mental handicap' and 'cerebral palsy,' but he really didn't tell us much. She was a little bit slower, but we didn't do anything differently. She was just included and loved. Did her chores, played with the kids. But she really wasn't walking properly, and two people came out to ask me some questions. When it was time for her to go to school, the doctor told us to take her to the city for some tests. I wish she could have had early intervention, but it's easy to look back now and know better. She was the apple of her daddy's eye." Arthur died in 1978 when Donna was 11. "When she was 25, this epilepsy thing started. She's on so much medication now, eight pills a day. It worries me. Donna is a very nice person, kind, and I'm so proud of her. She's really on the ball so many times. She always surprises me with what she knows. I know there's a couple of guys at the shop who keep an eye on her, but she don't seem too interested. She thinks of herself in a good way. She thinks she is pretty and good. I am happy about that."

Hillary Shaw, Woodland Hills, California

Seventeen-year-old Hillary is a poised young woman venturing into adulthood. She speaks candidly about having Down syndrome and often attends conferences with her parents. She has dated, and her parents have coached her not only on what she might do to protect herself and on how to act "appropriately" but also on how to enjoy relationships. Her room is a collection of her latest passions: posters, photos, clothes, and a prized new pair of red shoes. She goes to high school in Woodland Hills. She has discussed the difference between a "wish" and "reality" with her mother and is trying to understand that dreams are fun to have but that they may not always come true.

Lou and Michele Shaw, Woodland Hills, California

Divorced with one son, Lou met Michele, who was widowed and had one daughter, on a blind date arranged by a mutual literary agent friend. They soon married, and their daughter Hillary was born in 1978; Lou's recollections of the first hours of Hillary's life were revealed in a July 1994 *Exceptional Parent* article. When Hillary was 5 years old, Lou, a television writer and producer, wrote an episode of *The Fall Guy* to include a 10-year-old boy with Down syndrome, played by Jason Kingsley, who had already made appearances on *Sesame Street.* Lou, who created the television show *Quincy* and was writer/producer for shows like *McCloud* and *Columbo*, also wrote a mystery novel, *Honor Thy Son* (1994). The book, which won a National Down Syndrome Media Award and the Angel Award, featured a young man with Down syndrome. Active as peer counselors for new parents, board members of advocacy organizations, and conference speakers, the Shaws co-produced *Include Us!* (1996), a children's musical with an "everybody's different" awareness message. The videotape includes Hillary as well as Michele, who has played leads in many television shows and musicals, including *The King and I, The Music Man,* and *Tomfoolery.*

Lucky Smith and Tim Feser, Whitehorse, Yukon

Lucky Smith and Tim Feser are "a match made in heaven," says support worker Mona Sullivan-Curtis. "They're a great support for each other, and because Tim talks a bit more, he's a great source of information about how Lucky is doing, if anything's bothering her. Each seems to fill in gaps for the other person." Lucky, one of ten children, is a member of the Teslin Tlingit tribe and the Xoox Hittan clan and is a "Raven child," said her sister Clara. Lucky never went to school, but grew up on the trapline, where her mother taught her living skills. Because of her status as an Indian, Lucky receives financial support from Indian Affairs; Tim earns an income from his job at the workshop. The couple met in a group home, soon rented a small house in downtown Whitehorse, and eventually moved to a two-bedroom apartment. Lucky attends a living skills program in the afternoons, and Tim handles the saws to make stakes and core boxes for the mining industry. His father Ted and stepmother Pat are involved in the couple's life, and Lucky's supportive father, brothers, and sisters live in Teslin, British Columbia, 110 miles down the Alaska Highway. Lucky's mother died in 1981. Tim and Lucky travel by bus to visit family or invite them to their home.

Dawn Thompson, Vernon, British Columbia

Dawn, 31 years old, is a single mother of 6-year-old Courtney and 3-year-old twins Rebecca and Jacqueline. They live in a small logging and farming community in southern British Columbia. The children's father, Dawn says, has not been actively involved with his children since the twins were born, though there are occasional visits. When the twins were just 5 weeks old, Rebecca, who was born with Down syndrome, went back to the hospital with congestive heart failure and was taken by air ambulance to Vancouver. As the doctors treated the additional problem of pneumonia, they discovered a torn diaphragm and Rebecca had her first surgery even before her heart was repaired. Dawn, a former nurse, says with these medical emergencies, "I couldn't have cared less about the Down syndrome." Dawn depends on a respite worker who often spends several hours a week with the children. Dawn sells household products door-to-door, and their home is a noisy whirlwind. Because daily routines are so hectic, planning for the future is a luxury.

Shelly, Rebecca, and Brian Garner
Moose Jaw, Saskatchewan

Chapter 3

A Place to Start

How do you know you are loved? This question is one that will trouble us all of our adult lives. In fact, the more secure we become in our relationships, the more insecure we feel. How do you know after 25 years of marriage that you are loved, really loved? How do you tell the difference between habit and desire? Oddly, this insecurity fuels the drive toward intimacy and reassurance we will seek all of our lives. An older woman said once, "You know, all my life, even after my husband died, I have needed to know that I am cared about. Why do you think God played such a cruel trick on us? It seems like we were left with a hole in the bottom of our hearts so that old love dribbles through, never allowing the top to be filled."

Good question: How do we know we are loved? Perhaps we don't. As adults we depend on faith in another to trust other people's love. As adults, some of us simply are too cynical and careful to believe love. As teenagers, we don't care much about love. We care about the tingly feelings we get, and, in the rush of hormones, our hearts seem to get caught in the current and end up dislodged from the chest and left somewhere in the region of the genitals. For children, there is so much going on. So much learning happening. Love is something that pops into their minds; they run in to reassure themselves that there is a "big being" there who loves them, and then it's on to other things.

Ah, but infants spend their time learning about love. Oddly, some of the affectional patterns that are established during infancy translate directly into adulthood. A mother's soothing patting of her infant child is not done randomly. It replicates the heart rate of a woman at rest, which the child heard and felt in the womb (Morris, 1997). More than that, applause replicates the soothing pat between mother and child. It seems like we learned a pattern as infant and that pattern follows us throughout our lives.

Love should be entirely natural and completely guaranteed. The world would inalterably and radically change if every child, from now on, grew up loved. But it doesn't seem that loving infants is as natural as we thought. Some disturbing studies (Morris, 1997) have reported that parents (and indeed all of society) respond quite differently to infants based on their attractiveness ("Goo goo, she's so cute") or perceived desirability ("Goo goo, I'm so glad we finally got a boy"). Remarkably, it was discovered that parents talk less to and touch less children who aren't perceived as quite so desirable.

> *It took about 20 years before we celebrated Brad's birth. There was so much emphasis on the differences, the chromosomal abnormalities, the scientific explanation of Down syndrome, and that there would be so many things we couldn't do. [We were told] he would never graduate from high school, never go to university. What other baby needed to justify his existence or the fact that he could even go home with his parents or that he should be allowed in a normal world at all? None of the other babies in that nursery had to justify whether they were going to be university graduates.*
> *—Ethel Magnus*

In our lives, we have known many people with intellectual disabilities who work, love, and live lives of vitality. Seeing an infant with a disability isn't much different than seeing any infant. We see a little tiny being with a future of varied possibilities, a future of varied relationships, and a future full of love. We wonder, though, what parents feel when they look down at a child that seems so different from themselves. One parent said that she felt she had given birth to a "foreigner," someone whom she couldn't understand. More than that, she was assured by pretty much all of the professionals who swarmed around her that the child was, indeed, different.

"Special" was the word used in place of "different." Her child was "special," and she was feeling anything but special. She said that it would have been nice for just one person relate to her infant child as a *human* child. Of course, now that she knows her child, she has difficulty understanding why anyone would have called her "special" when they knew her name was Janet.

Karen Lord

My name is Karen Lord. Karen Michelle Hutchison Lord. The whole thing. That's me. I walk to my job. Every day. We're gonna have a party. At graduation. I wear a hat. Also a dress. White. I try a different job. In a day care. I like that. I take care of little kids. Sometimes I babysit. I like old little kids. I don't like diapers. Not very much.

I would stay here. With Mom and Dad. I got three sisters. Sarah, Krista, and me. And one brother, Jessie. He doesn't live here. All the girls live here. We don't fight... we do. Sometimes.

I am 16. I have a boyfriend. Yes, I do. Michael. He's handsome. Michael, he's crazy. For a date, we come here. My house. We have no parents. And we party. We have a dance, watch music. I like "Whoomp, There It Is." I like country music. I like Harry Chapin. Mom and Dad go out for dinner, to Charlie's. Maybe to their friends, having dinner. I have guys to the party. 14. And girls. I'm a girl.

I have apartment. All fancy. Pets. Dogs. I get Angus with me. He's our dog. He live in my apartment. My mom take my dog to the vet. He got a needle. He was okay. He took my mom to the vet. No. My mom took my dog, and he went to sleep, and he was awake, and he couldn't walk. He was limpin'. Had to carry him. He got to shave his hair off. He looked like a goof.

My apartment got four rooms. Gonna be one bedroom and a sink. And a living room and a bathroom. No, three bedrooms and a kitchen. And a stove and a living room. And a TV room. A stove. And a fridge. Do you like ravioli? I have that in the fridge in my apartment. I put pasta on the shelf. On the top. Do you have a freezer? I put the pasta in there. I put bread, jam, peanut butter, butter. Chips and pop. And dip. No vegetables. Yuck! And salad. And I can make a ravioli sandwich. No, actually, tuna salad. Do you like tuna? 'Cause I make tuna salad. Or lasagna. Or pasta. I have my friends over. My friends can help me with the pasta. Do you like garlic bread? I will make a salad. Caesar salad. And ice cream. And wine. And pop.

I'm not skinny. I'm fat. I do this, stretch. I walk. I go swimming. I am good swimmer. I take Angus for a walk.

My mom and dad are cool. I like them a lot. They are cool. My sisters. My brother. My mom is so kind. She doesn't yell at me. Dad, he doesn't yell either.

When I have kids, I name him Ben and Angus and Peter. George and Elizabeth. Margaret and I name my kid Sally. I play games with them. I like kids. My apartment is fancy. With balloons and stuff. 'Cause we party.

My family is cool. I like them. They my best friend in whole wide world. 'Cause I like my mom. I like her on Mother's Day. And Angus. He's a good dog.

You shouldn't fight. Just walk off. Don't get mad. I can drive a car. No, I can't. I like a jeep. No, actually a trailer. With beds. A camper.

I got braces inside my mouth. I get more braces in May. I like to go to Charlie's. The buffet. It's so good. We eat a lot. We pig out.

Down syndrome, I don't know what is. No idea. Is it talking different? You have to learn. Learn stuff. I read to them, to Mom and Dad. They like it. I like Robert Munsch. I like that book. I Have to Go Pee.

I go to Pathfinders. After there's Guides, Brownies, Pathfinders, Rangers. I flying over to Rangers. Then it's done. We play games. No boys. Only girls. Don't have to wear uniform; we wear uniform.

I cook. I make pasta. I make lasagna. Down at the mall, they got lasagna. It's good. For $1.99. I buy my lunch at school, and I buy my lunch every time. I buy large fries with lots of cheese and lots of gravy and ketchup and lots of mayonnaise. I like it. It's so good! All together. You should try it. It's so good. Lots of pepper, lots of salt. Lots of gravy. It's so good. I also buy chips and pop. Do you like salt and vinegar? Do you like dill pickle? Sour cream and bacon? I like it.

My wedding some day is so cool. Michael give me a ring, and he say, "Will you marry me?" I will wear a gown. White. It has a bonnet and a white dress and you know what that on your face. A veil. He wear a suit and tie, and Mom and Dad will come. My family. We have it here, at my house. We honk the horn, and I come out and they sing "Here come the bride, here come the bride, all dress and white!" After that they have confetti, and they throw confetti at us. Then we are married. We have apartment with balloons. His job is in college. Angus, too. Then we have babies. And parties. It's so cool.

Self-Love and Self-Acceptance: The Basics of Healthy Sexuality

We begin here. Yes, your child has a disability. This is not a "So what?" issue. Disability *does* make a difference, but not the difference that people seem to think. It doesn't mean anything more than that your child may take longer to learn some things than other children, and in some cases, a lot longer. It also means that she may have a visible disability about which others will make assumptions for her entire life. A physical or intellectual disability may involve adaptations and interventions. It also means that your child will require a greater store of love and acceptance in order to face some of what she will have to face. It's almost as if the heart will have to be very full so that it will take a lifetime for the "old love" to dribble through.

Why are we talking about this when the issue is sexuality? Well, to understand sexuality, you have to understand love. To understand love, you have to understand bonding. To understand bonding, you have to understand unconditional love. To understand unconditional love, you have to have felt it. Think logically and emotionally about the study finding mentioned earlier: Parents touch and talk less to children perceived as undesirable and unattractive. This is a hard fact to face.

It is important to remember that the images that people have in their heads about people with disabilities have been created in a society filled with prejudice, out of a past full of perceived "horrors," by a media bent on sensationalizing difference.

Dave's Story

I am an ugly man. I know that. I know that others who see me know that. I am treated like that daily. When I go out, I know that others will respond to me very differently from how they respond to others who are attractive. I have stood in line, clearly the next to be served, while the person behind the counter looks past me to offer service. I have been asked to leave clothing stores (I'm not kidding) by salespeople who tell me in patronizing tones that there is "nothing I would like" in their store. I am used to this now, and alternately it makes me laugh or makes me angry.

How do I know I am loved? By touch. By talk. These are the very things that can be deprived of children who, like me, are less attractive or less desirable. I thought about this last night. It had been a very hard day, and I lay down on the bed feeling lost, alone, and quite vulnerable. Without saying a word, the one who loves me (I hate ownership statements like *the wife, the hubby, the little missus, the big galoot*) came and lay down beside me. My eyes were closed, but I still enjoyed the feeling of closeness. Then a gentle hand touched my forehead, and for the next several blissful minutes, my forehead was stroked, my face gently rubbed, each one of my several chins caressed. Then some words flowed like honey; it doesn't matter what they were, but it matters that the tone was one of acceptance. I knew that I was loved.

Touch and talk, coo and stroke, murmur and caress—the very first lessons children need to learn is that they are valuable and desirable beings. The very parts of them that others will use to discriminate and deny need to be gently rubbed into acceptance the way a potter rubs a unique pattern into a bowl.

You're wondering about your child's abilities and your own abilities. At that point, childbirth is daunting enough. We were sitting for a day or so hardly able to look after ourselves. It was just too hard to get up and make a meal or even have a shower. Yet in the middle of all that, Nicholas was a vigorous, hungry little baby. He was the thread of sanity at that point. He was propelling us forward through enough time that it took to get over the initial shock and start healing.
—Elizabeth Popowich

Seeing is believing, right? We took Karen in to meet this couple in the hospital who were having such a hard time with the fact that their child had Down syndrome. I could see the mother just do a double take. Here was someone with Down syndrome who wasn't drooling and wasn't overweight and was actually quite civil and polite. She seemed to slowly switch her view from some vague

clinical view of someone with a mental disability to a more positive look at the whole person. There's an extra chromosome, and she does learn more slowly, true. But here's who Karen really is.
    —*John Lord*

A woman adopted a baby with a disability and was thrilled. Her baby was beautiful. One day when visiting, she was holding the baby and nuzzling the child's nose. She then used her thumb and stroked gently at her child's eyes. Almost like no one else was in the room, she said, "You have the most beautiful eyes; don't let anyone tell you anything else." A master potter was at work.

We wish this woman could have parented, even for a day, two women with disabilities who arrived at adulthood with a dismal lack of self-esteem. The first woman arrived with a trunkload of self-hatred. She had become self-injurious. She had to be in places where no shiny surfaces would allow her to see her own reflection. If she did, she would become agitated and begin to pummel her face with her fists. She hated who she was and what she looked like. The other woman would only whisper answers to questions. Staff members said that her family would always whisper about her and that when she spoke she was told to be quiet. She learned that invisibility was a desired goal. One woman needed intervention because of personal self-injury, and the other needed it because she made herself available to any man who would take her. A moment's desire, even if just for her body, would allow her to forget that she felt unattractive and undesirable.

It's important for new parents to realize their child is going to be all right. It's pretty overwhelming when you first learn your child had a disability. You can't see the forest for the trees for a while. The husband blames himself; the wife blames herself; they might blame each other. What did we do wrong? What did I do wrong? If you happen to be a certain religion, there may be some mea culpa going on. It's very powerful when the parents realize the child is going to be all right.
    —*Lou Shaw*

With Katherine, you don't really have a chance of getting away without getting drawn in. She's just there, and she draws you into her life and her day and whatever's happening with her. Bang, you're a part of her. I don't think I pay much attention to her disability; once you get to know her, it's really sort of secondary.
    —*Darryl Davey*

Touch and talk: These are powerful tools to begin an education about sexuality, selfhood, value, and worth. They are inherent elements of three major self-awareness concepts along the way to healthy sexuality:

I am loved.

I am welcome here.

My body is mine.

Touch

It's interesting that when something really moves us emotionally, we say we are *touched*. What we mean is that some *thing*, some *sense* reached right inside us and—well, there is no other way of explaining it—*touched* our emotions.

We were made to feel. The concept of touch, started at birth, grows from something physical to something emotional. Have you ever been out for a dinner with a friend and had him or her sit across the table from you? Over the course of dinner, you become wrapped up in a conversation, so much so that the rest of the world disappears and the only people who are there in the restaurant are the two of you. Soon you actually feel warmth flowing back and forth between the two of you. You feel embraced, but you never touch physically. What you were doing in that restaurant is a *very* adult version of what happens between parent and infant during a snuggle fest. We need to look at how people learn to show intimacy in ways that are quite abstract.

> *We visited him every single minute practically. We were constantly touching him, touching his toes. We had his bed so the sun would come through the window, and he'd blink his eyes, so we knew he could see the light. We'd tickle his toes and he'd jerk his feet, so we knew his reflexes were good. We bought a little tape recorder and hung the earphone just inside the isolette and we got him the three B's: Bach, Beethoven, and Brahms. Don wanted to get him The Who.*
> —Ronalyn Bradshaw

Dave's Story

Recently, I met for the first time a man in his forties with an intellectual disability. He said something nice; I said something nice. I could tell that he enjoyed the interaction. Then he wanted to hug me. My rejection of the hug caught everyone including him by surprise. You may think that I was mean, but I don't hug strangers. I didn't care that he had a disability. It was notable to me that his parents, who were there with him, were quite affronted. Good heavens, you would have thought that I had refused to hug *them!* Afterward, I took them aside, and the man's mother refused to speak to me. I think she thought that I "didn't really like people with disabilities" and therefore wanted nothing to do with an uncaring professional.

I told the man's father that I was not being cruel. In fact, I said, it would have been cruel for me to return the hug. I told him that after years and years of working with people with disabilities who had been raped and exploited, I couldn't give hugs any more. I told him that after hearing about the man with a disability who willingly followed some young men to a park and was target practice for martial arts and was beaten to death and that after seeing a woman with a disability refuse in a role-play situation to say no to unwanted touch, I couldn't let my behavior "lie" to people with disabilities. I couldn't teach them that all people are safe and that boundaries are unnecessary. I couldn't teach them that they could just hug anyone. I then said, "I am sorry that you thought I was mean, but

if your son is beaten or raped as a result of the fact that he didn't understand social boundaries, I wasn't part of the problem."

You may think that my response was harsh. And if you think that I upset
that father, you are right. He became very upset. At first he was upset with me.
He told me that he thought that I was being foolish and mean. Who would do
those things to a person with an intellectual disability? After getting home, I received a call from the host agency. They asked me if I would call my potential
hugger's mother. Ready for another attack, I braced myself and made the call. I
wasn't attacked. All the way home, they had talked about what I had said to the
man's father. Finally, the parents realized that their "boy" would hug anyone and
would give anybody anything and also that the world wasn't safe anymore. The
mom said, "You know, I would never let my daughter go out into public without
knowing how to take care of herself and how to size people up. I wonder why I
didn't think it was important for my son?"

Part of the reason that this mother didn't initially think that being cautious
with strangers was important for her son was because—don't think us judgmen-
tal here—perhaps she was unable to see her son as a *real* adult. We don't want
to lay any blame on the mother for this. First, society doesn't see adult people
with disabilities as adults. Second, some professionals never speak of people with
disabilities as having an adult future. The man's mother can be forgiven for giving into these two forces. A "real" adult has *boundaries* in a big time way. Part of
the journey the infant has to go through is the journey from being someone who
trusts absolutely to being someone who trusts conditionally. This can be a painful
journey, but it is one that must be made. It is also one that parents have to teach.

Don't even think it! A whisper just happened in your mind. You may have just
had an uncomfortable thought. You may have just thought, "I am not up to this.
This is too much. How do I teach things like boundaries and conditional trust?
Maybe all my feelings of inadequacies are right. Maybe I am not the best person
to parent this child."

Hold on! Look back at what that man's mother said. She said she knew that
her daughter, who did not have a disability, needed safety skills. Who do you
think taught her daughter those skills? We're betting Mom and Dad did. We're
betting they didn't say at any point, "Oh, God. Our daughter is becoming a
teenager and needs to learn how to establish boundaries and to be wary of trusting too easily. It's time to call 1-800-SOCIAL-WORKER." We're betting they
taught her naturally, over time. So touch, then, is important—starting as an infant and growing and changing, evolving within age-appropriate boundaries as
the child becomes an adult. But there is also talk.

*I don't think we raised Hillary any different than we did our older daughter,
who's now 22. The one thing that I know, though, that I remember, happened
when Hillary was about 2 or 3. She was sitting across from Mariah and copying
everything Mariah did. It was just like she was really trying to learn. She's always been someone who wants to learn. When she was 6 months old, I caught
her looking into a mirror, pushing her tongue in after we'd been working on
tongue thrusts.*
    —*Michele Shaw*

Florence Schulten, Ocala, Florida

It was my policy in my school that every child could make progress. If they came in with bad manners at the table or poor speech, that was the first thing we'd go to work on. I insisted that we were ladies and gentlemen before anything else. And we praised. Children need it. You can't just think, "Oh, she's doing fine." You have to tell her and let her know she's doing a good job, that you're proud of her. That's how children develop pride in themselves.

   —Florence Schulten

Talk

What is there to "talk" about with a child? Here's a story that we don't want you to find offensive but that we think is important. Dave was visiting a group home to do a consultation on communication with the staff. One of the reasons that he loves visiting this group home is that they have this enormous dog named Laura. She is a St. Bernard, which is one of the most beautiful breeds of dogs in the world. It acts like a cross between St. Francis and Mother Theresa. A gentle, big dog, it is a perfect pet for people in a group home. Visiting the home meant that Dave also got to visit Laura. She never moved fast, but she always managed, at some point, to gently lie her head on his lap and be petted. He loves dogs and could sit for hours chatting with and petting Laura.

Dave's Story

We were talking that day about communication. I was saying to the staff that they should be talking with the folks who lived in the house. I had noted that when I visited, the staff would be in one room talking with each other and the folks who lived there would be in another room, sitting quietly, waiting for staff to bring life and action into the room. I felt that the folks with disabilities were not quiet out of passivity but that they were quiet out of a skill deficit. Carrying on a conversation is a skill. They needed to up the amount of talk with folks in the house. Now, let's define *folks*. This was a home for children with disabilities. There wasn't a *folk* in the house more than 8 years old. One of the staff members said, "That's all well and good, but what do we talk to them about?" I went on and on about all of the things that could be talked about—and they took notes! There is a world of subjects to talk to a child about, and they took notes! They made a list!

(To my shock a week later, I visited the house and found that the staff had made the list into a little poster they kept up on the fridge. It looked something like this:

The weather

What happened at school

What happened on the weekend

Did you like dinner?

What do you want for breakfast?

It just seemed so gooney— but at least they were trying.)

After the initial consultation meeting, I went into the front room to sit and chat with some of the kids in the house. Laura dutifully followed behind me, probably for more pats but also probably because I still had a couple of cookies. After a time, the staff member who wanted the list came into the room and sat down across from me to continue a chat we had started in the front room. Laura, sensing that I would give her no cookies, went over to the staff member. The staff member rubbed Laura's face, saying, "What a good dog you are. I just love my Laura. Laura is the absolute best dog in the world. Laurasmaura, that's what I call her." She went on and on, talking with Laura and describing her—to Laura—as the best possible dog in the whole entire world.

This staff member, who felt she had nothing to say to a child with a disability, could carry on a conversation with a pooch for a long time. It took Dave a long time to process what had happened, and he felt foolish. The list that had been generated was a list of questions, the kinds of questions you would ask strangers. But the conversation between the staff and Laura was important. It was a constant flow of words that communicated nothing but value, worth, and love. Isn't that what we should be talking about when we talk to a child, particularly when we talk to an infant—any infant?

Sometimes it's still a little hard to get used to when people see us and the boys are walking together. Then Nicholas turns around, and you almost see the smiles sort of freeze a little on their faces. I guess not in a bad way, but they just freeze. Then they look up and take their cue from us. We could either smile back or grab Nic and hide him under our jackets like we're ashamed of him. We smile, and their faces go back to normal.

    —Greg Popowich

I think my biggest worry is that people won't accept Becca for who she is, that they won't allow her to grow. People have been very supportive, we've been lucky. I'd rather have people ask questions. One year, we were going to get Christmas pictures taken. There were eight of us, can you imagine? My sister was watching the kids, and I ran out to get something. On the way back, I passed two older ladies who were whispering, "I wonder what's wrong with that baby." I stopped and said, "They're my twin girls, and Becca has Down syndrome." They sort of looked at me, but it was okay. They were just wondering. People often just don't know. In some ways it's sort of like seeing someone with a birthmark or a burn; it's kind of hard not to look. So look. Get it over with. Then we're done. If you want, ask me.

—Dawn Thompson

I take Michael places with me. I took him to work with me. I took him to the saloon with me to have a beer. He didn't have a beer; he was too young, but I'd sit him up there and get him his chili and French fries. I used to be a cartoonist and considered myself pretty good, even got a letter from Walt Disney once. Now my boy's an artist. It's not something you can really teach somebody, but I help him and then we talk about what he's done. He's really trying. He's a good boy.

—George Creamer

It was a real worry for me when they moved away. How was I going to still be a real presence in the kids' lives? At the time, Erin was the only one who could read with meaning. Jim read but without much comprehension. Every week or two, I tried to make sure they got an audiotape from me. It sounds goofy, but I'd get storybooks from the library and read to them on tape. In an audioletter, I'd just talk to them about stuff going on with me and what I knew was going on with them. At first, it feels really artificial to take a break from work, go stand in the parking lot, and talk to your kids on a tape recorder. I'd take the tape recorder with me in the car and just talk to them as I drove. I just felt if my voice was there, I was with them.

—Richard Schwier

Remember the study that showed that parents talk less to children who are unattractive or less desired? This is true for many people. Watch a parent is pushing a buggy in the park as the child is lying in the buggy. When a person stops to talk to the parent, bends over, and sees a pretty little baby, that person coos and goos and says things like "such a pretty baby" and "look at the little snookums." We have been told over and over again by parents of kids with disabilities that this did not happen to their child. A person would look at their child and then look away quickly, as if she were embarrassed or, worse, as if she had seen some kind of monster. These looks are messages. We give children messages all of the time.

There was a trade fair set up in the mall, and a photo studio was calling for models, so we took [Rebecca] in. She loves to pose and smile for the camera.

Everyone just fell all over her, and she really hammed it up. It never occurred to
me that I shouldn't consider her a potential model.
    —*Shelly Garner*

What to Teach When

It's been more than 20 years since the World Health Organization called for an
understanding of human sexuality within the context of human relationships.
People with disabilities often learn how their bodies function sexually much later
in life than do their peers without disabilities if, indeed, they are ever taught at
all. Some people hold mistaken beliefs about their bodies, and ignorance leads to
misinformation and opportunities for sexual abuse (Ludwig & Hingsburger,
1993). People who have accurate information about sexuality are much less likely to be victimized than those who do not (Senn, 1988).

Keeping in mind the fact that every child is different, you may find the following list useful when you're deciding what to teach your child at different
ages. Remember to use the list as a general guideline, not as a hard and fast rule
that means disaster if the time doesn't seem to be right for your child:

The Early Years 3–9
• Differences between boys and girls
• Public and private places, parts of [the] body
• How babies are born

Puberty 9–15
• Menstruation
• Wet dreams
• Other body changes
• Ways to recognize and say no to inappropriate sexual touching by others
• How babies are made
• Sexual feelings
• Masturbation

Older Teens 16 and Up
• How relationships grow
• How sexual feelings happen and how they can be handled
• Homosexuality
• Difference between love and sex
• Laws and consequences of inappropriate sexual touching of others
• How pregnancy can be prevented—methods of birth control
• Sexually transmitted diseases
• Responsibilities of marriage, parenting (Maksym, 1990a, p. 107)

You can see that teaching someone with an intellectual disability about sexuality goes beyond merely getting her to correctly recite names for body parts or
to know how a baby is made. We believe it is important to integrate the physical, emotional, and social aspects of sexuality into what people are taught. People
also need to understand attitudes and values and learn practical skills in order to
respond in different situations. For example, when learning about her breasts, a
young girl needs to know that:

- Breasts have a functional and aesthetic purpose (physical aspect)
- Breasts are private body parts (social aspect)
- Since not everyone is comfortable discussing these things, it's important to find someone who is willing to answer questions and concerns (social aspect)
- [There are ways] to refuse unwanted advances if someone tries to touch her breasts (skill)
- That if someone tries to touch her breasts, she may feel bad about this (emotional aspect) (Ludwig & Hingsburger, 1993, pp. 5–6)

This guidebook is designed in a way that will help you, as parents, identify and practice what is important for your family. It can be overwhelming when you try to look at the big picture; from that vantage point, there are always things that you may have overlooked, didn't understand, or didn't even want to think about!

 ## Rest Stop:

Just for fun, make a list here of the fundamental principles or concepts you'd like your son or daughter to understand. Don't let any possible "no's" prevent you from writing down what you'd really like your child to know. Don't let language that might be embarrassing slow you down. Just jot down your ideas; you can edit them later if you need to. When you are done, read over your list. Can you say why each of your items are important?

What I want my child to understand	Why it is important

Sexuality and Sexual Functioning—the Facts

It's only been in the last year or so that she's starting to talk about her own sexuality and interests in boys. That's part of being 14. She's beginning to ask questions. She talks about relationships. The word sex pops up periodically, so we'll be dealing with her very honestly. She already knows that couples are not necessarily only male and female; she knows that, obviously, because she lives with us on a regular basis. Answering questions honestly is how we'll handle all her questions about sexuality.

—Bob Manwaring

We are back to *touch* and *talk.* As your child grows, new touch boundaries are established. Now you will need to talk directly about sexuality and sexual development. Diane Maksym urged parents to have open discussions and provide accurate information:

> All children show signs of sexual awareness: they touch their genitals; young children look at and touch other children; they masturbate; they giggle at someone of the opposite sex; they develop crushes; they want a girlfriend or boyfriend. Instead of worrying, we need to celebrate them as signs that our children are developing and growing like others...we're not suggesting that youngsters get the green light to behave in any way they wish. We just want to let you know that their feelings are normal. (1990b, p. 25)

Dr. Mary Coleman, co-author of *Medical Care in Down Syndrome: A Preventive Medicine Approach* (Rodgers & Coleman, 1992), said that sexuality is a field fraught with inadequate information and often misinformation. Each young person with an intellectual disability should be treated like any other person—that is, individually. The issues of contraception, HIV/AIDS, and so forth are usually as relevant as they are to everyone else (Coleman, personal communication, 1995).

There is a lot of information to cover. In order to know what to say, you can remember some simple facts. Here is a list of facts about sexuality and sexual functioning that you can look back on as you talk with your child.

1. Adolescence happens for kids with intellectual disabilities in exactly the same way it does for other young people. The same kinds of emotional, physical, and social changes occur in similar ways. The emotional aspect of adolescence can be more difficult for kids with intellectual disabilities because they may find that their sexual interest in others may be severely rebuffed. They may find that their parents are unwilling or unable to talk to them about dating, marriage, and parenthood. They may suddenly feel very alone and very undesirable. As such, the emotional "moodiness" that is associated with teenagers can be exacerbated.

2. Being unprepared for adolescence and its trauma has been tied to an increase in mental health and behavioral problems for people with intellectual disabilities (and most other teens). From refusing to go back to school where they feel their difference most keenly to severe depression and self-loathing, kids with disabilities have a difficult trip to healthy adulthood. (See the section called "Healthy Mind and Spirit" in Chapter 6.) But studies have shown, for example, that there are no significant differences in hormone secretion between young men and women with Down syndrome and their peers without disabilities (Pueschel, personal communication, 1996).

3. Sex education is vital for young teens with intellectual disabilities. There are several reasons for this. First, Sobsey (1994) suggested that the relative risk of abuse for people with disabilities is probably at least twice as high and may be five or more times higher than the risk for the general population. Sex education increases the likelihood that people with disabilities will either have the skills to stay safe or will report a victimization after it occurs. Both men and women with intellectual disabilities can have children. Unwanted pregnancy is a very real concern for young teens and their

parents. The issue of HIV/AIDS and intellectual disability is truly frightening. New studies show that the doubling rate of people with HIV in the population of people with intellectual disabilities is 22.5 months, the same rate as infants who are perinatally infected and people who are heterosexually infected (see Kastner, Nathanson, & Marchetti, 1992). It is important to note that the number of people with intellectual disabilities is low but that the infection rate among them is high. This means that we have precious little breathing time and that we have to make sure that people with disabilities get information because the danger is not just conceptual. It is real.

4. People with intellectual disabilities are capable of loving, marrying, and feeling sexual pleasure. With all of the doom and gloom reasons for sex education, there needs to be a balanced message. Sexuality and relationships are quite possible and desirable. People with intellectual disabilities have married successfully and have parented well.

5. If you heard that men with Down syndrome are sterile, that message comes from a different time. Many books state that there never has been a case of a man with Down syndrome fathering a child. For this to be a significant statistic, men with Down syndrome would need to be having sex at a normal rate. Because of years of oppression, restriction, and institutionalization, however, people with Down syndrome—and other intellectual disabilities—haven't had a whole lot of opportunity to have sex. There now has been at least one documented instance in which a man with Down syndrome has fathered a child (Sheridan, Llerena, Natkins, & Debenham, 1989). It has been said that men with Down syndrome have a low sperm count, but this is also old information. Unfortunately, no recent studies are available (Pueschel, personal communication, 1996).

6. There have been documented instances where women with Down syndrome have given birth (Pueschel, 1990). Although you may have heard that women with Down syndrome are infertile, this may not always be the case. At least 50% of women with Down syndrome are fertile (Pueschel, personal communication, 1996). Some studies that report that statistics showing low fertility in men and women with Down syndrome have to be looked at with some caution. Most fertility studies were done in institutions in which the people had never lived under normal circumstances.

7. The average age of menarche (the first menstrual cycle) has been falling steadily in America since the mid-1970s. It is now about 10.5–11.2 years of age. Young women with Down syndrome usually follow a similar pattern, with menarche ranging from 11 to 13 in some surveys (Elkins, 1995).

8. Women with intellectual disabilities have been known to have premenstrual syndrome (PMS) and suffer from the same symptoms as women without intellectual disabilities. The primary difference is that for women with intellectual disabilities, their access to adequate medical care may be limited and the issue may be seen as "behavioral" rather than "medical." It is important that behavior changes linked to menstruation be charted so that it can be determined whether the individual needs medical care, such as a pelvic exam, to determine whether other

problems exist or whether just the use of over-the-counter pain relievers would be helpful.

9. Studies regarding reproductive organs in some men and women with disabilities have found some differences. (Not all studies agree, however, so be cautious in reading about these differences. Remember, something that occurs *in general* may not happen *specifically* to your son or daughter.)

10. Some studies have suggested that women with some types of intellectual disability have slightly enlarged labia majora and underdeveloped labia minora. Some studies also showed that women with Down syndrome, for example, have a slightly enlarged clitoris. This again is old information, and more current research did not find this to be true (Pueschel, personal communication, 1996).

11. Men with Down syndrome tend to have penises with slightly diminished length but with slightly increased circumference. Some studies have shown that men with Down syndrome have smaller testicles than their typical peers. By and large, however, there is no problem with undescended testes in boys with Down syndrome as some older literature suggests. Occasionally, a boy with Down syndrome may have undescended testes, but the frequency is no greater than in the general population (Pueschel, personal communication, 1996).

12. Discussions about genitals, reproductive functioning, and sexually transmitted diseases for a particular "population" leaves one feeling like a whole group of people have been put under a microscope and studied like specimens in a laboratory. Let's not forget that no matter how the penis is shaped, no matter how "well formed" the labia minora, all people with intellectual disabilities are fully capable of loving others and enjoying the sensation that comes from being respected and loved.

Use this book as a kind of sexuality and self-esteem road map to help identify some main issues, a few paths you might like to explore, and some places you'd like to visit for a while. Throughout the book, you'll find "rest stops" or exercise breaks—like the one earlier in which you thought about some fundamental concepts that you want your child to learn. At these stops, you can make notes for yourself, jot down your own ideas, and make your own lists. What are the secrets of any good travel planner? Flexibility and the willingness to strike off down a new road, the ability to take a deep breath under pressure, and a sense of humor are always helpful, especially when your luggage gets lost!

Don't be afraid.
Don't pretend that all of this will take care of itself.
This book is a good start at feeling more confident and comfortable.
Put one foot in front of the other!

> *We wanted us to be an average family. Mom, Dad, and hopefully more than one child. I guess if I could take away that extra little chromosome, maybe Nicholas would have a more level playing field in many ways. But maybe there would be other things that would be missing, and maybe he wouldn't be the person who he is. I would miss that. That chromosome didn't take everything away, and*

maybe it added something. We realized right away, even at the tender age of 3 weeks, Nic was already a tremendous little teacher.
   —*Elizabeth Popowich*

Q

My wife and I are so uncomfortable with the thought of sex education for our son. We're not convinced he'll really understand it anyway. We're more concerned about making sure his behavior doesn't get him into trouble, even if it's just misinterpreted as sexual by someone else.

A

You may be concerned because when you think of sex education, what you are probably thinking of is *SEX* education. This is really a misnomer. Most of the educational curricula that have been developed for people with intellectual disabilities would more appropriately be called *relationship training* because they teach primarily about relationships and safety. Sure, there are one or two classes about genitals, but most classes are about friendships, social skills, grooming, manners, safety, and other neat stuff that kids need to learn. Go and take a look at some of the curricula that the educator wants to use. Don't be afraid to ask questions. The first question I would ask is "What age group was this curriculum developed for?" Many sex educators working with teenagers use teaching materials developed for adults. True, most also adapt the materials to their students, but you can never be sure that this will happen.

A wonderful, relatively inexpensive curriculum was developed for the Seattle Public School System. It is called *FLASH* (Family Life and Sexual Health; Stangle, 1991) and is brilliant and well targeted to young teenagers with intellectual disabilities. Check this one out; you might be very surprised at how it focuses on all of the things that you are probably concerned about: understanding relationships, developing boundaries, and making friends. By becoming informed about the curricula and realizing what is going to be taught, you may become more comfortable with the whole idea. You need to know, though, that most sex educators are very good at adapting information to your child's skill level. If your child has real limitations with learning, the educator may want to focus mostly on safety issues. If your child is becoming interested in the opposite sex and talks about dating, the educator will want to ensure that proper information about relationships is given. We also know from hundreds of studies that without sex education (relationship training), your son will be more likely to make a social mistake that will be interpreted as sexual. You need to ensure that "your issue" doesn't become his issue.

Q

Wait a second. Why all this emphasis on "touch" when you say people with disabilities are so vulnerable to abuse? Shouldn't we be respecting and encouraging our daughter's right not to be touched?

A

You are right. We need to respect all of the times when even our infant children don't want to be touched. We can usually tell by their facial expressions and—to be polite—their "little noises." What we mean about touch, though, is that research tells us that parents touch cute kids more than children who are "less cute." We worry that parents of kids with disabilities may fall victim to this trend. Children need to be loved by their parents. They need to be picked up, held, and tickled. They need to know that they are loved—exactly as they are. A man who is now in his fifties said he refuses to celebrate his birthday because "I was born bad, you know, 'wrong.' My mom and dad didn't love me. They didn't want me. I got sent away to a big institution. I lived there for over 20 years. I celebrate the day I got out of the institution. That is my birthday. 'Cause that is the day I knew that even if I was 'wrong,' I have the right to have a home and people who love me. So now I am 30 years out of the institution and been married for 10 years." This man's resilience is remarkable, but can you imagine who he would have been if for the first year of his life every touch had said "I love you"?

So, what we are saying is that from the get go, we respect times when children don't want to be bothered and fussed with. But we ensure that all the rest of the time is fair game for touches and hugs, tickles and kisses. A word of warning: A child's rejection of touch may be telling you something about his own sense of rejection. There are natural and fun ways to incorporate touch that aren't so upsetting to your child. Get creative: Everything from playing Pat-a-Cake to using "high fives" to show excitement can be used. But remember the bottom line: No means no. Self-awareness is the only way to tell what's really going on.

Q

My daughter is only 2! I don't think I need to think about this stuff yet. Come back when she's 14.

A

Your daughter is only 2, and you haven't started? Well, get cracking! You probably think we're kidding. Wrong. From a very early age, your daughter needs to learn about relationships, about ownership of her own body, about privacy, and about names for all of her body parts. The trouble is that when people think about sexuality or sex education, they always think about genitals. You are quite right; 2 is a bit early to start talking reproduction and the wonderful journey the egg makes down the fallopian tube. But it isn't too early to think about how to teach privacy, modesty, and personal boundaries. In fact, parents who don't think about teaching these things can inadvertently teach things they will have difficulty "unteaching" or changing later on.

For example, you can teach privacy from an early age by teaching dressing with a closed bedroom door and by teaching kids to wear housecoats when out of their bedrooms. From there, start teaching names for all of the body parts: arms, legs, hands, vulva (please teach *vulva* for female genitalia—the vagina is inside the body, and therefore *vagina* is the incorrect word for women's external genitalia) and so forth. Then you can teach about how some body parts are private body parts. *Private* means three things: It means that no one can touch it without permission, that no one can see it without permission, and that it shouldn't be shown to another person who doesn't want to see it. From there, you can start to teach about relationships, then move on to social distance. Let's get to work here!

Q

Our son is 22. He's a very friendly person, and people enjoy him. Whether or not we have people over, as soon as he gets lost in the conversation, or when he's watching television, he starts fiddling with his penis. I wouldn't call it masturbating because it seems quite absent-minded and is just sort of a pushing or rubbing through his pants or pajamas. We speak to him about it being private and okay in his room when he's alone. He says okay, but it doesn't last. We're afraid if we start sending him out of the room, he'll interpret it as punishment. But if he doesn't learn the appropriate place, he's going to upset and maybe frighten somebody. I worry about him going to a sleepover.

A

From what you describe, your son is just "fiddling." Given that he is 22, you would know if this was masturbation what with erections and sperm and all of that. So find something else for his hands to do. Get him something to fiddle with, like a Rubik's Cube, a worry stone, a small ball, or some other object, rather than send him out of the room. He probably doesn't understand your talk about privacy because he probably isn't even aware that he's fiddling. So redirect him to something else. Because you are introducing something here, try to find something "cool" for him to fiddle with. Introducing a childlike toy is probably not a good idea. So go in search of adult toys—there are lots of them out there.

Q

On her way home from volunteer work, my daughter, 24, usually stops in at a couple of stores near our home. One older shop clerk always makes a huge fuss over her, gives her candy, and talks to her as if she were 6. He means well, and she loves the attention, but how do we intervene without hurting anyone's feelings?

A

Is this older clerk the only person who does this? If he is, then maybe you should just ignore it. It doesn't seem to be worth a whole lot of confrontation if this is an isolated incident. There will be bigger battles to fight. If it's a common thing with many people, though, you need to look at what's going on. You might have to ask yourself how your daughter is presenting herself. Does she present herself as an adult? Has she learned to be a young woman? You mention she's 24; the transition from childish and childlike behavior to adult bearing and mature behavior can be very difficult for people with disabilities. If your daughter is "acting" like she's 6, she may be pushing the "pity button" that many people have.

   If you determine that this is happening because of pity or a sort of benevo-
lent prejudice among a lot of folks, well, then it's time to teach your daughter
how to speak up. Ensure that she's proud of the fact that she has her own
money. Teach her to say, "I work hard for my money, and I like to spend it,"
rather than to just accept gifts of candy. Besides, at 24, she should have learned
"never to take candy from strangers." She has to learn to say, "no," or, perhaps,
"no, thank you." Watch your own language and tone of voice; make sure you
have made the transition to parenting an adult, not a child. This is a harder
transition than you might think!

Chelsea, Thomas, and Denise Duffey
Mt. Dora, Florida

Chapter 4

Hold Me Tight

Some wit or wag once said that the four stages of parenting are

- Hold me tight
- Put me down
- Leave me alone
- Let me go

There is real truth to that statement. Chapters 4–8 explore some of the pleasures and problems experienced by families with sons and daughters who have intellectual disabilities in passing through these stages.

In *Shared Feelings: A Parent Guide to Sexuality Education for Children, Adolescents and Adults Who Have a Mental Handicap (Discussion Guide)*, Diane Maksym presented a straightforward "bill of rights" for parents who want to be effective sexuality teachers for their children. It offers some good reminders as parents wade through their children's development, a time sometimes made murky by old stereotypes about people with disabilities and even old myths about sexuality itself!

1. Mothers and fathers should both be involved in the sex education of their children.
2. Parents have a right to set standards of conduct in the family.
3. Parents have a right to privacy and time alone together.
4. Children have a right to facts about sexuality.
5. Children have a right to discuss sexuality with their parents.
6. Children have a right to privacy.
7. Children have a right to learn how to make their own decisions.
8. Children have a right not to be touched when they don't want [to].
9. Children should not be punished for their feelings.
10. Parents have a right to adequate support services. (1990b, p. 19)

Build Strength and Self-Esteem

Infancy for children with disabilities is different from infancy for children without disabilities. The major difference right now is not so much with your child but with others around him. You need to ensure that others *hear* how you speak to your child and how you expect him to be spoken to. We're not just talking about content but tone of voice as well. You may have never imagined yourself as a role model, but congratulations! Now you're one not only for your son or daughter with a disability but also for other family members.

The surest route to building self-esteem is to teach your child about having and meeting expectations. We are big advocates of having dreams or sometimes even exceeding them. One of the healthiest things that the mind does is to create a dream world wherein we are all exactly who we should be, where we should be, and doing what we should be doing. Yet, dreams are wildly misunderstood. Let's get this clear: Dreams are, by definition, unachievable. We often confuse the words *dream* and *goal*. These are two very different words. Goals are what we work toward with a reasonable degree of hope for success. Dreams are what we work toward and never really expect to achieve but are fun to have anyway.

When I hear that parents of kids with disabilities should be realistic, *it makes me think they're saying that you shouldn't dream about winning the...lottery but it would be okay for you to dream about winning some turkey raffle. You should be happy with that because it's more* realistic! *What's wrong with having some high hopes?*

   —Greg Popowich

I have difficulty in expressing a dream that I may have for Brad because Brad has demonstrated his ability to have his own dreams. All the things we have dreamed that he might be able to do, he can do. But those are our *hopes. His dream is to dance, and he has showed the world he can do that. We've allowed Brad to be independent just like the other boys. Each has to make their own mistakes; every one of them has left their marks on our vehicles, their own distinctive dent in some fender or bumper. There's the odd fence post or tree missing. But each has to be allowed to try and fail. I guess my hope for Brad's future is that he gets the same opportunities to develop his talents and interests as anyone else.*

   —John Magnus

We're betting that if you are like us, you had a dream or hope for yourself that lodged somewhere in the region of your heart when you were between 7 and 12 years old. Here you are now, an adult, and you know that you will never, ever achieve that dream. But it's still there. More than that, we're betting that every now and then when you drive to work, a magical thing happens. Your body takes over doing the routine aspects of the drive, and your heart and mind become free to wander (ever arrive at work and not remember driving there?), and during that time, that dream in your heart dislodges and overtakes you. That little taste of your dream is still sweet.

   Right from the start, you need to talk about your child as an individual with a future and with potential. When people offer sympathy or pity on the birth of a child, you need to cut them off at their metaphoric knees. Do not allow this outpouring of pity to occur. Do not allow people around your child to begin to talk about your child as "hopeless" or "futureless." Let them know that *you* see your child as a child who will grow into a competent adult. Let them know that *you* intend for your child to be treated like a legitimate member of the family. Let them know that *you* intend for your child to go to school, go to work, get married, and live independently. And let them know that *they* will not speak of or to your child as anything less than a child.

Someone gave a talk about [how society views disability] and said it was sort of an ABC equation. A is the event, B is the belief system in our society, and C are the consequences of those beliefs. So, you have a child with a disability. If the belief is that this is a tragedy, then the consequence is that you'll spend your life basing everything on the belief that it's a tragedy. Or you can make inroads into that societal belief and change it to one that says this is a child with different abilities who may need support but he is a child and a wonderful gift. If we see

Peggy Hutchison and John
Lord, Kitchener, Ontario

*the child as a way to help people grow and if he brings out the good in people,
then the consequences are so much healthier.*
    —*Elizabeth Popowich*

*When people ask about Karen, I don't even talk about Down syndrome. I talk
about Karen. She meets people. She's a wonderful part of our family. I would
hope families would remember to see their child that way, but it's often a struggle. They get hit with the clinical stuff first, then the disability system stuff falls
into place with a thud. Because we've seen people get trapped, Peggy and I made
a conscious effort to see that Karen would be a part of our family and a part of
community life, the day care, the Girl Guides, whatever classes she wanted to
take, part of our lives in every way.*
    —*John Lord*

    This need to show how others should interact with your child goes double if
a professional is less than encouraging about your child's potential. When parents are told by professionals that their children should be "prepared for the reality of their disability" and encouraged to "dream realistically," parents need to
look professionals in the eye and tell them to back off. We need to coin a new
word. *Dreamicide* is the word we should use to describe the mass murder of the
dreams of people with disabilities. We often hammer at children's dreams with
the club we call *reality*.
    This may seem a bit harsh, but pity can kill initiative, self-esteem, and per-
sonal growth—for *you!* Yes, it does the same thing for your child, but on hard
days you will wonder, "Why do I bother? The kid's got a disability, and nothing
is going to change that." We know that at the end of the day, yes, a kid with a
disability is still going to have a disability, no matter how good a parent you are.
But we also know that a kid with a disability who grows up with expectations, a
sense of belonging, a sense of purpose, and a sense of hope is going to go further
than any dour predictions made by pitying relatives or friends.

*The doctor said, "We're pretty sure he has Down syndrome." Well, jeez, what's
that? But he was great about it. But what I remember most about that night*

was another guy who was there. His wife just had a baby, too. His baby had a birthmark on her leg, and this guy was hounding the doctor about whether they could do surgery on his kid to get rid of it. There I was, happy that the doctor was trying to save my kid's life, happy with what I got, not knowing if he'd live. Here was this guy, whining about a little birthmark on the inside of his daughter's knee. Then they brought my baby out in the transport unit, wrapped up in silver foil. He looked like a baked potato.

—*Don Bradshaw*

I used to be kind of on the defense when [Michael] was little. To me, he was beautiful. So when people would stare, I always thought to myself, "Why are they looking at my boy?" I had a couple of run-ins that I hate to admit now. I said to one little kid, "What are you looking at? You're not so good looking yourself!" Well, I could have smacked myself in the mouth as soon as I said it. But I've developed a tougher skin over the years.

—*Peggy Creamer*

Dick Sobsey, a parent of a son with disabilities, offers a list of suggestions to help parents and caregivers promote the kind of interactions and environment that will encourage self-esteem and a positive sense of the future in your child:

1. Begin early. It is much easier to develop self-esteem in young children than to repair damaged self-esteem in older children and adults.
2. Support and encourage the development of affectionate bonds between yourself and the child.
3. Whenever possible, encourage learning through reinforcement and minimize the use of punishment.
4. Accept each individual for who he or she is. Avoid focusing on the things that he or she cannot do.
5. Do everything possible to build your own self-esteem. We need to feel good about ourselves before we can help others to do the same.
6. Interact with the child. Avoid domination.
7. When correction is necessary, focus on building the desired behavior and not overly much on eliminating problems.
8. Arrange for the child to have opportunities for success.
9. If things go wrong, seek solutions, not someone to blame.
10. Do at least some things just because they are fun. Encourage your children to do the same.
11. Seek out the people who make you feel good about yourself and your family.
12. Celebrate the positive things in life. If they are rare, that is even more reason to celebrate them. (1994, pp. 198–199)

So, as you teach others around your child how to think and speak about your child, you also teach your child. You will need to recognize and celebrate your child's growth milestones. You need to pick up the phone and shout for joy into Grandma's ear when your child says that first word. When your child takes that first step, get out the video camera. All of these are things that parents celebrate. That your child has a disability doesn't exempt you from the celebration. The celebrations are just as important. Your child, no matter what her age, needs to see excitement and approval in your face while taking her first step into the future. Let your child overhear you when you talk about how wonderful she is and how well she is learning new things. All children love to eavesdrop on their parents, so use the opportunity to build pride.

I've gotten into arguments with people who talk about the research going on into a "cure" for Down syndrome. I look at it this way. I have my daughter Hillary. I like her. I like who she is. I don't think I want to give her something or take something from her that would change her into a different person. If they offered us a potion, I wouldn't give her a teaspoon of it.
    —Lou Shaw

If you find something the person is interested in, you must encourage them. The feeling of accomplishment adds to life. I play the violin. I used to play for square dances but not much any more. But if I wanted very badly to learn and nobody helped me or thought I couldn't learn, I would be very sad. The minute someone believes in you, you can lick the world. Everyone has a soul. Everyone has ability. Everyone wants to learn. You just start.
    —Florence Schulten

When interviewed for the videotape documentary *Your Baby Has Down Syndrome* (Cohen, 1994), Karen and Donald Lucas of Pittsburgh, Pennsylvania, said they were firm about teaching their son Danny that anything is within his reach. "If he wants to try something, we'll try it," said Don. "Until he shows us he can't, we'll give it a good shot. If he comes to me and says, 'Dad, I want to learn to drive,' the last thing I would say is 'No, you can't.'"

The concept of not being able to do something because of disability is one that will not see much light in Danny Lucas' home. This is a child whose sense of self-worth is being nailed down solidly by his parents as he grows from infant to child, from child to teenager, and from teenager to adult.

"What you think of your child is reflected in the child," said Karen Lucas. "If he knows what you think of him is good, then he feels better about himself. If he feels confident in himself as an adequate human being, he can go out and be what he wants to be. Even when he was little, I *never* said to him, 'No, you can't do that' or 'You can't learn that.'"

I had one girl with a disability who learned to ride a big quarter horse. I have a beautiful picture of Phyllis riding like the wind, with her hair blowing back. Every time she hit the saddle, she would sing that Dale Evans and Roy Rogers song, Happy Trails. Now, she didn't sing too well because she couldn't carry a melody to save her soul, but on that horse she was no longer a young woman with a disability. She was Dale Evans. She would ride that horse, and she felt so free. You could hear her singing, completely off key, as she rode in the pasture. I go into a dream world now and then where I imagine myself as a marvelous tango dancer. What's wrong with that?
    —Florence Schulten

Rest Stop:

In the box below, list at least three things someone has said to you that made you feel stronger, prouder, more successful, or better looking! Describe how you felt physically and emotionally when those things were said.

Things people said that made me feel stronger, prouder, better looking, and so forth	How the comments made me feel

One of the basic elements of self-esteem comes from the comfort in being part of a valued social circle. To have and be a friend is a powerful motivator for anyone to learn and grow. In British Columbia, families compiled a list of suggestions and strategies that have been helpful in creating and nurturing friendships and connections for their children. While every family situation is unique, these families offered these ideas as some place to start:

- We can teach simple social skills such as greetings or how to invite someone to play. We can assist our children and teens in making (or receiving) phone calls.
- We can interpret for our children, helping others understand their needs or style of communication while helping them understand other peoples' intentions and overtures.
- We can ensure our children have opportunities to give to others, whether it be cards, letters, greetings, phone calls, invitations, or tokens of friendship.
- We can encourage our children to make decisions, have opinions, and state their likes and dislikes.
- We can try to give our children as typical a routine day and lifestyle as possible to minimize differences.
- We can find environments in which our children can succeed, using their interests and strengths in different settings.
- We can discuss our children's friendships with them at home, talk about what it means to be a friend or to have a friend, and ask about particular friends and what they like to do together. Or, we can ask whether there is someone they would like to get to know better.
- We can follow our children's lead in making choices of friends, activities, interests, habits, or social style. (Rousseau, 1995, p. 14)

Being sure that we have our children's best interests in the forefront of our decisions will ensure success, even if the process takes a little longer.

> *We recognized early on that the more people he knew and the more people who knew him, the better. With any child, the more contacts and the more friends you have, the more people there will be to see you through. If people get to know him, they're not going to write him off based on a stereotype. I want both of our boys to grow up healthy and happy and to have someone they love, lots of people they know, but someone special for each of them, too. I want it all!*
> —Elizabeth Popowich

> *It's very hard to think about what you want for your child when they're still so young. It's hard to know what to expect. We want her to be healthy. For us, health means being able to be active and talk and grow. She's an individual and she has so much growing to do. We don't know what she'll be like or what she'll be able to do. Who knows?*
> —Denise Duffey

Parallel Talk: Say It!

There are some facts about intellectual disabilities, which apply starting from birth, that need to be understood. One fact is that people with intellectual disabilities have difficulty learning from context. Dr. William Cohen (1994), Director of the Down Syndrome Center at Children's Hospital in Pittsburgh, said that "how far someone's likely going to get in life is going to be somewhat different than if they didn't have [a disability]...It affects people's cognitive abilities, but we know there's a range. But there's a range in typical people, too."

Most of us are probably very good at picking up subtle social cues, and we have learned to see the world around us and select relevant information. People with disabilities struggle with this for their entire lives. A type of communication that helps with this is called *parallel talk*. This is a flow of words that just describes what's going on. It is a very easy task when learned but can be a bit difficult to get used to. The more you do it, the easier and more natural it will become.

If you were about to take your child out to visit your parents, using parallel talk you would just describe to your baby what you are doing. "I'm picking you up now, and we are going to go and get you dressed. I picked out some of your favorite clothes. Let's see. Oh, look, I've got your yellow shirt." You will note that this is pretty natural stuff and that parents often do this with their children. Parallel talk gives vocabulary and context. It will be a tool that you will be able to use for many, many years to come. As you play with your child, work with your child, or even go on a drive in the car with your child, parallel talk gives you something to say and involves your child in your life.

Teaching your child with an intellectual disability is not a great deal different from teaching your other children. Generally speaking, as a parent, you should model the kind of behavior you want: Say things out loud, encourage and expect growth, and praise, praise, praise. Be consistent; it's difficult for anyone to learn a skill or behavior if the rules—and the consequences—keep shifting.

*When she was about 8, she came in with a ponytail and she had done the rub-
ber band by herself. I don't know where she learned how to do that, and she'd
done it behind her back. She probably listened while someone else was doing it
and remembered. I told her right away I liked her hairstyle and that she'd done
a good job. It's important to notice when your child does something well. You
need to say so.*
    —Michele Shaw

Greg Plosz, a teacher, is the parent of a 22-year-old daughter and 20-year-
old twin boys, one of whom has an intellectual disability. Modeling and talking
have been common practice in their household for the last two decades. "It's not
good enough to hope that Jay will just *get it* the way Laura did or the way Dave
does," said Greg (personal communication, 1998). "When we wanted to move
Jay along to be interested in more age-appropriate things instead of *Barney* and
Mr. Dressup, I spent time with him watching sports and going to hockey games.
With his clothes, his brother and sister were always there to lead the way, but we
all make a real point of telling him when he looks nice and why." Greg said it
takes some learning for parents to get used to praising as much or more than they
correct. "If we're all going out for dinner, we talk about what we're going to wear
beforehand, not at the pressure point when it's time to head out the door. I say
out loud to Jay, 'Well, we're going out for a nice dinner, so I'd better go shave so
I look good.' You just learn to be more encouraging and positive. That makes you
a better person anyway."

Develop Values

*People always compliment us on the fact that Michael is such a polite, well-
mannered person. He's very religious, very spiritual and so am I, so maybe he
got that from me. He's the only one of my kids who goes to church regularly,
and he takes up the collection every week. I think I instilled in him some of the
values I felt were important. Sometimes it's good, and sometimes it's bad if
you're very accepting and trusting because it can open you up to ridicule, but
you're still a better person for it.*
    —Peggy Creamer

Your child will develop not only a theoretical sense of values but also action-
oriented values by watching how you treat other family members and people
outside the family and how you expect to be treated in return. Take your child
along when you're doing a favor for a neighbor; let her help you take in the mail,
shovel the walk, or deliver groceries. On a walk to the grocery store, stop and pick
up litter and talk about why it's everyone's job to keep the neighborhood clean.
Speak kindly of others, and encourage your child to do the same. If something
goes wrong, avoid angry finger-pointing and blaming others. Show your child
how problems can be worked out through discussion. You can do some things
consistently to encourage your child to absorb what is valued by your family:

- Treat others with respect and consideration.
- Recognize and praise the good behavior of your child, her siblings, and her friends.
- Encourage curiosity, independent thinking, and problem solving.
- Encourage self-expression.
- Be consistent in approving or disapproving of certain behavior.
- When you discipline your child, let her know it is the *behavior,* not her, that you disapprove of.
- Give reasons for your decisions.
- Keep the promises you make to your child.
- Your home and school are the laboratories where your child learns values by observation, by limitation, and by reward and punishment.
- Approval or positive reinforcement is more effective than punishment in teaching values.
- Show your child you love her. (Down Syndrome Association of Los Angeles, 1995)

Getting your kids to value what you do doesn't just come from them hearing about it; it comes from them watching how you live your life. The disadvantage you have as the parent who doesn't live with them all the time is that you want your kids to experience you first hand. You're a two-dimensional reputation. For someone like Jim, who needs concrete experience, and the other kids, too, I worry about who I am to them. You try to exhibit your values when you are together and hope over time you build a history of real experiences. Part of Jim's way of dealing with people is to overlook the stereotypes and see you as you really are. Maybe he's got the answer.
  —Richard Schwier

If you're a young parent, it won't be long before you realize that your child is an absolute miracle. If you're a more seasoned parent, you might begin to wonder what all the fuss was about in the first place. As this happens, you will face one of the most difficult questions that people ask themselves after they first discover that those who are *different* are not particularly different after all. You will begin to ask the question, "What is normal, anyway?"

Dave's Story

I would like to tell you of a religious experience I had. I was on a lecture trip to New Mexico. On a weekend off, I went to Acoma Pueblo near Albuquerque. This may be the most holy ground that I have ever walked on. The small village is built high in the sky, 400 feet up on the mesa, and nonnative visitors are not allowed to be unattended.

Our guide took us up the mountain, and our first glimpse of the community was a group of small houses that looked like they were formed right out of the earth. I was blinded by the simple beauty and how the native architects had built structures in such harmony with the ground, the sky, and the horizon. We walked through the streets and then turned a corner and saw an absolutely huge cathedral built in the Spanish style. It was so out of place that it took my breath away.

We walked into the building and were told of how the Spanish had forced natives into labor and how the logs to build the huge structure were hoisted up the side of the mountain. Many natives perished during the building of the cathedral. We walked out of the cathedral, and I found myself next to the guide. I told him that I couldn't believe what I saw. He misunderstood me and asked if I found the building beautiful, like all the other tourists madly snapping pictures of the church.

I told him that, no, I did not find it beautiful. I found it at best odd or unusual. It seemed lost and out of place. It was a building that did not belong there. He looked at me and asked if I understood native ways. I said no but that I did understand when things don't fit. He said that the Spanish wanted to consecrate the ground. Then he said, "Holy is not what is created. Holy is what was created." Pow! This was a revelation. When we talk about *normal,* we always assume that there is a norm and that the norm is determined by counting. The more of one thing there is, the more *normal* it is. How weird. If we apply the guide's thinking to the situation of disabilities and norms, we would say, "Normal is not what *is* created. Normal is what *was* created." Therefore, it is normal to have a disability. No facial operations, educational programs, or parenting strategies can create normalcy. Your child *was* already created as he or she should be. Nothing more *is* necessary.

This is pretty powerful stuff for a Saturday off.

Donna Serblowski

I have lots of cousins. Six brothers, one die. Four sisters. My family is good. I like them. They are good people, my family. I have lots of pictures, albums.

I have my room here. At Mom's. I have my room in Cudworth, just myself. I work at the shop. At my work, do bottles. Recycle. I get some money. Buy clothes. In the store. I like new clothes. I like red.

Come home on weekends, I rest. Get home Saturday. Stay home Sunday. See my mom. She is good person. We play games, puzzles. Go for a drive, visit, my sister's. Go downtown Bruno. I vacuum. Help my mom. I straighten up the kitchen! She is messy, my mom, sometimes. I straighten up for her the kitchen. Pick strawberries. A bunch of strawberries. The birds eat them, such a nuisance. Mom makes good stuff. Food. Potatoes.

We get along, all my brothers, sisters. Kenny is good to me. He is always my brother. Janet is my sister, too. She is a good person. And Elaine. My brother is on the farm. And Elaine is on farm. In Regina. Edmonton. My brothers and sisters.

Got a wedding in August. I go with Mom. I never have boyfriend. Nope. Just me. Sometimes I like one. He look like a normal person. Black hair, I like that.

I take my medication. Twelve o'clock. Five o'clock. I have seizure. I fall down. Then I am sleepy.

I am happy. Sometimes sad, I cry. I don't know, just do.

I'm a good person. Great person. Very nice person. I am pretty, nice hair. Sometimes I get hiccups, too.

Parent Support: Find Allies

*In the delivery room, I remember saying to Greg—and he agreed—"Promise
me no matter what you're thinking, even if you feel it's stupid or not worth
mentioning, let's talk. Let's talk about everything."*
     —Elizabeth Popowich

Remember Dick Sobsey's 11th suggestion for helping your child to develop
self-esteem? "Seek out the people who make you feel good about yourself
and your family" (1994, p. 199). If most of our interactions are positive, even if
there are a lot of unanswered questions about our child's opportunities and
potential, we tend to build positive self-esteem and to gain confidence in our
own abilities.

*We have supper together now and then; we have birthday parties with all of us
together. It's healthy for the children to see everyone together getting along. I
think sometimes parents of kids with disabilities tend to find ourselves so involved in the kids' lives that disconnecting is very painful. There are some families who never do it, who can never let go. There are a lot of older parents who
never reached out and are very worried as they get older about what will happen to their children.*
     —Bob Manwaring

Though families may seek support at different times, you may want to make
early contact with other parents who have kids with intellectual disabilities. You
might just be surprised to find a group of parents who are supportive, fun, and
all incredibly proud of their children. Oh, yes, you will also find anger, frustration, and deep, deep resentment, but this is almost always targeted at schools,
relatives, governments, professionals, and society in general. These meetings are
both social and supportive. Some parent support groups also have newsletters
and other means of keeping up to date with what is going on. Check the
"Recommended Resources" section at the end of this book to find a group you
can write to for information or a World Wide Web site you can visit.

*I want parents to have the self-confidence they need to drive the system and to
create a vision for their child's life. Your vision doesn't have to stay within the
narrow boundaries of what is already offered for "the disabled." I encourage
parents to learn so they know what they're dealing with. It's like getting on a
train. You need to have an idea of your destination, even if the landscape
changes as you travel. Your vision may even change a million times, but don't
be afraid of change. The parents who are stuck are those hanging on to the old
ways because they worked hard to get there. New things come along, and you
must be open to them.*
     —Gayle Foy

Parent organizations can do much more than simply provide you with facts
about disabilities and lists of services available. Most important, perhaps, is that

these parents have experienced some of what you are facing, no matter what your age, the issue, or the stage of your child's development. Even if you're traveling the path well, they may be able to reach back and point out the shortcuts and the quicksand. And sometimes its helpful to have other parents point out the obvious: The disability "is powerless to trespass into our children's personalities...each one's personality is as unique, fascinating and vital as any other child's" (Down Syndrome Association of Greater Cincinnati, n.d.).

Shortly after I came out, I contacted a group called Gay Fathers. We get together twice a month. One of the interesting things about the choices I've made is that when it came to a gay relationship, I didn't know the rules. Or are there rules? The girls have just sort of learned with us as we go along. I had separated from Joyce for about a year and a half. I remember thinking, here I was, a guy with three kids. Who was going to be interested in me?
—Bob Manwaring

Although other parents may be struggling with their own battles, they can also remind you to enjoy your child, yourself, and each other. Loretta LaRoche is a diminutive Italian grandmother who appeared on television with a program called *The Joy of Stress: How to Prevent Hardening of the Attitude* (n.d.). She reminded people to laugh, find the humor in themselves, each other, and their children, and said that there are too many magical moments in this life to waste it with too much self-pity and self-flagellation. If we approach it right, she said, we are brought back to earth, time and again, by our children. When she feels down, she explained to a group of parents, she often goes to visit her young granddaughter for "treatment": "The last time I went, I found her standing in the living room, stark naked...in high heels. And she was applauding herself. When was the last time you did that?"

Some Canadian families offered a list of practical suggestions that will not only ease anxiety about the connections in the community for your children but also help you as a parent share concerns and ideas and surround yourself with positive people:

- We can expand our own circle of friends to model a full social life and to broaden our network of personal support. We can examine how we support relationships for typical children and ourselves.
- We can inform ourselves about such topics as group dynamics and social skills.
- We can ask for help. We can talk with other parents to share strategies and ask people at school, as well as family, friends, or neighbors, for support.
- We can make friendship development a family priority.
- We can understand the natural cycle of friendship. For all of us, friends come and go and change with time. It will be no different for our children. (Rousseau, 1995, p. 15)

Don, Riley, and
Ronalyn Bradshaw
Saskatoon, Saskatchewan

One of the most important things is family support. We have exceptional support on both sides. Everyone accepted Riley exactly the way he was from the beginning. Everyone fell in love with him. My dad wrote me a letter when Riley was born; I still have it, and I cry whenever I read it. He wrote how proud he and Mom were of me.
　　—Ronalyn Bradshaw

Another great wellspring of support and comfort for parents is sometimes overlooked. Grandparents and other extended family can be an important element in the network that parents build around themselves, and although every family has its unique dynamics, grandparents can be tapped for their child care skills, moral support, and understanding. Even in a relationship that is distant or strained, the needs of a grandchild with a disability may be what draws a family back together. But, like parents, grandparents need information about their grandchild's needs, the specific disability, disability issues, and new philosophies. Occupational therapist and social worker Anita Unruh is an associate professor at the School of Occupational Therapy, Dalhousie University. She offered strategies to "strengthen and support the relationship between family and grandparents. Often what has been helpful for parents may also be useful for grandparents" (1995, p. 41). These strategies may be useful to keep in mind for other family members, too:

1. Recognize that grandparents need time to adjust to the birth of a grandchild with a disability and may need opportunities to express their feelings and concerns.

2. Provide opportunities for grandparents to obtain information and ask questions. Grandparents may be interested in pamphlets and books about the child's disability.

3. Encourage grandparents to attend medical appointments with the child's doctor. Arrange to have some time set aside for grandparents to ask their own questions about the child's needs.

4. Invite grandparents to attend appointments with your child's therapists to learn about special care strategies. Grandparents may be especially interested in how to encourage play and social interaction, particularly if the child has difficulties in these areas.

5. Talk to grandparents about what support or assistance from them would be helpful to the family and manageable within the grandparents' available time, energy, and resources.

6. If possible, introduce grandparents to other children with disabilities and their families.

7. In some situations, it may be helpful to seek specific help for parents and grandparents through family counselling. (1995, p. 41)

I told my Dad that Nicholas had Down syndrome, and his response was really no different than if I had told him Nicholas had ears. They were concerned about how we were handling it. But they thought since he was their grandson, he was perfect already! One grandmother was particularly wonderful. She said Nic was our boy, he was just fine. She wasn't in denial about the disability, but she said, "Be fierce in loving this baby, and don't let anyone tell you different."
　—*Elizabeth Popowich*

As you are making your community connections, you will also want to forge a really good relationship with your doctor. This can be difficult at times. Waiting-room delays before appointments can be frustrating, especially when you have several rambunctious children in tow and a gazillion other errands to run. Also, with all the medical jargon that may come your way, it's important to remember that there is a difference between fact and opinion. It is a fact that people with certain kinds of disabilities sometimes have medical complications involving the heart. It is an opinion that their heart doesn't work the same as others do.

Remember that doctors, like anyone else, are not always totally free of prejudice. It is interesting to note that minorities are now choosing doctors and therapists who come from within their minority group. There seems to be a sense that, as a patient, one is vulnerable anyway, so why enhance that vulnerability by choosing a doctor who is clearly different from you? Women discovered a radically different health care when they started to see female doctors. All of a sudden, they had "symptoms" rather than "complaints." You need to talk to your child's pediatrician and ask pointed questions regarding his attitude about people with disabilities.

My own family doctor, whom I loved dearly, looked at me and said, "Why don't you put her in an institution? You want to help children who can be helped. She's going to be a handicap to you. Do what's best. Put her away and concentrate on your other children." I'll tell you what. My daughter was a blessing to everyone who knew her for 31 years. She was a blessing to me the day she was born, and I thank God for her every day. She showed me a way of life that I might have missed if I had given up the school. She taught me things I could not possibly have learned without her. I haven't the faintest idea what I would have done otherwise because I haven't given it a second thought. She showed me my life.
　—*Florence Schulten*

You may think it's odd to be so particular about finding a doctor who has a positive attitude, but just as you want your child surrounded by family and friends who see your baby as a real child, you also want your doctor to do the same. Viktor Frankl, a German psychologist who survived the death camps of Nazi Germany, used his experience in the camp to develop a new branch of psychology. It is considered a humanistic psychology, as he insists that health care professionals of all types see their patients as human. In fact, he says that doctors who do not recognize the humanity of their patients are not doctors, they are veterinarians. Make sure your child has a *doctor.*

A key is to find a doctor who understands that you know a lot about your child. Find a doctor who wants you as a partner, an equal partner. We've had doctors who, too, were wonderful for certain stages in Hillary's life, but then who couldn't handle the next stage. So then we change. There are doctors out there now who are interested in the person and her family and who don't see the person as a syndrome or a definition of disability they've read.
  —Michele Shaw

The doctor insisted that I leave the hospital without the baby and that John and I should go to Banff for a romantic holiday. He didn't want me to leave the hospital without having my tubes tied. I told him I wouldn't make that decision then. He said lightening could strike twice in the same place. He told us to give Brad up for adoption, go home, and look after the one child we had. That way, he said, Nolan would never have to be known as the brother of a freak. This man was the director of family medicine.
  —Ethel Magnus

The nurses wouldn't come into our room. They wouldn't talk to me. Finally, a nurse said, "Oh, you're the people with the Down syndrome baby. We could tell which one she was in the nursery." That wasn't what we needed to hear. We needed someone to come in and say, "What a cute baby!" because that's just what she was.
  —Tom Duffey

Part of the reason you need good medical and health care professionals with good attitudes is to guard against something called *diagnostic overshadowing.* This means that once the doctor, for example, is aware of the disability, there is a tendency to blame everything that happens on the disability; therefore, the diagnosis literally overshadows everything else. When a child has a temper tantrum, it's because "the kid has mental retardation. What do you expect?" It is not because "the kid is frustrated."

Diagnostic overshadowing is a particular danger in the area of sexuality. We know parents who, surprised that their child discovered this really neat toy that God conveniently placed within reach, talked to their doctors about their child's "masturbating" as an infant. (This kind of body play is a healthy part of infancy and is different than adult masturbation [Klass, 1999].) Rather than tell the parents that this is entirely natural for young children, a doctor told one parent that her "retarded daughter was oversexed, like a lot of retarded people are." Our advice? Lose this doctor real fast.

> *There are too many doctors out there who just think, "These kids are retarded, so why bother?" Using that sort of thinking, we wouldn't be doing heart surgery or vaccinating people with disabilities either. One doctor said to us, "You parents of these kids set your goals too high." I remember looking over at Tom in tears saying, "What does he mean?" I guess if we wanted her to live, that was setting our goals too high.*
> —Denise Duffey

> *When the doctor asked us what we thought we could possibly want for her, we told him we just wanted her to drive a Corvette and balance her checkbook.*
> —Tom Duffey

A good rule of thumb is to remember that doctors and other health care professionals are human. They may be knowledgeable about disability and current issues, supportive, and open to new ways of thinking...or they may not. In *Making Life Right When It Feels All Wrong: How to Avoid Being an Emotional Victim with Lovers, Mates, Bosses, Friends, Family*, Herbert Fensterheim and Jean Baer said,

> Because doctors do to some degree have the power to "make it better," even to make sickness disappear, many people project onto them an all-knowingness and powerfulness...regarding them in the same way they regarded their parents as children. Even though the public perception of doctors is changing (witness the use of informed consent and recourse to second opinions), many of us still feel a need to act passively and placate our doctor...Just the same, we must not let our anxiety and concern with self—sometimes legitimate, at other times exaggerated—combine with unreal expectations to turn the doctor into our victim. (1988, pp. 144–145, 147)

> *Our daughter has a big job ahead of her in educating the medical community. One doctor was showing interns around while we were in the hospital. He took one look at her; she was having some respiratory problems then, and he announced, "These kids are always this bad." He walked out, and the interns were still just standing there, looking sort of embarrassed. I said, "You just got a lesson in how* not *to be a doctor."*
> —Shelly Garner

> *There was one nurse who came in quietly one day, and she told me about a person she knew who had a mental handicap. She said, "I just want you to know the person is doing just fine and living independently." That was in 1972. She said, "This might not mean a whole lot to you right now, but maybe there will be a time when you look back and will be encouraged by the fact that there are young people who are doing well." I didn't believe her at the time, but it was very nice of her to say.*
> —Ethel Magnus

If you're searching for a doctor or other health care professional, check with other parents. There is usually a pretty good grapevine of information. Many parents are quite open about their preferences and their reasons that a doctor may be better during one stage of your child's development than another. Don't be afraid to educate your medical or health care professional about your child and how you want him to be "treated." Treatment means more than just a medically focused perspective. You want your child to be treated as a whole human being.

Q

My wife and I have had some close friends for many years, and they also have a child with disabilities. Lately, when we come home after visiting or when we're cleaning up after a party, my wife and I talk about how exhausted we feel—defeated, almost. When we talk about what we're trying to put together for our daughter, they always seem to have some reason why it won't work. How do we help our friends understand we might want different things?

A

Remember that old joke about the guy who goes to a doctor, contorts one arm up behind his back, and says, "Doctor, it hurts when I do this." The doctor says, "Then don't do that." We think what you're describing falls into this arena. There's no law that says you have to be close friends with people who don't share your beliefs and values simply because you both have a child with a disability. People change. People make new friends. They see the world in different ways. That's all right, but if being around these people is making you and your wife chronically uncomfortable and tired, then don't do it. Sometimes old friends drift apart. You don't have to make a big deal out of it, but if you're pressed to explain why you don't get together much anymore, say that you have some fundamental differences in how you view your children. We know of one parent who was finally advised by a counselor to avoid contact with some rather, in the parent's view, bitter and pessimistic friends. The counselor's said, "They're poison for you!" Indeed, once the father started spending less time with them and more time with some people who shared his philosophies about his child, he felt rejuvenated and energized. The truth, honestly put and gently given without accusation, might be the best way to handle it. You have to be the judge, and maybe when you're feeling stronger, you might offer your friends some new ideas. They just might be feeling bitter and defeated because what they once wanted was too far beyond their reach.

Q

My parents love their granddaughter immensely and are always interested in what she's learning and doing. Because of the time when they grew up (they're in their eighties), they really don't understand inclusion or why we don't send our daughter to a special school. Though they've never said it, we can almost tell they're thinking, with only good intentions, "Wouldn't she be happier with people of her own ability level?" We suspect they think our expectations are too high and probably unrealistic.

A

If you can sit down with them (maybe you already have) and explain what you mean by *inclusion,* your parents might get a better understanding. Like a lot of people, they may see something on the television or in the newspaper about inclusive education that features a stressed teacher or school administrator talking about kids being dumped into classrooms with no support. Explain to your parents this is not inclusion. Have you ever given your parents any good books, videos, or other information about your child's disability and your philosophy? They might welcome some good reading material that helps them form a better picture of their granddaughter's life and what you plan for her future. Advocacy organizations often have new parent information packages that would be suitable; some even prepare grandparent packs. Your parents sound like they are genuinely concerned about your daughter's happiness and satisfaction with life. They are simply drawing on their own memories for ways to achieve that; those ways might have been very progressive in the 1940s and 1950s. Give them a new way to look at things. Check the "Recommended Resources" section at the end of this book, and start your gift giving early this year! You might even give them their own copy of the book you're holding right now, with our best wishes.

Hillary Shaw, Woodland Hills, California

Chapter 5

Put Me Down

Build Boundaries: Balance Risk and Growth

From the moment we are born, there are things to learn. Remember parts one and two of the major self-awareness concepts along the way to healthy sexuality:

I am loved.
I am welcome here.

The third major concept is modesty. Modesty is indeed the first blush of understanding that the body is owned by the self and that others don't have access to it. Modesty really is a claiming of the right to control who sees your body. This is the first step to understanding the right to control who touches your body. Now separation begins:

My body is mine.

When looking at what kids learn as they grow, modesty is the first concept that is directly tied to sexuality. No one really knows how kids learn this, but they do. Around the age of 5 or 6, most kids want the door to the bedroom closed when they are getting dressed, and a naked run through the sprinkler is as offensive to them as spinach with cheese sauce or a fish taco. This concept is amazing when you think about it. All of a sudden, like a thunderbolt out of the blue, a boundary is built between parent and child—and the child builds it. The building of healthy boundaries is one of the most important jobs the child has during the "put me down" phase of development.

Modesty: Public and Private

A lot of kids with intellectual disabilities have difficulty learning modesty. It is probably because they may not get the same opportunities to build the barriers. Because it may take longer for a child with an intellectual disability to learn how to dress, toilet, wash up, and do other intimate tasks, the parent may have to spend more time in the room with them. You need to be aware that your child has two things to learn: the skill being taught, and the concept behind the skill. For example, with the skill of dressing, the concept is that dressing is a private act. It can be difficult for parents to juggle teaching dressing as something private because there are so many other things to do during a day. Who has the time to close a door and stay in the bedroom with a child? Actually, who has time to do this in the bedroom? Why not just do it in the kitchen while making breakfast?

> *One word that Hillary really seemed to understand early on was the word* appropriate. *That became the perfect word as we were teaching her. If we said, "Hillary, that's not appropriate" or "That's very appropriate," she really understood that from an early age. Parents have to try different things to get across the concept.*
> —Lou Shaw

Modesty is going to be the most difficult skill you have to teach, and it is going to take the most time, so you need to think about how to organize your time. You probably hoped this book would give magic answers to difficult problems, but there are some realities. Try this activity:

 Rest Stop:

Think of all acts that occur behind closed doors. Make a list:

Things that occur behind closed doors:

These are things that you need to teach very carefully.

It is unnatural for a child to have neighbors, babysitters, and other virtual strangers teaching him intimate things as he gets older. It is true that typical kids have others teach them, but because they learn quickly, they are probably younger, so they don't really sense the weirdness of having a babysitter help them dress. Kids without intellectual disabilities probably need fewer trials to learn, so they don't have this kind of privacy intrusion often or for very long.

 Rest Stop:

You need to determine a very limited number of people who are going to teach intimate skills. Make a short list:

People who can teach my child intimate skills:

The reasons for teaching modesty are complex. Think of it in the context of our culture. We teach our children to appreciate their appearance, to take responsibility for their hygiene and for their clothes and other possessions. We teach them to tidy their room (sigh) and to help with household chores. We teach them that it's not polite to fart or burp at the dinner table, especially when Grandma and Grandpa are visiting ("Well, okay, it was funny that first time, but cut it out, and I mean it!"). We teach them that going to the bathroom is a private act and that when you can do it by yourself, it means you're growing up. Modesty also means that you close the door and that other people are not to come in and out while it's your turn. We teach all of these things to our children so that they will understand the "rules" of our society. It is the same with knowledge about public and private.

Your child has to have the concept of modesty before hitting the school system. If she learns to dress in the kitchen and learns that it is okay for strangers to see her naked, this is going to lead to problems. This is a fact, not an opinion. One professional who works in a sexuality clinic said that that almost 100% of the calls received by the clinic from schools and from parents of young kids are about the modesty issue. Schools are outraged when a girl with an intellectual disability drops her pants in class to show everyone her nice new underwear. Or how about the boy who casually pulls his penis out of his pants to show everyone the "boo-boo" he made with his zipper? Schools think that these kids are "dangerous."

Is this an overreaction? You bet. But doctors aren't the only ones guilty of diagnostic overshadowing. Many schools do it all the time. Part of this "jumping to conclusions" about why a child has behaved immodestly probably has to do with the myths regarding sexuality and disability. There are two competing myths regarding the sexuality of kids with disabilities. One myth is that they are sexually innocent. Another myth is that they are sexually deviant. Interestingly, when a social-sexual mistake is made, people almost always jump to the second myth. As such, kids need to get to the school system with a healthy sense of modesty.

> *Katherine can be very definite about a lot of things. She sometimes needs assistance, but she wants her privacy, and she'll say, "Get out of here!" if you're intruding on her space. She has a mind of her own. She knows a lot about her body. She's definite about privacy.*
> *—Darryl Davey*

You can teach the distinction between public and private most effectively through modeling, explanation, and persistence. When you teach the skills of personal grooming, for example, do so in a private place (National Information Center for Children and Youth with Disabilities [NICHCY], 1992). Close the bathroom or bedroom door and tell your child...that this is a private behavior, so we close the door (Edwards & Elkins, 1988). If your child makes a mistake and, for example, touches his genitals at the supermarket while you're weighing the cantaloupe, immediately say in a calm voice, "Touching yourself is private. We don't touch ourselves in public." If it's not possible to take your child to a private place, then try getting him to focus his attention on something else and discuss appropriate behavior when you get home.

It's also important that children and teenagers be given privacy. Not only does this allow them to understand the difference between public and private, but it also acknowledges their right to have and enjoy time alone (NICHCY, 1992). Allowing privacy is reinforcement of the concept of public and private behaviors and provides the guidelines for decision making related to social-sexual activity that your child must make throughout her life (Edwards & Elkins, 1988).

I remember walking into the bathroom one day. I didn't think anyone was in here, and suddenly there's a bloodcurdling scream, "Aaaahhh! I'm naked!" and she jumped behind the door!

  —Lou Shaw

Karen has quite a positive feeling about her own body. She's quite fit and has a good physical self-image. As she grows older, we've had to balance being comfortable with your body with the fact that you can't really walk around in the nude. It wasn't an issue for her, but it was for other people. Other kids her age would be quite self-conscious [in the locker room] in gym class, and she'd get changed facing everyone. She's not very modest, but that's partly a function of our family. We've been quite open, but since many others aren't, we need to talk to her about it.

  —Peggy Hutchison

Teaching modesty does not mean that you need to be harsh in your reactions to your child as he or she makes mistakes while learning this skill. For example, if you are working on teaching your son about wearing a bathrobe when he comes out of the bedroom in the morning, you can expect that while he is learning the skill, he is going to forget and make mistakes along the way. This is why it is called *learning*. Don't be so tense about this that when your child comes out of the room in the morning stark naked, you react by yelling, scolding, or berating him for the mistake. It is just a mistake, and he is in need of gentle correction. There are many concepts in your child's education that he (and most children without disabilities) will not "get" on the first try. Keep at it. Be consistent.

Now she'll go into the bathroom and before she closes the door, she'll announce that she wants her privacy. We haven't really gone out of our way to teach her that sort of thing. When we were up at the Institute in New York, they wanted to make a videotape of her and they wanted to take some pictures without her clothes on. She made all the men get out of the room. She'll change her swimsuit in front of us, but she has very strong ideas about her body. Maybe more kids would tell their parents to get out of the bathroom or that they don't like their parents dressing them, but they can't say so. Chelsea will speak up. When she was little, she was into body parts. And I mean every body part!

  —Denise Duffey

The danger in teaching modesty is that your child may mix up *private* and *dirty*. It is absolutely important that your child does not come to see her body as bad or hideous or ugly. Remember, your child may have a physical difference and could attribute your reaction of horror to the physical difference rather than to inappropriate nudity.

A woman who has a huge scar on her cheek said that when she was growing up, she had really chubby cheeks. She said that her parents teased her about it, and she felt that they hated her because she looked different. One night when her parents were in bed, she got her father's razor and hacked at her cheek, trying to cut it down to a size where her parents would then love her. This is a tragic story, and it should make us even more sensitive to the journey that kids with intellectual disabilities have and the danger that they may pick up messages of disappointment from accidental interactions.

But parallel talk can come to the rescue! That last story probably scared the willies out of you. It wasn't meant to, but we can imagine parents becoming paralyzed with fear about what messages they may unintentionally send to their child. Well, don't worry. If you have been using parallel talk, then you know exactly what to do. You would go over to your little naked jaybird and say, "Whoa, remember the rule? You need to have your housecoat on. Look around. Yes, we're in the front room. This is a public room. Come on now. Let's go back into the bedroom where it is private and start again. When you came in here, you probably saw Mommy's face change. It was because I was surprised to see you naked."

Something new has been added to the parallel talk. Notice the description of the emotional event and the focus on the connection between the behavior and the emotive event. Here is another fact about people with intellectual disabilities: They have difficulty reading emotional expressions and often misinterpret them. As such, adding to the parallel talk a description of your emotional state gives your child information, and there is little worry that your child will mistake shock or surprise for disgust or disappointment.

As your child is learning basic skills (dressing, toileting, and bathing), begin teaching the names for body parts. Start with arms and legs, move to facial parts and then teach the private parts of the body. Although you want your child to be comfortable using the words for private body parts, make sure that she understands that even the words are special. Use a slightly different tone of voice, lean in a little bit (but don't whisper or violate too much personal space), and talk about the fact that these parts are private parts. Teach her to always remember that *private* means "don't touch without permission" and "don't look without permission."

Not only are there public and private clothes and behaviors for different places and occasions, but there are also private and public body parts. You can have some fun teaching this idea, over time, using dolls. Choose a male and female doll with removable clothing. Get anatomically realistic dolls (we like *Teach•A•Bodies* not only because they are realistic but also because they look pleasant; see the "Recommended Resources" section at the end of this book for more information). Have your child determine whether the doll is a boy or a girl, a man or a woman. If your child doesn't know, show her how you can tell (facial hair, penis, breasts, pubic hair). Have your child give the dolls names.

Pretend with your child that the doll wants to go shopping. Have your child decide what the doll wants to buy—make it interactive. When the doll is naked, ask your child if the doll can go to the store. *No? Why not? You're right, she should wear clothes because other people will see her, and the store is a public place. Let's put some clothes on her so that she can go to the store. Her body is private, so we will cover it up.*

Put the doll's underwear on. *Now is she ready to go to the store? No? Why not? She covered up her private parts with clothes, so why couldn't she go to the store yet?* You are also teaching the concept that underclothes are private clothes and are not for everyone to see. The "outside" clothes, like shirts, pants, dresses, hats, and shoes are public clothes.

You can also use these dolls to teach your child what kinds of clothes should be worn for different seasons, different temperatures, different weather conditions, and different social events. Which clothes are appropriate for church, school, or a movie? Let your child guide some of this learning, and remember to keep it fun. Your daughter shouldn't panic when she sees you bring out the dolls. (Karin still has "mathaphobic" attacks about the old multiplication flash cards!)

At this point, don't worry about explaining what all of the body parts are for—there's enough time for that later. Right now, it's important that your child know the names of body parts and begin to understand private body parts and personal modesty.

As with all children, these societal subtleties are taught over time as the child grows. Don't panic over slips. If your child forgets the private versus public rules, just go back and do a refresher. No part of social-sexuality education is a one-shot, one-lesson proposition!

Karin's Story

Each year, my family looks forward to the annual Mexican party with friends Earl and Linda, gourmet cooks who gather friends together for a wonderful potluck. In the days before the party one year, we reminded Jim about the art of making conversation, how to execute a hearty handshake, how to eat with your mouth closed because dip on someone's silk blouse doesn't generally endear the spitter to the spitee, and how to mingle. In essence, we gave him a crash course on how to work a party crowd. We didn't want to be shadowing Jim for the evening, nagging him there about, well, all of the things we could nag him about in advance. By the way, being equal-opportunity naggers, we included Jim's younger sister Erin and younger brother Benjamin in this crash course on etiquette.

Jim has always been a friendly person and is never shy about meeting new people, but his making-himself-understood skills have waned. So we arrived at the party and set the kids loose amid university colleagues and their partners. Jim did beautifully. He shook hands. He smiled. He passed around trays of hors d'oeuvres. As he moved around the room, he generally spoke in sentences about his interests instead of giving the one-phrase Star Trek or Beatles statements as he is sometimes wont to do. He would announce, "I like Star Trek things," which would guide the party conversation and occasionally identify a fellow Trekkie.

Jim followed our advice to smile and mingle so well that later I saw with horror from across the room that Jim, still smiling and waving, was in the guest bathroom, sitting on the toilet with the door open so he could still be part of the party, still satisfying our pre-party nagging. As I moved inconspicuously across the room (in actual fact, I probably lunged with arms outstretched), he saw me approaching and a huge smile spread across his face. As I reached for the door knob, he whispered loudly, "I doing good, Mom!"

And indeed he was. On the way home, we congratulated the kids on how well they had handled their first faculty party—and we made plans to discuss bathroom rules. Jim turned to Erin and Ben and said proudly, "I am a man."

Jim's issue was more than just the fact that he had a less than the best understanding of body privacy. There is also the issue of assertion and the ability to think about rules and when they do and do not apply. The rule "mingle at a party" is quite separate from the rule "close the bathroom door," but choosing which rule applies takes thought, a decision, and the assertive ability to follow through. And sometimes missing a few minutes of a good party is the sacrifice we have to make to take care of more urgent—and personal—business!

It's important to gear your conversations with your child to a level of information he or she can understand. As your son or daughter grows, however, remind yourself to grow with him or her. Think of your other children and how much they dislike being spoken to like a child—sometimes even if they still are one! Claire Canning of Rhode Island candidly discussed the strategies she has used with her daughter Martha to teach about some of the more sensitive subjects: "She knows she can always tell her dad or me if anyone violates her privacy. I always stress, too, that our discussions are private and are not intended for everyone to hear" (1990, p. 273).

His disability has never stopped me from correcting him when I saw him doing or saying something he shouldn't. Even to this day, I'll say, "Now, Michael, you know better. Think about what you're doing." I've been pretty tough on him. I've always said, "Michael, don't say something dumb just to keep your mouth moving. Think about what you want to say." His relationships with people have always been good because he just loves everybody. He's had some relationships with girls, some a little more serious that others. He's had a habit of patting women on the rear end, but we've talked and he seems to know where the line is now.
—Peggy Creamer

As your child grows, remind him of the basic concepts behind public and private:

- Public is where and when there are more people than just you.
- Private is where and when you are usually by yourself.

Your child should grow increasingly more aware of what is a public place and a private place, a public act and a private act, and a public part of his body and a private part of his body and when it's okay for people to touch his body. Try asking from time to time about these concepts:

- Is brushing your teeth private or public?
- Is your classroom at school public or private?
- Is your bedroom public or private?
- When is it okay for people to touch your arm?
- How about your penis (or breasts)?
- Point out pictures of people in magazines: Are these people in public or private situations? If the people are touching, do you think it's okay? Why or why not?

Rest Stop:

Jot down some ideas here you might have of ways to reinforce public and private.

Ways to reinforce the concepts of public and private:

   Make up scenarios about a person's behavior, like wearing nothing to school or brushing your teeth at the dinner table. Little pop quizzes done in a relaxed and teachable moment (as opposed to drill sergeant interrogation) will give you a good idea whether your child understands these important concepts and where you might need to focus more teaching.

When [Chelsea] was about 3, she and I went into a restaurant. I was tired, I think, so I wasn't saying anything. I must have been thinking about something else. She was so prissy when she was 3, and there she was, sitting up so proper at the table. She looked around the restaurant for awhile, then at me. She leaned forward and whispered, "Mom, let's talk about something." I had to laugh. She saw other people in the restaurant having conversations, so she knew we should be doing what everybody else was doing.
   —Denise Duffey

I certainly hope that both boys will have friends, girlfriends, wives, sex. I'll say it! Sex! I guess it starts with feeling comfortable with themselves. We both recognize that they are sexual beings right from the start. We've tried to be open and correct, even with things like terminology. There never has and never will be any suggestion that you can't touch any part of your body. It's just there are some parts you don't touch at the dinner table!

—Elizabeth Popowich

Risk Reduction and Assertiveness

He's vulnerable. We have to teach him to be streetwise. But we have to realize that we're involving him in a community that isn't always inviting, isn't always safe, so with what we want goes risk. What's an acceptable level of risk? How do you look after someone who needs some level of looking after? Yet, if you're protecting him all the time, he'll never grow the way he should and you cut him off from the potential of so many connections. Jim's very confident and bold and friendly. He can go farther than a lot of people his age I know simply because he's not afraid.

—Richard Schwier

There's been quite a bit of streetproofing education going on at school. Katherine did have a bit of a scare recently. She was out on the sidewalk; I was on the front porch. A man followed her down the sidewalk and came right up to the gate here. He had had a few drinks, and I went down to talk to him. Through his drunken state, I finally got the story that he had once worked with people with disabilities, and he noticed Katherine, followed her home, and wanted to talk about it....Katherine got quite scared about it, but I think she learned that you have to be a little bit on your guard with people. I really don't know how we're going to teach her that there are some people out there who aren't very nice. She often greets people with a hug, and we talk to her about those issues of vulnerability.

—Bob Manwaring

An uncomfortable truth is that people with disabilities are sexually abused in huge numbers. Although we will talk about this later in the section in Chapter 6 on abuse and exploitation, all parents need to prepare their children for the real world. The real world has some really awful people in it. We know that you know this, and we know that as parents, you don't even want to think about it. But you have to do this. *All* parents of *all* kids have to think about this subject.

Part of the best defense against abuse and exploitation is to teach your child to be a confident and assertive person. This will take practice, and the best practice is real life. Parents must realize it's virtually impossible to teach children about abuse and exploitation in a vacuum. It must be taught in the wider context of sexuality, sex, relationships, and values. Dick Sobsey, sexual abuse expert and parent of a child with a disability, recommends booklets from the Sex Information and Education Council of Canada and *Being Sexual: An Illustrated Series on Sexuality and Relationships* (Ludwig & Hingsburger, 1993), among other good materials, but he emphasized that individualizing the teaching and making your child feel that she can talk to you about anything is most important:

> You do run into parents who've never dealt with sexuality, yet they will say to their children, "Don't let anybody ever touch you." But then they take the kid to the barber or the doctor who, of course, touches them. To a kid, that's like saying, "Don't let a piano fall on your head." Sounds like a good idea, but what exactly does that mean? In what context? (personal communication, 1995)

Teaching your child about exploitation, intimidation, and sexual abuse without putting it in the context of sexuality, being male, being female, public and private, and relationships with others simply presents a concept without the foundation. Although we deal with the specifics of sex education and sexual abuse later in this book, Sobsey suggested that the first thing to do is try to facilitate a network of connections or at least an individual or two who are real friends for your son or daughter. Along with that should come information about developing bodies and changing emotions. None of this will happen in one or two lectures about the "birds and the bees." Learning about sexuality, sex, and the risks and pleasures of being human happens over time.

> *I don't like to add to the myth, but Nicholas is a very happy guy. It's one of those good things about him that I hope we can temper with what's appropriate and what isn't. He's a very gentle person, but he's not above shoving his little brother and taking what he wants. We've never hit them, and there's no hitting between them. I don't want him to lose that genuineness and openness. I would never want either of our kids to think they weren't permitted to touch and hug and hold other people, but they need to learn about the appropriate and consensual ways.*
> *—Elizabeth Popowich*

For a lot of kids, including kids without disabilities, parents talk a lot about "good touch" and "bad touch," but that assumes the kids have some good touch in their lives. How do you tell the difference if it's a matter of deciding between "bad" and "worse"? Within the family, you need to create as much communication as you can. *Never* create a situation in which your child feels there's anything he can't tell you. If you do, telling about "bad touch" will almost certainly fall into the category of things your child thinks he cannot tell you. Usually, a child will start to confide before what is happening becomes overtly sexually abusive or before it becomes obvious. Your child may not even be particularly aware that the situation may get to be uncomfortable. But he may say, "Oh, Mr. Jones across the street wants me to come over again." If you've established a dialogue and a comfort, you can get more information and hopefully work through with your child what's going on and help him recognize a potentially risky situation.

> *You worry about any child being sexually abused. You worry about girls, when they're older, being used. I haven't really talked to her about that yet, but I will. In the meantime, she's learning to be assertive. She knows her body is private. I*

don't want to scare her about people, but she has enough standoffishness about strangers that I think she'll have a better chance.
   —*Denise Duffey*

I worry about her vulnerability about friendships. We see her get hurt by kids who tease. She can be very hurt by someone she thinks is a friend. One time, a kid we thought was her friend phoned and said she'd meet Karen down-town at the movie theater. Karen got all dressed up and went down. The kid was in her grade eight class, and they both had gone on to different schools since then. Karen was so excited to be seeing her again. The "friend" simply never showed up.
   —*Peggy Hutchison*

How to Teach "No"

You'll love this one. You need to teach your child how to say no to you and to other adult authority figures. Pick yourself off the floor and stop laughing; We're not kidding here. I don't mean teach your child how to throw a tantrum, pout, or scream, "You aren't my boss." (Just how did your child learn to fling peas across the room while screaming, "I hate peas," anyway?) We mean that you need to teach your child how to effectively and maturely say no to things that vi-olate his rights, his boundaries, and his beliefs. Saying no firmly without a tem-per tantrum is a skill that your child needs to learn (and is one that many adults haven't really learned either!).

Begin by being careful of how you ask and what you ask of your child. It is very important to keep *choices* and *demands* quite separate in your head. If it's a choice, that means your child can either say no or select a preferred option. If it's a demand, that means there is no choice. Some people will tell you that every-thing should be a choice. We couldn't disagree more. The reason we as adults maintain our jobs, our relationships, and our self-control is that we have demand tolerance. We all have to do things we don't want to in order to get a paycheck, a kiss on the cheek, or a feeling of responsibility. Part of growing up is learning that in some issues there are no choices and that we simply have to follow the rules or suffer the consequences, as in "I may want to play my new CD really, re-ally loud and sing and dance along with it, but if I live in an apartment or if I love someone who is trying to study, then I won't." The rules are "consider others" and "I have to follow this, or I will either lose my apartment or wind up sleep-ing on the couch." It's okay for your child to learn that sometimes "because I said so" is reason enough.

Consider the following scenario: You ask your son if he wants to go visit Grandma. Because you asked, your child figures this is a choice, and he says no because he knows Grandma is going to make him sit on her lap while she fuss-es about him. You then say, "Don't you think you should get your coat on?" Your child still figures this is in the realm of choice and says, "Nope." What do you do next? You have to make him get up and get his coat on.

Now ask yourself, "What is my child learning?" You are teaching your child, by example, that when he says no, he will be forced to do what he doesn't want to do anyway. He is learning that saying no is meaningless and powerless. This is not what you want your child to learn. So, by ensuring instead that demands are demands and choices are choices, you aren't stuck in this position. This isn't to say that you can't build a choice into a demand: "Do you want to wear your blue coat or your black sweater on the way over to Grandma's place?" Choice and demand can co-exist, and it really does make life a little nicer for everyone.

 ## Rest Stop:

Now actively teach your child to say no. When you offer a yellow shirt and your child can say, "No Mom, I want to wear the blue shirt," or can tell you by some other means that he would like to wear the blue shirt, your child will demonstrate a good command of "No." If you insist and your child says, "Okay, yellow," or throws a massive tantrum, this shows a limited "No" skill and you have some teaching to do.

By purposefully planning times when your child needs to say no, you can ensure that he learns that no means no. This is easier than you think:

You: Michael, do you want to wear your blue shirt or your yellow shirt?
Michael: Um, blue.
          [You hand your son his yellow shirt. Michael should be at a point at which he can comfortably restate his preference.]
Michael: No, blue.
You: Okay, blue. You look handsome in blue.

Now it's your turn. Make a list of everyday choices relevant to your child, and teach him or her to pick one option or the other. Make sure you can follow through on the choices!

Choices my child can make:

If your child has difficulty with temper tantrums over issues like these, then this isn't the best way to teach. Think of temper tantrums as a poor way of saying no. This means that your child may have to learn better ways of communicating her desires before you can effectively teach these skills. Be careful, though, that your child isn't in a situation in which she *has* to throw a temper tantrum to be heard. If you need more help with your child's behavior, you may want to find resources in the library on how to deal with temper tantrums.

One mom complained that her son said no to everything, and she thus figured that he had the "No" skill down pat. This isn't true because her son isn't discriminating "yes times" (like when there is no choice about a matter) from "no times" (like when a situation is getting dangerous). Saying no all of the time is as bad as saying yes all of the time. It indicates a lack of skill. So practice, practice, practice!

Dreams and Expectations

Dave was giving a lecture in northern Ontario—it was just a "couple of minutes after the general meeting" kind of talk. Just before speaking, the organizer introduced him to a young couple who had driven for miles and miles just to be present. Before Dave could say anything more than hello, the woman said, "Mr. Hingsburger, we drove all this way because we wanted to thank you." Surprised, he asked them what he had done that was deserving of thanks. She said, "You saved our lives." This was a pretty big statement given that he didn't know these folks from Adam. They agreed to talk after the speech.

Dave's Story

We met again in the hallway, and they purposefully waited until everyone else had left. Then they told me that they had read my book, *i to I: Self Concept and People with Developmental Disabilities* (1990) and had thought a lot about the "dream stuff." They had a son with Down syndrome with a hole in his heart who told everyone that he wanted to be a fireman. All of the professionals had told him that he was not going to be a fireman. How many firemen with Down syndrome or holes in their heart do you know? (There are a lot of people with huge, figurative holes in their hearts...but that's another story.) The professionals told the parents that they should "get him ready for his future now." They surely didn't want to set him up for disappointment. "Let him know, gently, that he will never be a fireman and that he should think about other things he can do," said the professionals.

Well, the parents discovered that there was no "gentle" way to let their son know that he couldn't be a fireman. So, they had to cope with his temper tantrums and his tears as they would confront him—at 6 years old—with his disability. The education of their son in curtailing his dream did not go well. Then they read in my book that dreams are acceptable. They read that professionals can be wrong. Then they went out and bought two smoke alarms for their house. They put them up in the right spots, and they marked on the calendar that once a week, each battery would be checked. They bought two fire extinguishers, one for wood and one for electrical fires, and they marked on the calendar one time per month that each would be checked. Then they bought a big bell and scheduled family fire drills and put them on the calendar, too. The change in their son was incredible. He would run home from the bus to get into the house to mark off the calendar and see if it was a "fireman day." When it was, he would be in sheer heaven. His favorite were the fire drills during which he would get to ring the bell and direct people exiting the house. He was a happy little boy.

His mom started to cry when she told me that one day they had a fire. It wasn't a big fire, but it was definitely a fire. Her son was thrilled. He looked at them as if to say, "Mom and Dad threw me a fire! *I love these people!*" He was in total control. He sent Mom and his sister out of the house to call 911, and instructed Dad that he had grabbed the wrong fire extinguisher. By the time the fire truck arrived, the fire was out and the son was gleefully ready to tell the men in the fire suits what happened.

They were so impressed with this little boy that they called the local newspaper who came and took a picture of him in the fire truck. A caption ran in the weekly paper, "Son saves family from fire." What about his disability? It was never mentioned. Can you imagine the impact on the community, seeing a picture of a kid with Down syndrome looking out at them as hero from their morning paper? Later that month, the son received an award from the fire hall. He has friends there now whom he stops and visits sometimes.

"You saved our lives." No, these parents grabbed onto of a concept and did so much with it. They were able to see how to make an abstract thought practical, given their family and their circumstances. Dreams are important.

In San Francisco, there is a place called the Glide Church. The minister, a black man married to a Japanese woman, has created a community. People of every type congregate to celebrate community. The service is so inclusive as to embrace all, whatever the ideology, sexuality, or religious beliefs. The only thing they do not welcome is hatred. People sit together in rows of black, yellow, red, white, gay, straight, rich, and poor. There is an usher with intellectual disabilities and the woman handing out the bulletin uses a wheelchair.

The minister says that the main tenet is "If you don't believe that the person sitting next to you belongs here, then you don't belong here." He then goes on to give a rousing, inclusive sermon. The demons of hatred, division, and evil run from the room. Once he said, "Love without honesty is sentimentality; but honesty without love is brutality."

The nastiest people we know call themselves "honest." We have to be careful. Yes, a boy with Down syndrome probably can't be a fireman. True, a hole in the heart is going to be a significant disability in regard to physical work. But we should let someone with either characteristic dream a bit. When your child comes forward with a dream, feel honored that she has told you, and let that dream give your child's life meaning. It's even better if you can find a way to let her taste a corner of the dream.

Chelsea Duffey

My dog is Wizard. He is Wizard B. Oz.

Someday I have my own apartment. Yes! Because I'm gonna get married and move out. I get married to a husband. He's black. He's brown and he's red and he's white. Oh no, he's 4 years old now. That's me at my school. I was sitting down there so my butt would show.

My apartment. Gonna be lots of clothes. Wizard will live there. Not my bird. He will stay here. Maybe sometime, my mom and dad will come. Yeah,

*maybe they can come on Sunday or Monday. I make them ham and broccoli
soup and ham and meat. They can stay overnight. Maybe the whole week.*

*I work at a bank. I would pay money. I guess I would like to have a baby.
In my tummy. I would, I guess. I will marry, well, because that just is. My hus-
band will work in Orlando. I work at a bank. I just love at a bank, just like
Susie does.*

*For breakfast my apartment, well, French toast and sausage. I want to go
to high school. Dad says not yet, then I get to have it. I am 7. When I get married, I gonna be 8. My husband is going to be 4.*

Beyond dreams there are expectations. Children with disabilities, like all
people, have a desperate need to belong and feel necessary. They must have expectations. They must have things that they do to fulfill their role in the family.
Along with the study that showed that parents touch their kids less if they are
seen as unattractive, another showed that expectations were lower. This study
was not about kids with disabilities, just about the way that "pretty" people are
expected to succeed and "ugly" people are not. Although many kids with disabilities are the cutest we have seen, a similar phenomenon can happen.
Diminished expectations lead to diminished achievements.

*I think you can crucify a person by expecting far too much or expecting too little.
I never pushed a child beyond what they could do, but we tried all sorts of different things and different ways. If a child couldn't learn arithmetic, we
switched to spelling. If spelling was beyond a child, we'd try something else.
Maybe art would be the thing they would be wonderful doing. I never gave up.
But it has to be interesting. I get so irritated with these places where people sit at
tables and do boring things all day long, sorting this and sorting that. It's
ridiculous. That's not life. People need incentive.*
—*Florence Schulten*

Karin's Story

When my stepson Jim was about 13, the kids were with us again for the summer. Jim talked constantly of being a doctor when he grew up, specifically one
who wore a white jacket, black pants, and black shoes. He was (and still is) very
concerned and helpful when someone isn't feeling well. One evening before bedtime, I was washing up a few dishes. The glass in my hand suddenly shattered,
and I cut my knuckle quite badly. I wrapped my hand in a paper towel, but the
bleeding didn't stop. Jim wandered in, saw the blood-soaked paper towels and
demanded to see the damage. I showed him, assuring him it was fine; he said,
"No, we go to hospital. To doctor!" Richard came in, confirmed Jim's diagnosis,
and away we went to the medi-clinic. Jim was out of the car first, took me by
the elbow, explained to them at the reception desk what had happened, and
handed over my health card. He waited with his dad and brother Benjamin while
the nurse put me in a back room. The doctor arrived and patched me together. I
mentioned to the doctor (without mentioning Down syndrome) that my son had
handled the emergency very well and, to reinforce his dream of becoming a doctor, asked whether she could speak to him. Leaving me with the nurse to finish

up, the doctor went out to the crowded waiting room and called for Jim Schwier. (Richard and Ben looked up from their magazines, a bit puzzled.) Jim walked up and quietly conferred with the doctor who—without missing a beat—explained to him what she had done with my finger and that my bandage should be changed daily. They shook hands, and she thanked him for taking such good care of his stepmother. He said, "It's my job. I be a doctor," and she wished him luck with his career. My cut finger was definitely Jim's highlight of the summer.

By setting expectations that weave a child into a family, the child knows that she has a place and something to offer. Children need to know that if they were not there, things would not get done. They know, then, when they hear on television (and they *will* hear) that people choose to abort babies with disabilities, that they are here because they are wanted, that they have things they can do, and that they would be missed. All of these messages are necessary to combat some of the negative things that will be said about their *even being alive*. It's amazing how this knowledge can make a difference. One father said that after watching a news story about a child with a disability who was murdered by a parent, his son looked up at him with great gravity and said, "Would you do that to me, Daddy?" The dad said that he didn't know what to say because he was crying, so he grabbed his boy, tickled him, and finally said, "Of course not. Who would do the dishes then?" Crisis was averted, giggles reigned, and hurt was healed.

> *Karen has a responsibility for her own behavior, too. Parents need to be very firm about that. We can't always depend on other people being firm and expecting things from her. She has to learn to be responsible for the way she acts. Our job is to insist that she does do the things she knows how to do.*
> —John Lord

Expectations that your child will participate in the family will also build respect between your child and his siblings. It is easy to understand why some kids resent their brother or sister with a disability when they see their sibling snuggled up on the couch with Mom or Dad while they have to do the chores. Excuse us, but this needs to be said: The resentment they have has nothing to do with disability and everything to do with favoritism. Don't tell us that the other kids should feel lucky that they don't have a disability and that they should be tolerant of their brother or sister with special needs. *There is no special need to watch television rather than do dishes.* Kids with disabilities the world over hate us for saying this, but their brothers and sisters are right. Get the kid off his butt, and get his hands into dishwater.

> *If he did something bad, he got a spanking like the others did. When he was little, I remember I had planted flowers out front one spring. He and my granddaughter, who was about his age, got into them and dug them all up. I was so mad! Someone said, "Well, he didn't know." I said maybe not, but from now on he will. He had to be treated like the others. But he's a very gentle person, and I think I've only really gotten mad at him four or five times in his whole life.*
> —Peggy Creamer

Nobody likes an ill-mannered, obnoxious person. As a parent, you have to insist on good behavior because as life goes on, the child with the handicap will have to be better behaved than someone without a handicap. If you are handicapped, people expect a flaw. It's not fair, but it's reality.
    —*John Magnus*

For many parents of children with intellectual disabilities, a universal lament is "But it takes *so long* for him to do the job. He should learn to do it and feel a sense of accomplishment and responsibility, but it's easier and faster if I just do it myself!" Believe us, we understand. But pitching in with chores like the rest of the family is *so* important, not only for your son or daughter's developing work ethic and self-esteem but also for the message it sends to family, neighbors, teachers, and strangers.

When Brad got to be semireliable in doing the chores, he knew what to do, maybe with a little help. But he'd be lagging behind in getting started. I'd just think, "Let me just go do them quickly myself. I won't have to nag anybody about it. I'll know they're done properly." John would say, "But Brad should go with you." Sometimes I'd think, "But it'll take twice as long!" It's been a big commitment of time, but it's so important. It's just that sometimes you feel like you don't have enough time in the day.
    —*Ethel Magnus*

With 10 children in our family, we had a paper route for the Indianapolis News/Star that's been handed down from one child to the next for years. Everyone got it at age 10. I announced that Chris was going to have his turn. When my husband kind of laughed, I said he's got to learn responsibility, what it means to earn money, to work hard. We hadn't ever heard of supported employment; I just said to his brother, "Okay, Chris needs to learn the route." Each step of the way, Brian would explain to Chris they had to deliver here, here, not here, here. A week later, they walked together and Brian would say, "Okay, Chris, now you tell me which houses get the paper." After a while, Brian walked behind just to check. It took us 6 months to teach 12 houses. He delivered in the winter. He'd fall asleep in driveways. He'd complain it was too cold to go. Our response was the same as it was for all the kids, "Too bad, Buster, you dress up warm and go do your job." The next spring, it was time to teach the other 12 houses on the route. It took 1 day to teach him. Brian turned over the route and Chris had it for 5 years. There was an enormous amount of learning and responsibility taking in those 5 years. When he hit 15 and got a job at the nursing home, he already had a sound work ethic. When he got the Kroger [supermarket] job, it was 40 hours a week plus school. He did well and never complained. He was so excited and kept saying, "Mom, 40 hours!" Now he works full time in the mailroom at the American United Life insurance building in downtown Indianapolis. Everything he had before was a job; this is his career.
    —*Gayle Foy*

When we see a person with an intellectual disability who is doing a job, greeting people, offering assistance in a store, and is dressed and groomed well, we are impressed with her confidence and competence. When we see someone with an intellectual disability being led by the hand by a parent or worker, seemingly not thinking for herself, who looks unkempt and lost, or who acts inappropriately and immaturely, it reinforces every stereotype about the person with an intellectual disability as being the "eternal child." That's the message being given to teachers, employers, and neighbors.

Many years ago, I went back to Denmark to visit my family. On the Swedish ship, the Gripsholm, I met a young deck steward who was very charming. Everyone wanted him and, although he couldn't make change, he was wonderful. He had Down syndrome. It so impressed me that then, 30 years ago, this young man had such a wonderful job. To me, boring work around a table is punishment. An awful lot of people would take exception to that, but it's what I've always thought. This young man's pride in his job and the fact that people enjoyed him was proof to me.
—*Florence Schulten*

 Rest Stop:

Take a minute and think of the two best teachers you ever had. Which two did you most admire and respect? They could be elementary, junior high, high school, or college instructors. Write down their names. Think of the main reasons why you still remember them.

Names of my best teachers:	Why were they the best?

Now think of the two teachers who demanded the most of you, who had high expectations, and who insisted you try harder. These teachers knew you could do better, and they didn't let you get away with sliding by or making excuses.

Are the names the same?

At camp, where some of the counselors are young, you sometimes get someone who will let Karen get away with things. If everybody is doing a morning dip, and she's whiny and says she can't do it, counselors might say, "Oh, well, that's okay." Wait a minute. If everyone is doing a morning dip, Karen does a morning dip. Her disability isn't an excuse.
   —Peggy Hutchison

I don't think Jim should expect people to be good to him simply because he had Down syndrome. I'd be very suspicious of anyone who was. Jim's responsibility as a member of our family and neighborhood is to be a person whom people enjoy being around. That's the job of all our kids, disability or not. Our job is to help them become decent, self-confident people. Jim's disability alone is no more reason to like him than it is to reject him.
   —Karin Melberg Schwier

So, determine what your child can do for himself, and keep changing your expectations as he grows. Having expectations and encouraging your child doesn't mean you're a tyrant. Remember those two teachers you admired and why you felt that way. You admired them because they made you believe you could accomplish anything. Nothing was out of your reach. But they also encouraged you by demanding that you do your best. Be that kind of teacher for your child.

Even if your child's reach at the moment is relatively short, help your child believe he can do what he puts his mind to. How about making a list of tasks you expect your child to do:

Feed the hamster	Answer the telephone	Bring in the paper
Set the table	Take a message	Deliver the paper
Put own clothes away	Dust	Make eye contact
Make the bed	Vacuum	Say good morning
Brush the cat once a week	Hang up jacket	

 Rest Stop:

Make your list of things you expect your child to do. Better yet, make a list with your child and other family members.

Things I expect my child to do:

There are a million things in your household that your child can take on as her responsibility. Start small, and work up. Remember the confidence you're helping to build and the message of self-worth you're helping your child give to others. And don't let your child fake incompetence! We know plenty of people with intellectual disabilities (including adults) who will wordlessly hold out their arms so a parent can put on their coat for them—when they're perfectly capable of doing it themselves. Watch out for con artists!

I put the children up on the horses and, to my chagrin, my own daughter started to scream, "Mommy, mommy! Get off! Get off!" I paid no mind and put the other children up. We got the horses going to see how well the children could keep their balance. By that time, a crowd had gathered. People thought I was a kook! One man cussed me out and threatened to put me in jail for child abuse. Loretta continued to whine. Finally, we stopped, and I said, "Okay, honey, you can get off now." She sniffed for a moment and then she said, "Mommy, do it again." Once you give in to a child before they really try, you teach them there are things they can't do. If you don't expect them to risk, they learn very quickly there is something to fear.

—Florence Schulten

We do expect Hillary to be responsible. She makes her bed every day—well, almost every day. She hangs up her clothes conscientiously. She sets her own clothes out every night. She's fully self-sufficient. I've tried to teach her money, and I don't know if that's ever going to work. But she gets money, and she spends some and saves some. She is so tight! If we go somewhere, she won't spend a penny.

—Lou Shaw

There are so many things he's got to learn, and I do worry because he's 22 and should have some of this stuff handled by now. He's got to learn to eat properly, how to initiate conversations, to look people in the eye, dress appropriately, not fart in public; all those things are critical. But we can't work on all of them at the same time! I think that's where two parents can balance each other. We agree that if we try to do everything, we'll just wear him out and ourselves, too. Let's pick out two or three things at a time. Jim's got to have room to breathe

Loretta Schulten
(picture taken in the 1970s)

and be himself. You learn how to behave by watching other people, by being in public. It makes us more aware of how we're teaching him.

    —*Richard Schwier*

Out of his paycheck, Chris gets spending money every week, and he pays us rent. Not much, but he does pay it so he learns that as an adult, that's an obligation and a responsibility. It's difficult to teach him money skills. Not long ago, he got his check but hadn't cashed it yet. He was still supposed to have some of his cash allowance left. He wanted to rent a movie. We got ready to go and his dad said, "Well, where's your money?" Chris said, "No money. I get my check." Well, he'd already spent all his cash and the bank was closed, so we said if his money was gone, he couldn't afford to rent the video. We wanted him to learn the lesson; if you spend your money, there will be things you can't buy. It was a very teachable moment, and it really sunk in. It might be painful, and he was a little mad, but we'd been telling him this for a long time. Sure, we could have paid for the video, but he has to learn.

    —*Gayle Foy*

She goes everywhere with me. As many people as I can introduce her to, she's going to know. I kind of see that as her job in life, to educate the community. I'm not going to go anywhere and apologize for her. "My child has a disability, and I'm really sorry to bother you, but could you please take her in this class if it's not too much trouble?" She is going to be part of things, and people will just have to cope if they've got a problem. That's all there is to it.

    —*Shelly Garner*

Expectations are about more than chores. They are also about social skills and grooming. Your child needs to be part of the social group called family. Your child needs to go out with you, be seen with you, and hear you talk about him or her with pride. That means that they need to learn grooming skills and greeting skills.

Grooming and Greeting

I think the key is that we didn't do things much differently with Hillary than we did with our older daughter and my son earlier. We always thought it was important to have appropriate manners when we went out, or when you were at the table at home, for that matter. That's true for any kid.

    —*Lou Shaw*

It's very important Brad feels good about himself. I've encouraged him to get his hair styled, and he quite enjoys it. We've tried various haircuts, and now I've backed off and let him go on his own. He's started making his own appointments, and I'll occasionally remind him by saying something like, "Since you'll be dancing at the concert this weekend, how about getting your hair done?" He always comes out happy as a clam. It's important for your child to do what other children are doing, whatever happens to be cool.

    —*Ethel Magnus*

Rona's the fashion coordinator. We hate the old stereotype look for people with Down syndrome. Bowl haircut, plaid pants, mouth hanging open. Rona insists Riley looks cool. You can't ever think, "Well, the kid doesn't care anyway. We'll just dress him in a dirty tea towel and he'll be happy." You've got to help them not stick out. We help Riley blend in. He's got the shoes that light up, even though he's usually in his chair. He gets cool haircuts. Rona shops at the GAP. His teachers and other kids are always looking to see what stuff Riley has on. When you're a kid, how you look is important. His teeth have to be clean because people get grossed out by scummy teeth. Why put up barriers for him?
—Don Bradshaw

Sometimes teaching grooming and self-care skills calls for a deep breath, a smile, and a release of a parent's own inhibitions, but because a child with an intellectual disability can learn well by modeling and repetition, parents find themselves teaching practical skills by performing them with the child, then pulling back as the child learns. Of course, you should not teach some things to your 21-year-old in the same way as you teach your 4-year-old. Parents can adapt their teaching for their child's age and level of understanding. Claire Canning, a parent of five, wrote one of the best descriptions of why good grooming and self-care skills are vital to a child's self-esteem:

First, I cannot overstress the importance of good grooming in adolescence, perhaps more than at any other age. Cleanliness is essential to acceptance by peers and society in general. Although I am by nature a more private person, my practical side told me that the best way to teach Martha cleanliness was to shower with her. I have always tried to make it a happy time, stressing how wonderful it is to feel clean and naming body parts properly as they are washed. Because hair becomes oily with adolescence, I have stressed the importance of frequent shampoos and proper rinsing.

Over a period of several months, Martha learned to shower and shampoo herself, to regulate water temperature, then dry herself, and to carefully wipe the shower. If she stays in the shower much too long, I use an automatic timer wrapped in a plastic bag as a reminder that she has been showering long enough. She blow-dries her own hair, and neatly cleans the bathroom when she has finished. I have found that if I check her carefully just once a week, I feel very certain that she is totally clean. We also clip fingernails and toenails weekly. Because in our country it is accepted practice, I help Martha shave her armpits and legs each week. Deodorant is essential. Skin moisturizers and powders are nice finishing touches, and Martha delights in using them.

A nice adjunct to good grooming and more attractive appearance is a well-styled haircut. Approximately every six weeks, we go to an excellent and very personable hair stylist for a haircut and styling. Martha feels a warm friendship for her hairdresser, and regular haircuts give her increased pride in her appearance.

Make-up, too, can improve one's self-image and is a fun reward of becoming a young adult. Martha delights in having me help her apply a little eye shadow, blusher, and lipstick when she is going somewhere special.

It is worth the time, energy and expense to dress our teens...in attractive, current clothing. It is so important to their appearance and acceptability in society, superficial though such aspects may be. Occasionally, her sisters or sisters-in-law shop with us, so that they can keep us abreast of the latest teen trends in fashion....It is ironic that our children are judged by their appearance when they, themselves, are so beautifully nonjudgmental of others. They are truly attracted to others if they are kind and good....We can learn valuable lessons from them. (1990, pp. 270–272)

Many cosmetic company representatives offer in-home or in-store "makeovers" and will give suggestions about make-up application. Your daughter might enjoy inviting a few friends and relatives to a make-up party in your home, led by your area cosmetics salesperson. Pay attention to what girls and young women your daughter's age are wearing. Ask for help.

He's taking initiative around the house. When people get the idea they're not capable, it's easier to just do nothing. He's always been very good at dressing, shaving, that sort of thing. I was always very careful to let him do whatever he could for himself. But he needs help with some decisions, like about which clothes match. He will ask for advice, and I think that's because I encourage him to make his own decisions.
—Peggy Creamer

Dads, older brothers, cousins, and uncles can play a role in helping boys and adolescents develop self-awareness about appearance. Watching Dad shave not only provides some good instruction over time as a boy nears puberty but also offers a chance for some quiet time together. Going on a shopping trip for personal toiletries, choosing a cologne, hair gel, an electric razor, or even a nice tie for a special occasion can impress on your child that he is growing up.

For boys and girls, the novelty of purchasing then using their own shampoo, bubble bath, soap-on-a-rope, shaving cream, and other toiletries can provide the incentive for adequate time and attention in the bathroom, tub, and shower. Gentle reminders from family members and praise, when earned, can do wonders.

If you're struggling to find a solution to a problem with teaching grooming and self-care skills, mention it (discreetly) to someone with a fresh outlook. Two heads are better than one when sorting out a answer, and sometimes the best ideas come from people who can see things from the outside.

Karin's Story

As Jim got into his teens, there was a time when he went from being pretty careful about his appearance to not bothering to look very closely in the mirror. He showered, but there was room for improvement. He preferred to stand under the running water and sing Beatles tunes rather than be bothered with annoyances like shampoo and soap! We thought of making a list he could take into the bathroom as a reminder. We considered laminated pictures of someone shampooing and scrubbing. We wanted to respect his privacy and not give mixed messages about people seeing him naked in the shower. We tried a number of things.

We mentioned it to Jim's hairdresser, Samantha, who is an open, free spirit if there ever was one. She adores Jim and always puts a positive spin on her outlook about him. When we said we were trying to think of a way to get him to shampoo thoroughly, Sam took a sip of her herbal tea and said,

"Why don't you put on bathing suits and get in the shower with him?" Voilà. We continue to keep Sam on our list of "people to ask" when we need a fresh approach.

Part of presenting a confident air comes from being fit. Many people with intellectual disabilities tend to be or appear to be overweight. In the past, parents and professionals tended to assume that this was "just part of the disability" (this is yet another instance of diagnostic overshadowing). Giving children sedentary activities (including eating!) were also sometimes easier for caregivers who didn't see many other recreational or leisure opportunities in the community.

Unfortunately, once a child is overweight, a vicious circle may develop: The overweight youngster will be less active, will perhaps watch more television, engage in snacking, and become more obese (Pueschel, 1988). It's important for families to reduce fat and starch intake, keep an eye on the kinds and amount of foods consumed, and set by example an enjoyment of regular exercise. In fact, during a session on obesity and nutrition at a conference on disability issues, the presenters offered a gloriously uncomplicated piece of advice to parents: "A daily walk is the simplest way to insure daily exercise" (Roizen, Luke, Sutton, & Schoeller, 1995). Family walks with the dog plus an open invitation to others in the neighborhood to come over to play badminton, swim, or just play outside not only encourage exercise and activity but also makes fitness a regular part of daily life. It also lets your child be seen as an active, visible community member.

I remember in graduate school, we did a placement where I had to go into a school and observe a special education class. There were a lot of people with Down syndrome, and what blew me away was that, without exception, every person was overweight. I remember looking at the literature on fitness and education and all it said was people with Down syndrome tended to be overweight and less fit. It's so exciting to see today a younger generation of people because we realize how environmentally driven all those assumptions were. It wasn't anything genetic. It was low expectations.
—John Lord

Michael just loves to get dressed up and go out. There's a place in Lawrenceburg, Indiana, that we like: Whisky's. He knows how to handle himself in a real nice place. One time I picked up my fork, and he said very quietly, "Mom, that's for your salad." We've traveled a lot, and Michael is always getting cards and letters from people all over the world we met who were just so impressed with him. Not just because he has a disability but because he's a nice young man. One day we were in a store, and the woman at the cash register said to him, "My, what a handsome young man you are." He smiled and said, "Thank you very much." Later he told me, "Mom, people are always telling me that."
—Peggy Creamer

Parents can model the "social niceties" valued in our society. A firm handshake, a "hello" with a smile, and the pleasantries often exchanged in greetings and good-byes are important for your child to learn. The secret, as with so many things, is practice, practice, practice! Siblings and their friends can be enlisted to help teach a good handshake and eye contact during conversation. Expect your son or daughter to be part of the action; if a server asks you what your child wants to order, don't answer for him or her. Ask the server to ask your child! If you know the servers or clerks in your favorite restaurant or store, ask for their help. Learning to order a meal or buy socks are important survival skills, and this competency will enhance your son or daughter's confidence.

> *I hate it when people say, "Oh, they're all so happy." What Nicholas is is gen-uine. He can be genuinely happy, and he can be genuinely grumpy. He's quite aware of things that make us happy, too. When I come home from work, he meets me at the door with this wide open smile and he takes my hand and says, "Tell me about your day, Mom." We have a nice long discussion about my day and his day and Dad's and Lucas' day.*
> —Elizabeth Popowich

> *How come when he meets me at the door, he just says he wants to go to McDonald's?*
> —Greg Popowich

 Rest Stop:

Write down just a few things your child does now that are positive and image reinforcing (says hello, smiles, waves, says thank you when the clerk hands over the bag). Add one thing you'd like your child to practice. What's a reasonable learning time for this? When do you start teaching?

Things my child does that are positive and image reinforcing:		
One thing to practice:	How long will it take to learn?	When do we start?

Role playing can be a fun way for your child to learn how to respond in different situations. Many kids enjoy playing "dress up," "church," "house," or "the office," taking on various roles of family members or people in the neighborhood and community. Build on this pretend play to add to your child's arsenal of responses. Get your child to think, to anticipate, and to have a Plan B for when something unexpected occurs—these are important survival skills.

> *Integration teaches people to act like their peers. If someone is acting like a twit, they're a twit not because they have a disability. They're just being a twit. Kids soon learn that you don't make friends and keep them by being a jerk. People aren't going to want to be around you; friends will come and go depending on the kind of person you are. When kids grow up together and go through school side by side, they see that everyone has their own strengths and weaknesses. One is good at sports, one can really draw, one can tell great jokes, one is a good listener. You need to put people in proximity to spark something.*
> —Greg Popowich

For years, Karin and her husband Richard have focused on their son Jim's conversation skills, important because of his stutter and hearing impairments. With a CD playing, Karin will ask Jim if he'd like to dance, and as they seesaw around the living room, they make small talk. They arrange for him to take a turn asking her to dance. She asks him how his brother and sister and grandparents are doing; he'll answer and ask about her parents. They chat about the cats, the weather, and movies. This small talk also happens waiting in line at the theater or sitting in the doctor's office. Sometimes the small talk is just silly (and doesn't take the place of more substantial conversation), but Jim often uses this skill with family, friends, and people he has just met: "So, how's your brother?" "So, how's your job?" And he's not a bad dancer, either!

 Rest Stop:

Make a *small talk* list of three or four conversation starters your child can practice. If your child does not speak, are there responses like a smile or eye contact that you can work on? A big part of this exercise is the message of worth and value you send your son or daughter: He or she is someone worth having a conversation with!

Three or four conversation starters:

You only have to look in the "Meetings" or personal ad section of your local newspaper to see that there are many people struggling to become better and more at ease in meeting people and handling social situations with confidence. One important and sobering motivator is that just about every self-defense and assertiveness skills course offered to the public lists in its top five tips good eye contact and a straight, self-assured posture to deter potential attackers. If you think your child could use some help, contact one of these groups or even a local public speaking organization. Perhaps your son or daughter could attend a meeting, either alone or with a friend. The groups may offer some general rules or suggestions, and you can modify these. Then practice, practice, practice the ideas with your child.

Talking About Disability

She's very eager to talk about Down syndrome with people. She's eager to let you know she knows all about it. She doesn't see it as a bad thing at all. She knows it takes her longer to learn things, but she's quite open about it. We've never treated it as anything to avoid discussing.
   —Lou Shaw

Michael knows he has a disability. He sometimes sees people in the workshop or group home, and he says, "Mom, I feel sorry for them." Not because they have disabilities, but I think he realizes he has something they don't have. He has a community and a job and his own home. I can see Michael living on here, maybe with someone else, after George and I are gone. He's so proud of doing things for himself. He cuts the grass. He and George do the dishes every night, and I hear them out in the kitchen, cutting up. That's their time together, and I've tried to back off a little bit and let them have time together, just the two of them, to be men.
   —Peggy Creamer

Teaching about grooming is the most natural time to talk to your son or daughter about disability. It is absolutely important that your child knows what his or her disability is and what it does and does not mean. This can be difficult emotionally for parents, but it is essential that children learn about the disability while still quite young. Don't worry if your son or daughter is older. You can still teach; maybe you have already. The disability is a part of who your son or daughter is, and just as your child has a right to know and understand his or her own body, your child also has a right to an understandable explanation about his or her particular disability.

When looking in the mirror, your child can be asked to make sure that she has picked clothing that matches. Talk to her about how her eyes or other physical features might look different from other people's. Make sure that you're pointing out a real difference but also that it doesn't mean a whole lot. When you are in different parts of town or have friends of different cultures over for supper, point out to your child that these people have different eye shapes, too and that the eye shape doesn't matter. Get her to notice people of different heights, weights, statures, sexes, and races. Talk to her about how looking different doesn't mean that you can't be pretty or handsome. Wouldn't it be strange if we all looked and sounded exactly the same?

Remember that the development of a good sense of self happens over time with a lot of reinforcement along the way. Many parents realize that their son or daughter needs support to understand not only how he or she is the same as other children but also to appreciate his or her differences too. Chad Pierro (1994), who has cerebral palsy, says it is wise to do so because "with this knowledge, children will be comfortable with who they are and who they can be." Karin's stepson Jim will occasionally notice someone who also has Down syndrome on the street or in a store. The first time he noticed, he was about 12. He said, "My face. Just like me." He was delighted with Karin's response: "Cool, eh?"

As your child learns grooming skills and as you are beginning to talk about the disability, mention that she might take a bit longer to learn than some other kids but can still learn. Point out things that she can already do alone, and get her to realize that she is a *learner* and that by sticking to something long enough, she will learn how to do it. It is best to conceive of an intellectual disability as a serious learning disability. That's all it is. You don't have to give much more information about it when your child is very young. What you do need to do is talk about how some people can be mean and use mean words. Your child needs to be prepared for what will be faced. Your child needs to know that you are there for her and that you love her *no matter what hateful people say*. Do all of this while chatting naturally while getting ready to go out to a fun event.

> *I thought from time to time as Brad was growing up about having a lesson on his disability. I remember thinking there wasn't much point to getting into great detail about it with Brad or his brothers, other than to explain what it was. Kids don't mind nearly as much as adults expect them to or as much as adults do. Brad makes the observation now and then if he sees someone else with a disability that they look like him.*
> —Ethel Magnus

As your child gets older, you can add more details. Much of this discussion will depend on your child's level of disability. Check the "Recommended Resources" section at the end of this book for sibling materials. You can adapt some of these for your son or daughter with a disability.

Hillary Shaw

Having Down syndrome everything is slow to learn. You have a disability inside. Everyone is different inside. Sometimes they speak Spanish. Sometimes they speak Japan or Chinese. Sometimes I don't understand their speech coming out. Having Down syndrome is to have disabilities. Sometimes it is like change syndrome. It is up syndrome and down syndrome sometimes. In different ways. It is okay to have Down syndrome.

Yeah, I have a boyfriend. His name is Jason. He lives in New York. Jason is a very special person. I am, too. Someday I would get married. Maybe to

Jason, and we will have children. I'm going to have him. I wish. It's not a wish, it's gonna be true.

I read Clan of the Cave Bear. *It's good. I read it every day. See this poster on my door? His name is Jonathan Brandis. He is like my boyfriend, too. He is cute. He is on TV.*

It is like the Disabilities Act. I have a disability. My friends at school, they have disabilities, like Mindy and Jessica. They have to try themselves and be careful because they have disabilities. Sometimes there are hard things, like homework, and we have to have patience.

I would like a boyfriend who has good manners and be appropriate. Good manners in school. We could play games like Monopoly. It would be okay to have a boyfriend who has Down syndrome like Life Goes On *and Chris Burke. He has Down syndrome. One time, we went to dinner, and the boy was acting silly. That is not appropriate. I don't like that. I would like a boyfriend who can play basketball or dancing. I like a date, and we could go to a movie and go to dinner. I wear my white and blue polka dot dress. Yeah. Sometimes I would like to have a boy kiss on the lips if we have our own children someday. That's is for married. A kiss is okay. But not on private parts.*

If he wanted to kiss me and touch me on private parts, I just say "Stay away of my American body. It's mine. My body." That means I am America.

A boy at school, he try to tell me to lift up my shirt. I said no and tell the principal. That's very inappropriate. Very embarrassing. I tell my mom and dad.

I go to dances at my school. Ernesto likes to dance. I don't like makeup. I don't like colors on my face.

I cook, I do. I cook with my mom. I make turkey. I try and make pancakes. Sometime I make Lou some pigs in a blanket. That is good. I make eggs lots of onions. When my mom cooks, my dad and I do dishes. My dad washes. I put them away. And also, I can clean the whole house.

Money is hard. I spend money from my parents. Sometimes I get a video. My dad's crazy all the time! It's true. Sometimes I say to my dad, are you the boss around here? He says yes, he is. I say you're fire.

Sometimes I got consequences. My mom says that all the time. That's like I'm in big trouble. I don't like consequences. I don't get in trouble. I tell the truth, and I'm not in trouble. That's tradition.

I grow up and live in a house like this. By myself. I am 20 when I get married. After high school. I work hard in school. Fractions is hard. I do Chisanbop [a way of doing math using the fingers]. I can do math. My mom and dad practice with me. My homework sometimes.

My dad is the world's greatest father. He is a writer. For Fall Guy. *He does* Quincy. *My favorite is the* Fall Guy *opera. Dad write that show. My mom sings in it. I like it. Sometimes my dad wrote a songs. He write a book. Sometimes he has good ideas.* Include Us, *that my dad's new video. I am in it, too. "Everyone's Different," that's a song in it.*

My sister lives with Bob. Her boyfriend. Bob is a nice looking guy. My dad has grown a beard and a moustache one time. At the wedding for my mom and dad. My mom's 50th wedding. My dad had black hair.

When I get married, I wear my pink dress. I have my hair long, just pretty. I am just perfect like this.

Relationship Boundaries

From toddlerhood to adolescence, children need to learn to understand relationships. That is, they need both to label them and to understand how those relationships make a difference regarding social behavior. Around the age of 8, most kids have relationships down pat. They understand, for example, that Mom and Dad are married, not related. They understand the difference between brother and sister and husband and wife. The most difficult concept is that of "fictive kin." This means that they understand the friend of the family whom they call Auntie Ling-Mei is not really an aunt like Auntie Jean is. They know Auntie Ling-Mei is a good friend of Mom's, and they call her "auntie" out of respect for that closeness. Given that kids with an intellectual disability have a learning disability and that people with intellectual disabilities have difficulty "reading" a social fabric, they are not likely to pick this up without some kind of teaching.

In teaching about relationships, you need to also teach about behaviors that are appropriate with people in different relationships. Most agencies that serve people with intellectual disabilities have or are able to get a wonderful system called *Circles* (Champagne & Walker-Hirsch, 1986–1993; see the "Recommended Resources" for more information). You may want to get this system and take a look at it. Even though *Circles* is set up to be taught in a group, its concepts are easy to adapt for one-to-one parent–child teaching. If you can't afford to buy your own set, you can probably get away with teaching the concept by drawing ever-widening circles on a big piece of paper or you may be able to borrow it from your local parent or self-advocacy organization. The program is set up so that the learner is shown a drawing that has a large, darkly colored circle in the middle. Then there are several circles that surround the middle circle. Each of these circles is defined by the behavior that is appropriate. The circles are the "close hug" circle, the "big hug" circle, the "handshake" circle, the "wave" circle, and the "stranger" circle.

Chris delivers mail to the secretaries in the building. The one to sign for a package wasn't at her desk, so he asked another secretary to sign. In the meantime, the first one came back, and the one he was dealing with said, "Oh, Chris, your girlfriend is back." She doesn't realize that Chris just might take that literally. We want him to have a good working relationship with people, and we have to teach him how to treat women on the job. It's not the same as high school or a social relationship.

—Gayle Foy

The fact that we have a breeding farm makes the conversation very natural. As things happen, I've tried to explain to Brad and relate it to men and women. Brad's had a few crushes and some sad and hurt feelings. He had quite a crush on the valedictorian at school. But the other boys have had their crushes and broken hearts, too. We try to help Brad understand that if someone hurts you or has been unkind, maybe that's not the kind of person you want to be around. Not that it always changes his feelings, but we try to help him think about it.

—Ethel Magnus

John and Ethel Magnus
Salt Spring Island, British Columbia

The principles of *Circles* are intended to help people with intellectual disabilities identify relationships and gain control over those relationships, their own bodies, and their own feelings. The principles include

- You are the most important person in your world. You are the center of all of your circles.
- No one touches you unless you want to be touched.
- There are very few people who hug you—close family or a sweetheart only.
- There are a few more people with whom you might exchange a far-away, friendly hug, such as a friend, on occasion.
- You shake hands with acquaintances, if you know their names.
- You wave to children and to others you know if they are too busy or too far away to shake hands.
- You talk to community helpers only about the business at hand.
- You do not talk to or touch strangers, and they do not talk to or touch you.
- You are the most important person in the world. It is your decision how close you want others to be to you. (Champagne & Walker-Hirsch, 1992, p. 2)

Circles helps to bridge the gap between knowing and using information by connecting cognitions related to social and sexual development and practice to a sense of self-control, autonomy, and powerfulness (Champagne & Walker-Hirsch, 1992). The principles outlined are obviously not carved in stone. For example, a police officer or security guard may be a community helper *and* a stranger. Even though one of the principles is to not talk to strangers, speaking to a police officer is not the same risk as talking to someone lurking in the dark shadows of a back alley or even to an unknown man or woman offering candy and a car ride. The principles establish the social interactions that generally relate to the people who are most likely to come into contact with your child in a variety of situations.

She needs to be accepting of herself before she's accepted by others. She needs to know she's worthwhile. I want her to be a self-sufficient person who can stand up for herself. I don't want her to let other people push her around, and I don't want her to feel bad because someone else is ignorant.
    —*Shelly Garner*

One family had a wonderful time with the *Circles* concept. They made up their own chart by placing their child's picture in the center of the circles. Then they took pictures of Mom, Dad, and Sister and placed them in the "close hug" circle. Auntie Gladys and Aunt Solvieg, along with Uncle Nels, went into the "big hug" circle. They took a picture of the child's teacher and teacher's aide as well as the babysitter and placed them in the "handshake" circle. The letter carrier agreed to have his picture taken, and he, along with a friendly bus driver, went into the "wave" circle. The child then had a *map* of his life, and his parents could talk about relationships and touch.

What the family noticed right off was that other than family and paid support people (whom they insisted should *not* be allowed to have a hugging intimacy with their child), their child had no other friends. Their goal was to increase the number and type of relationships that their child had. This concept was very workable for them because right from the beginning they were able to teach their child about relationships and physical boundaries. As they increased people in their child's life, they found themselves noticing real growth. There was a celebration when they took a picture of the bank teller and added her to the "wave" group. This meant that their child was now banking on his own. They said that their son's *Circles* map was kind of like the notches on a door frame that marks physical growth.

She has a friend, Michael. It was a bit confusing for her for awhile because she couldn't decide if he was a boyfriend or a friend. We tried to help her with that, but we weren't sure either. One of the teachers at school said she thought maybe there was more going on than just friendship and we shouldn't be so naïve. We like him. They spend a lot of time together.
    —*Peggy Hutchison*

I hope she does find someone someday with whom intimacy will be appropriate. She does want a boyfriend very badly. There are school dances. She has one friend, Ernesto, and we've double-dated. He comes over and we'll drive to a movie; sometimes they'll go see a movie they want to see, and we'll go to another one in the same complex. We'll have dinner. We started off with separate tables, and now they've wanted to sit with us.
    —*Michele Shaw*

Using *Circles* is fun and easy. The program can easily be adapted for home use and used as an ongoing teaching strategy. Some families have asked for the school to host *Circles* as a training module for all students. Clearly, the issues involved in teaching about relationships and boundaries are important for all children. Interestingly, some resources and practices, like *Circles*, which is aimed at kids with intellectual disabilities, are better than some others on the market for typical kids. That's because the approach is simple, clear, and engaging.

Karin's Story

Sometimes it seems difficult to even figure out who is or might be part of Jim's circle. And sometimes we make this stuff too difficult when the answer is right before us. Richard and I gathered together some photographs of Jim's half year with us (he is the ultimate Canadian snowbird and lives in California with his mom during our winter). We wanted to make him one of those personalized calendars for Christmas. We thought we'd write in all Jim's relatives' birthdays and anniversaries so he could see what was happening to significant people in his life on any particular day while he was away from us.

As we filled in the birthdays of siblings, grandparents, aunts, uncles, and cousins, we also thought of some co-workers, the guy at the video store who always says hi, the butcher Jim used to work for who moved to Vancouver, and that guy at the YMCA who took Jim to the Foreigner concert last year. As we filled in Jim's calendar, we realized what we had was not only a good way for Jim to keep in touch with people, but also a pretty good start on Jim's circles.

You can do the same thing by asking yourself: Whom does—or would—your child send a holiday or birthday greeting card to? If your child was on a trip, who would get postcards? Then ask yourself, if there is no one, why not?

 Rest Stop:

Use the space here to start a list of "contacts" for your child. Don't be bashful or feel embarrassed that you're forcing your child on someone who might not know him or her well. At this point, it's just a greeting card, and everyone loves getting mail!

Contacts:
What will be the purpose of the contact? (Get birth date, address, telephone number, and an "okay" to be in touch.)

How and when will the contact be made?

On a daily basis, parents can support their children's appropriate social development by building on the connections in the neighborhood and at school. Use ordinary activities to support your child or teenager's opportunity to be around others, but also use them as a chance to teach others about your child. It is critical that parents appreciate that friendship building is a responsibility that can be shared:

- We can invite children over to play, and include them with the family on regular outings and holidays. We can make our homes welcoming and fun places to be. We can create environments that attract other children and teens by having snacks available and fun activities to do. We can also create special occasions for parties (birthdays, Halloween) and invite our children's peers and their parents to attend.
- We can welcome our son or daughter's teen friends to watch videos, providing snacks and a space for them to hang out. Some families have invested in sports equipment that attracts other kids to their house or yard—trampolines, climbing frames, or basketball hoops.
- When friends come to visit, we can model appropriate communication, demonstrate how to adapt games to enhance inclusion, or simply structure activities that promote equality and encourage positive communication and social interactions between all children when playing.
- We can demonstrate techniques that help make our children and teens feel comfortable and safe in new situations.
- We can minimize adult involvement by letting the kids be together as often as is advisable or by pulling back on our verbal involvement so kids can sort out situations on their own with the comfort of knowing we are there if needed.
- We can offer opportunities for other parents to learn about the individual needs of our children and teens so they can be more comfortable and confident about inviting them over. Offering our homes for meetings or potlucks provides opportunities to meet other parents. And we can offer support to other families in their attempts to include our children by letting them know we are available for support when needed.
- We can be a bridge to friends by playing with other children in the community: starting a baseball game in the park, bringing out the badminton set, joining in the hockey game in the parking lot, pushing other kids on the swings, or playing hide and seek. We can choose games that easily include our children and then facilitate their participation.
- We can stay in touch with our son or daughter's peers, observing where they hang out, what activities they enjoy, and the trends in clothing, music and hairstyles they follow. And we can talk with kids who are the same age as our son or daughter, asking them for their ideas and input.

- We can build on today's successes by thinking of ways to encourage our children and young people to want to be together again. (Rousseau, 1995, pp. 14–15)

Some of the most wonderful offshoots of integration and connections with community aren't the most obvious or immediate. This summer, he went into the video store here, and I noticed a young man watching him quite intently. He finally went over to Jim and said, "Are you Jim Schwier?" Jim said he was. Turned out Doug and Jim had gone to school together in the second grade. Doug remembered him 12 years later. Now, every time Jim stops in for a video, he and Doug have a talk about movies.
—Richard Schwier

 ## Rest Stop:

Record some things you've successfully arranged in the past that brought your child together with neighborhood children or classmates. Or, write down one activity you'd like to try:

Some successful activities we've tried or would like to try:

It's difficult to cover the bases with a subject like sexuality and relationships, which involves children and adults with a wide range of intellectual capacity, behavior, language level, and family expectations. But clearly, there are many young people with intellectual disabilities who are very much the same as their age peers without disabilities. Teenage girls develop crushes and get giggly about the cute boys at school. They put posters of rock singers and soap opera hunks up on their bedroom wall. There are also people with (and without) significant disabilities who don't seem to show much interest in these sorts of things. Parents need to be in touch with their children for clues about their sexuality. In addition, as Dick Sobsey says,

If your son or daughter doesn't have any opportunity to be around people of the opposite sex, or their own sex, for that matter, of about the same age, it makes sense for parents to create those opportunities. Watch what happens. Some people without disabilities have a greater need for more social connections; some have less. You have to find that out about your own child. (personal communication, 1995)

She's so into boys. Her whole class is boy crazy. That's just what all the girls talk about. Typical conversation among all her 7-year-old friends is "I'm going to marry him." "No, you're not, I am." She's right in there picking out which boy she wants.
    —Denise Duffey

The curiosity and interest is there. He's got a stack of magazines that irritate me to no end, but I think it's pretty normal. I tell all the boys that I just don't want to see them, and if I find them lying around, I'll burn them. If they're important to you, then look after them and keep them in your room. I think that's fair. They're all adult men, but I'm still their mother and I still have my opinion. So we all respect each other's privacy.
    —Ethel Magnus

Jim's never had a girlfriend, or boyfriend, for that matter. I'd really like to know what sort of person he thinks is attractive. At this point, he seems to like both Commander Riker and Councillor Troi on Star Trek. In the fall, a Victoria's Secret catalogue came in the mail. I was flipping through the bras when Jim walked by, stopped, looked, and said very seriously, "Karin, I need that," and took it to his room.
    —Karin Melberg Schwier

As your son or daughter grows up (as was the case with all of us), there are a number of powerful drives going on. Some of these are a part of normal and healthy sexual development, learning how it feels physically and emotionally to be male or female and what it means socially to be a man or woman. Some of those drives involve the need to be social and develop friendships and relationships. All of it is a process of discovery. In her book *Shared Feelings: A Parent Guide to Sexuality Education for Children, Adolescents and Adults Who Have a Mental Handicap,* Diane Maksym (1990a) asked what children are learning when they learn about sexuality and what *sexuality* means. She explained,

- Learning about sexuality means being held, cuddled, [and] stroked by parents and caretakers
- Learning about sexuality means finding out what it means to be a boy or a girl
- Learning about sexuality is being curious about your body
- Learning about sexuality is running, playing, [and] wrestling with friends in the neighborhood
- Learning about sexuality is coming to terms with the physical changes of puberty and wondering, "Am I normal?" (pp. 19–21)

The more a parent tries to isolate a person or suppress the process of discovery, the more frustrated the drive becomes. If you find out your daughter was kissing your neighbor's son in their rumpus room, you'll be tempted to shriek, "That's it! That's the last time you're going over there! You'll never see that boy again!" A more reasonable solution may be a discussion about sexual behavior and an agreement that the boy is allowed to come over to your house while you're at home or that you'll chaperone them someplace together.

> *We've worked on her self-esteem, but it's pretty well intact. She's got a good one. One of the difficult things to teach someone who has a natural inclination to be affectionate is where to draw the line. It's cute when they're little to hug, but people get into some trouble and can make other people uncomfortable. We had an interesting thing happen the other night when the son of my closest friend was over. We were watching a video I'd just finished. He's quite a good looking guy, and he was sitting beside Hillary. She put her arm around him, cuddled up close and, because they don't know each other well, he was uncomfortable. I was by the piano, and Hillary looked up; I just shook my head. Very gently, she took her arm away and just sat next to him. I was so proud of her, and I told her later that I was proud she was acting more appropriately with Alex.*
> —Lou Shaw

> *At American United Life, Chris is around businesspeople, working with secretaries when he delivers mail and packages. We had a little slip recently. He was riding in an elevator when a very attractive woman got on. She was wearing bright lipstick, so Michael said, "Nice lips." She didn't say anything. As he was leaving the elevator, he smiled and said, "Nice breasts." She wrote him up for sexual harassment. The personnel department wasn't sure what to do, but I asked them what would they do with anyone else? We had a meeting. Chris realized it was a totally inappropriate thing to say, and he'll never do it again. Had the woman told him he was being rude, he would have realized then and stopped immediately. So we have to do a bit of awareness training, with him and with the people he works with every day.*
> —Gayle Foy

Talk with your child about friendships and dating:

- What's the difference between friendship and dating?
- If you don't feel comfortable about dating yet, do you have to?
- What are some options, like group dating?
- What can you talk about on a date?
- What are some things you can do?

Try some role playing; enlist your other children.

> *Our friend, Jean Edwards, knew a woman who wanted a boyfriend, and Jean said, "Why don't you make a list of the things you'd like in a boyfriend?" The woman said, "Well, I want him to be taller than me. I want him to be cute. And I want him to know how to rollerskate." Well, Jean just happened to know someone who was tall and cute and knew how to rollerskate! They got together, went on a few dates, and, sure enough, they got married and it's a happy marriage.*
> —Michele Shaw

There's always some teasing that goes on between siblings, but encourage your other children to take their brother or sister's blossoming interest in dating and relationships seriously. By helping them understand that their sibling is a developing, healthy, sexual person, the whole family is more likely to see him or her in a positive and respectful light.

> *I think your other children look to you for clues about what their brother or sister's life might be like. Even when I was still "Dad's girlfriend," and Ben was only 6, he asked me out of the blue, "Will we have to take care of Jim for his whole life?" I told him I hoped Jim will find someone, get married, and with our help they could look after each other. He thought for a moment, then said, "Cool."*
>
> *—Karin Melberg Schwier*

> *I think all of his brothers are quite different than they would have been had it not been for Brad. They have a sensitivity and a willingness to be themselves. They've seen what people say can't be done actually done over and over again. They have a sensitivity—and that doesn't mean being sympathetic—but they have a sense of inclusion and supporting people to do what they can do.*
>
> *—John Magnus*

Parents can develop a sense of responsibility in their child by giving freedom in a progressive way. If your daughter has never been anywhere without a chaperone, start slow. Maybe the couple could go for a walk for 15 minutes, but make sure they understand they're to be back in 15 minutes. Maybe you'll drop them at McDonald's for a half hour and pick them up at a set time. If that works, let the reins go a little over time. They could go to a movie; you could sit at the back or in the theater next door, and you can all meet at a designated spot by the door when the movie lets out.

 Rest Stop:

What are some independent activities you might let your child try? List them, even if doing this makes you nervous!

Independent activities my child might try:

There's a place called Monty's [a strip bar] in Victoria, and Brad had gone there with Nolan and his friends. Well, he thought it was pretty hot stuff. They're all adults; I don't necessarily approve, but they can go if they want anyway. Brad was very late getting back to the island on one occasion after his dancing lessons. I got on the phone to Monty's and explained my situation, and they were very helpful. None of the men in the family could believe I could call a strip bar and get so much information. I think it worried them all! Brad finally came strutting home off the ferry a few hours later. It turned out he'd stopped by McDonald's, taken his hamburger over to Monty's, and ate it while he watched the dancing. I can't imagine them letting anyone into a strip bar with a McDonald's bag, but he did it.

—Ethel Magnus

A lot of parents discourage their children from being overly friendly. I've always wondered why we teach people that it's not appropriate to hug, almost to the point where people are scared to ever touch each other. Maybe it's very appropriate that we hug and very inappropriate if we don't! I sometimes look at Katherine and the way she views the world; she sometimes seems to enjoy people and has a better time of it than her sisters do. She seems to enjoy her life and is much more vibrant. I sometimes watch her quietly while she's dancing or acting out scenes from plays, and she gets so much enjoyment out of it. I wonder what's wrong with that. She just dives right into relationships. What's the big deal if she gets on the bus and strikes up a conversation with the driver or the person next to her? Maybe we're all too tense. She and I used to go to the young people's theater, and at the end of the show, the actors would come out and ask for questions from the audience. It's not always easy for people to understand Katherine, so when it was time for the questions, I would start distracting her. I eventually realized that I was doing it because I was embarrassed and worried about me. I wasn't letting people experience Katherine. People have always been good to her and have tried to understand her, but I was more worried about being embarrassed.

—Bob Manwaring

Q

My husband and I are trying to teach our 10-year-old son "Peter" about modesty and public and private. His little brother is only 2 and runs around in a diaper or scurries around naked after his bath. Peter thinks it's okay for him to run around, too. Teaching him is a real challenge. Any tricks on getting him to cover up?

A

Teaching about privacy is complex. It's probably a good idea to simplify the concepts and to put in some visual cues to remind everyone about "privacy rules." First, separate his clothing into private and public drawers. Mark each with a symbol; many parents use a picture of an open door for public and a closed door for private. Others simply use a piece of red tape for private and green tape for public. (Avoid using a happy face for public and a sad face for private. Your child may well assume that private means sad or mad.) Now, on the doors of public rooms of the house, place the public symbol. On the private rooms, place the private symbol. Explain that in public rooms, we wear public clothing. To reduce the confusion, you may want to put a public symbol on the diaper. It's probably a good idea to stop Peter's younger brother from running around naked. It may not seem fair, but fair sometimes isn't the most important issue.

By focusing on private and public, you take away any concerns about teaching that the body is dirty, bad, or wrong. It also allows you to generalize later on to other issues. From topics of conversations to words to behavior, there's a lot to know about public and private. Starting at the beginning, you will be able to build all the various layers of subtlety that is involved in understanding privacy.

Q

How soon should my child start doing chores around the house? I mean cleaning her room, caring for the dog, and helping set and clear the table. We have another child, too.

A

This is a simple question. You start your daughter doing chores at exactly the same age as you would with your other child. There can be a tendency to delay assigning chores because of the disability, but this can breed resentment in your other child and it can diminish self-esteem in your child with a disability. You may be thinking that because the chores are complex, your child just isn't "up to learning them yet" and that you should wait until she is "ready" to learn. Your daughter is *always* ready to learn. You just have to be ready to teach.

The teaching tools you need to become aware of are the *task analysis* and *backward chaining*. Let's take making the bed as an example. To do a task analysis, you need to break the task down into its component parts. Just go at it one step at a time, and write down each step of the task. Now, backward chaining is teaching the child the task from the last step back to the first. This procedure prevents frustration, builds on success, and teaches sequencing. To do backward chaining, go into the bedroom with your child and use that parallel talk to describe what you are doing. Let her watch you make the bed all the way up to the final step, pulling the comforter over the pillows. Now get her to help you do the last step. When it's done, praise her for the made bed. I know, I know. You did most of the work, but what you are doing is connecting a finished product with praise and approval. Do this until your daughter can do the last step quite independently. Depending on your child, this process may take a long time. Keep at it until she's got it. Now, back up and teach the second-to-last step, add the last step, and then praise her. Keep adding one more step until you have taught the entire task from start to finish.

One of the nice things about this procedure is that it takes so little time to do. If you try to teach bed-making as a single task starting from the beginning, it is going to take a lot longer to do it, let alone teach it!

Q

Our son is 5 and has taken to showing his penis to neighborhood kids because they all shriek, laugh and run around, then come back for another look. We've told him that this is not nice and that his penis is private. But I think the other children's reactions just egg him on, and he thinks it's worth getting in trouble with us. Any ideas?

A

Yes. Supervise, supervise, supervise. This must stop now! Right now. Put down this book, and get to planning so that for the next several weeks, he is never, ever in this position again. If you can't afford a babysitter, call your social worker, counselor, or whomever and start lobbying for some funding. This is very serious.

First, your child is being victimized because of his disability. This is unacceptable. Second, your child may be learning a behavior that will get him in very serious trouble in just a few years. This, too, is unacceptable. Spend time with the other children; try to be with and near your child in the yard when the other kids come by. Make yourself invisible. Then, when he's about to drop his pants, intervene. Quickly, gently but firmly, stop him. Right in front of those kids. Let them know that this is over. Should you hear them egg him on, get right down by your son, look at him; don't look at the other children, and say to your son, "No! Tell those kids no!" Get him to say no himself. Never look at the other children. Focus on your son, and have the words of power come out of *his* mouth. The other children will figure out that Mom or Dad is on the scene now, and they'll get a new message, but it must come out of your son's mouth. If this doesn't work, get help. Go to the other children's parents to explain what's happening. Talk to a social worker. Get advice from a children's aid worker. Talk to people who can give you some direction and support.

Q

My ex-husband and I have pretty different views on parenting our daughter, who has a disability. I think he does far too much for her, and she learns just to sit there and seems so much more dependent than she is. I don't think he sees her as an adult, even though we've had this discussion many times and he says all the right things. My expectations are very different. Do you think this is difficult for our daughter? She seems to act like a capable person in one home and like a child in the other. It makes planning for her future in the long term very difficult.

A

This is not only about disability—it is also about divorce. Keeping this in mind will help keep this in perspective. It doesn't sound like it is as difficult for your daughter as it is for you, but it might lead to problems in the long run. Sure, she's learning that people have different expectations for her. She's living up to one set and down to another; this is not great for consistency, but kids are pretty adaptable. Right now, maybe you need to communicate enthusiastically to your ex-husband about the things your daughter can do when she's with you. "Hey, did you know that this week Jackie learned to put the dishes away? Cool, eh?" This gives information, but without confrontation. Consistent messages about capability may seep in sometimes. If possible, have your daughter demonstrate for her dad her new skill. Have her show her dad the shoes she tied when he comes to pick her up. Better yet, when she has learned to do something wonderful, like bake a cake or cross a street by herself, make a movie, and have her give her dad the video. He'll watch it, and she'll want to see it over and over and so will he.

Just remember, almost every set of divorced parents has these kinds of problems. It's better for your daughter to have parents who are civil and who speak respectfully to one another than to have parents who are fighting. The difference for people with disabilities whose parents are divorced is that they're not as likely to assert themselves and make their own dreams known. So educate your husband about his daughter, subtly, and see if things just start changing on their own.

Q

I try to encourage my son, who is 12, to be less dependent on me. He gets quite worried if I'm not home when he comes home from school. He insists on going everywhere with me, including sometimes standing outside the bathroom door. We've tried having him visit overnight with school friends with disastrous results. How do we make him feel more confident and less tied to me?

A

Does he have anyone else in his life that he considers friends? When you say "school friends," are these really "friends" or just people who know him and are willing to have him visit? We don't mean to be callous, but in many so-called "inclusive" settings, people with disabilities seem to be more like the classroom pet than like equal classmates. This is not inclusion. We know of one situation where a young woman stayed at a friend's place because the teacher asked, "Now, who wants to take care of Joanna for the weekend?" You could substitute "Joanna" with "the gerbil" and the sentence would still make sense. So check and see if your son really has friends. Be brutally honest with your answer to this question. You don't want your son to arrive at adulthood with only "friends" who are really volunteers or paid support people.

Alternately, your son may have friends but may have had a disastrous visit because an overnight was just too long. Start with half an hour. Drive around the block, go for a coffee, and then go get him. As he gets comfortable with that time away from you, slowly increase it to an hour, then a couple of hours, and so forth. Ease him away from you. It's important to do this slowly and gently, but with resolve. He needs to go through this; he will survive (and so will you!). Don't stop the process because he begs and pleads with you. This is a natural reaction to the transition away from parental company, even if it is painful for him now. He will survive.

Jim Schwier

I am Jim Schwier. James C. Schwier. Captain James C. Kirk Schwier, just like Star Trek! My house Visalia. We move. Culver City. New house, 1904, Visalia. Two houses. My dad, Karin, Sakatoon, 908. Canada. We share a room, 1904, Ben. Me and Ben my brother. My stuff and his stuff. He touch my things, my Star Trek stuff. My sister Erin at college. Her driving a car. College. San E-ego with her friend Debbie. She take her stuff.

Dad and Karin, we get marry San E-ego. Ben and me have rings. Erin wore her clothes. I wear my clothes. Ben has wear his clothes. A suit, just like Dad. Me and Dad, for me has a tie. Dad, Karin at Saskatoon. Charlie my step-father, long time ago, at...my school. I am little kid. Long time ago, me and Erin and Ben and Charlotte my mom and dad. Yellow house. Long time ago, I am little boy.

I miss Momo and Bobo. Fred and Mom. My father's father and mother. Grampa and Madelyn. I have sleepover at my Grampa. Thanksgiving. Madelyn's friend, Mary Wickes. She say hi to me. Madelyn's work for "I Love Lucy." Madelyn's friend, John Ritter. I have lunch with him. He say hi to me! My Uncle Ned his work "Murphy Brown" on TV. And Helen and the kids. I go to sleep over with them Seattle. They miss me.

Long time ago, I be a doctor. White jacket and white pants. My black shoes. My black socks. Just like Dad. Just like Grampa. Same ones.

Saskatoon, Country Butcher my job. My boss Jason. The butcher my apron on. I clean and I stir lemon juice on. I put meat in it. Sukyaki. I roll it, sticks. Things. Put lemon juice on it. Stir it. I dust windows. Bottles off in the basket, put it in basket. Put Windex and wipe it off. Put it back in. All clean, all of it. I am happy Schwier for my boss Jason. My buddy.

It bugs me school. I go to Y, my new friends. I do sweeping. My reading book. I do business stuff, labels on it. I go home, take the bus. By myself. I got my key. 1301 Visalia and 908 Saskatoon. Both ones.

Q

We want to plan ahead. What major areas should we at least be getting some information on now while our child is young?

A

There are a number of areas to consider in teaching your child about sexuality and safety. The book, *Just Say Know! Understanding and Reducing the Risk of Sexual Victimization of People with Developmental Disabilities* (Hingsburger, 1995), outlines a "ring of safety" that comprises a number of teachable skills aimed at teaching about sexuality, boundaries, decision making, and assertiveness. Each of these areas is important.

Unfortunately, a sex education class is not enough. You need to be teaching other social and assertiveness skills. If *Just Say Know!* is not available or if you want more immediate information, call the police. Talk to the officer who does "streetproofing" training and make an appointment to take a look at what is being taught and how it is being taught. These folks are very approachable, and their material is excellent. You may be able to begin today to teach some skills that will grow with your child.

Q

How do I teach my child to regularly use deodorant? I don't want to nag him every morning, but unless I do, he doesn't use it.

A

Ah, adolescence. Your hormones start running, your face explodes, and your pits start smelling; what a time! The body changes that occur at adolescence are difficult enough and on top of that, some of the "oppositional behavior" (the Obnoxious Teenager Syndrome) that comes with hormone changes can be difficult. But it is survivable. There are three things to consider in teaching about deodorant (or other hygiene related issues): choice, process, and result.

Before you pass out at the word *choice*, this is not about "the right to stink." This is about "the right to smell the way you want to smell." Sometimes adolescents with disabilities are just given a deodorant that Mom picked up at the local drug store. As your child is maturing and becoming an adult, why not take your child to the store and let him sniff his way to armpit bliss? Deodorants come in a variety of scents and a variety of means of application from spray, to stick, to crystal cleansers. Let your son pick one he likes. And it doesn't matter if you like it! Remember, he has to develop his own tastes and feel involved in the decision. Besides, picking up a scent that is liked is reinforcing just in its usage.

Second is the issue of process. Many people with disabilities have difficulty sequencing tasks. That means that they learn individual steps but have difficulty doing the task in its entirety. Take a picture of your son doing his morning "sink routine" (don't include bathing or showering; pictures of your son nude would be inappropriate). For example, take a picture of face washing, face drying, teeth brushing, mouth rinsing, shaving, applying of deodorant, and whatever else is necessary. Put these pictures in a plastic casing that can be tacked up near the sink and mirror. Have your son do his own check before he leaves. Rather than come in and do the evaluation, have him do it himself. Point to the pictures, and have him check to see if it is done. Soon he won't need the pictures or the reminders.

Results! We all like results. Make sure that you talk to him when he has put on his deodorant. Tell him he looks and smells great! In one situation, a mother and child fought about deodorant every morning. It was quite a scene. We suspect that the child enjoyed all of the foo-for-rah and indeed noted that when the child *did* put on deodorant, Mom just seemed relieved *but didn't say anything!* It became clear that the child was learning that the only way to get Mom's attention was to do something that bothered or upset her. Don't fall into this trap. Learn to praise that which you want to occur more frequently. Make a big deal out of the fact that he remembered how to do his morning routine. Make him feel that it was worth the effort to remember it all.

Q

My daughter seems more comfortable with her mouth open. This makes her disability look much more severe than it really is, so people expect less. (Also, I worry about respiratory problems.) I want her to think about how she looks and remember to close her mouth, especially when she's around other people. Any ideas?

A

There is a technique called "video self-modeling" that is wonderful for teaching people new skills and how to present themselves to the world. What you do is make a movie about your daughter. Call it "Looking Great!" Have her put on nice clothing, and then make a video of her using manners at the dinner table (remind her before taping to keep her mouth closed). Do several different scenes, like visiting Grandpa in the front room, shopping with Mom, and going to church, and before taping all the scenes, remind her to keep her mouth closed. At the end of every scene, have her look at the camera and say, "I'm looking great!"

Now that you have the video, show it to her only twice a day, even if she insists on seeing it more often. When she is watching the film, remind her about all of the things she is doing right. "Look at how straight you are sitting. Oh, there, look at that nice smile. You look so pretty." This way you are teaching her to see herself in a particular way. You are also no longer emphasizing the tongue or mouth. You are focusing on the "reason" behind why she should keep her mouth closed.

No, you aren't done yet. Now you have to go in search of your daughter when she's "looking great." When you see your child sitting in the front room watching television and her mouth is closed, pop your head in and say, "You're looking great!" Reward her when her mouth is closed, and keep catching her when it is. Between the reinforcers and the teaching tool, learning should occur.

Q

My daughter, 21, has developed a crush on her stepfather. She almost always follows him from room to room. If we go to a movie, she'll spend most of it staring at the side of his face, which is quite distracting! We've tried a few strategies to remind her of the roles and that he's not her boyfriend, but she persists. We've been married for 12 years, so he's not a novelty!

A

It's time for honesty. Sometimes we are so careful about the feelings of a child with a disability that we let him or her do things that hurt our feelings or make us uncomfortable. First, determine whether your daughter is looking for clues about how to respond in various situations. Maybe she doesn't "get" the movie and is looking to someone for hints about how to act? (Does she usually sit next to your husband in the theater?) Some discussion and modeling around this can be helpful. If you don't think this is it, you are doing your child no favor by not challenging this behavior. Have your husband flat out tell her that she makes him uncomfortable when she follows him around. He doesn't need to be rude or harsh in his language, but a clear message of discomfort is necessary. If she persists, then ask her to leave the room after one warning or have your husband leave the room. Now, it's your turn. Tell her you don't like it. Be clear and don't try to save her feelings. Her behavior is not just silly and childish; it's one that could get her into trouble. If she doesn't learn about roles and boundaries at home, she will be at risk for similar mistakes with people who could take advantage of her. So...be blunt—kind, but blunt. Put your foot down hard on this.

Q

I'd like my daughter to be a strong, assertive person when she grows up. When we talk about sticking up for yourself and not being afraid to speak up, she takes that like it's okay to be mean and bossy. She's 7. How do I help her understand that people can be strong without being loud and aggressive?

A

When you've taught your daughter, could you teach a few other people we know? This is tricky. Teaching assertion, not aggression, is difficult. Role plays and practice sessions can be really helpful. In situations where your daughter is just playing, try to enter into the play and act out some situations. "Hey, Rachel, your dolly just took my dolly's toy. What should my dolly do?" Act out the solutions. Don't forget you are a role model. Trouble is, parents use skills without explaining them. Imagine for a second that you have to tell a waiter that your tea is cold. Say to your daughter, "My tea is cold. I want to tell the waiter. How do you think I should do it?" Then do it properly. Show her that it's okay to speak up, politely, for herself.

Failing this, if your daughter has difficulty, it may be that the issue isn't assertion, it's anger. If your child has problems with anger management, there are some really good teaching strategies out there. Look for them, or check with a counselor for some good anger management strategies and resources, such as the *Habilitative Mental Health Care Newsletter,* which is now called *Mental Health Aspects of Developmental Disabilities* (see the "Recommended Resources" section at the end of this book for more information).

Wallis and Donna Serblowski
Bruno, Saskatchewan

Chapter 6

Leave Me Alone

Build Bridges

All parents dream of guiding their son or daughter down the path toward independence and self-sufficiency. Encouraging your child to "stand on his or her own two feet" means independence and, one day, a successful life without you. Parents of sons and daughters with intellectual disabilities need to be aware that building the bridges from childhood to adulthood, from dependence to greater independence—and interdependence in the community—may take more deliberate construction. There's a reason that the Eternal Child Myth got started! Parents need to help—sometimes forcefully—their children cross over to become men and women. Otherwise, let's face it, it's a lot more fun and less responsibility to stay a kid!

The fact that your child has an intellectual disability does not mean that you aren't going to experience Hormone Hatred as your child goes into adolescence. There is a time, just before puberty, when kids start to demand greater space from their parents. Parental closeness, emotional and physical, becomes embarrassing, and parents really feel an emotional wrench as the child pulls away, often with great force, from the parent–child bond. Given that this is the child's job, if the child doesn't do it, the parent isn't likely to. That means that parents of kids with intellectual disabilities need to begin to move away from their children.

Dr. William Schwab (1992) referred to the natural process of a child's becoming more independent as *launching*. It happens when a child lives away from the family home, it happens economically when a child is financially self-sufficient, and it happens in decision making when a child assumes autonomy in directing his life. The experience of adolescent launching can be substantially skewed by the presence of disability. Parents need to help their sons or daughters "launch" themselves into the teenage and adult world by supporting more independent experiences and choices.

When the three of us go anywhere on the bus, she won't sit with us now. She'll go find her own seat. She likes being independent. I think that's really good, and she's exercising her ability to do things she wants to do. It's good to see.
—Darryl Davey

Stand back, bite your tongue, or sit on your hands; do what you must to allow your child to mature. Has your teenager been given the opportunity to go shopping at the mall with a friend or relative—without you? Has she ever done volunteer work—without you? Has she ever traveled to visit a relative on a plane—without you? Teenagers and young adults with intellectual disabilities need a variety of experiences not only to broaden their own view of the world and its possibilities but also to give them a more mature message content in their communication and to be perceived as more mature people (Horstmeier, 1990).

Being a teenager around 16 or 17 is a funny age for her. On one hand, she wants to go to camp during the summer and be a camper. But all her peers are

*going to camp in staff roles. We've compromised, and she'll go to one camp as a
camper and we've negotiated for another where she'll be an assistant counselor.
She flips back and forth. Am I still a kid? Am I a woman? It sometimes comes
out in behavior. She'll get stubborn and won't do things. One minute, you're
having high expectations and treating her like an adult. The next minute, she
thinks you're treating her like a baby, so she gets mad.*

    —Peggy Hutchison

    Some of the more obvious things a parent might consider to help a child ma-
ture may not be so obvious because you and your child live together day to day.
Make every effort to see your teenager as his chronological age, and avoid the
tendency to add, "But he really acts as though he's 8 or 9." Of course you need
to use common sense about your son's level of development, but if you start
teaching yourself—and others—to see him as a teenager or an adult instead of an
infant in sheep's clothing, you'll have an easier time helping him become more
independent. Discourage babytalk. Allowing your child to refer to you as
"Mommy" or "Daddy," to wear clothing that is not age appropriate, and to act
childish reinforces the eternal child stereotype not only with others, including
potential abusers to whom he will seem more vulnerable, but also with your
family. All children take pride in the fact they are "growing up." The point is not
to stifle a fun-loving spirit, but your child may need a few more reminders and
support from you to leave childhood and "baby stuff" behind.

*It's hard to wean him off baby toys, especially when he enjoys them so much.
You can't take everything away. If we go on a trip, we'll maybe take his elephant along, but he has it at bedtime. At worst, he'll be 40 years old with
a stuffed elephant on his bed. He won't be taking it with him to the bank or
the store.*

    —Don Bradshaw

*When my father was about 79, he fell while he was fixing my car. He really
hurt his back and couldn't move. Hillary was 5; Mariah was about 12. Lou
and I found Dad and helped him to the house. He was really in excruciating
pain. Lou got on the phone to 911. Mariah was crying hysterically. Hillary
disappears. She comes back with a wet washcloth for Grampa's forehead.
Nobody taught her that. She just knew Grampa wasn't feeling well, and she
just figured it out. I sometimes think people can be much more mature than
we give them credit for being.*

    —Michele Shaw

 ## Rest Stop:

If you haven't kept up with current trends in clothes, make-up, and bedroom accou-
trements for your son or daughter, or if you think your child might need some peer support in this area, who are some same-age peers you could recruit to help with the job?
Neighbors? Nieces? Nephews?

Same-age peers who could help make my kid a "hep cat" (oops, maybe we need a little help with this, too):

Brad Magnus

I like having my brothers here. Less work for me! I feed animals. The horses and the works. Everything. I can be a little lazy.

I dance 3, 4 hours, 7 hours. Every day. Sometimes like 15 hours. I weight, what do you think? I weigh 177 my lowest. All is muscles. Sometimes my usual weight used to be is 195. Then I just keep eating! Now not so much food. I look good.

I love the farm. I try to help my brothers, sometimes. They are okay. Sometimes they are sloppy. Their rooms is so a mess. I am the perfect one. I clean my room perfectly clean. I do everything alone, by myself. Sometime my brothers come in my room. They don't make mess in my room.

I do like Monty's, but I better not get into it! Sometimes I drink a beer. I like to go by myself. Nolan is good. It's so fun. Nolan is so easy to get along. Duncan and Chris are little brothers. I am okay when they go away. University. More work for me though. I miss them. But I go in to Victoria once a week. My dancing lessons. Sometimes I stay over with Nolan and Duncan. At school. Victoria. I go in myself on the ferry. Only one bus goes to town from the ferry. Sometimes I am late.

I like it here. On the farm. I make it a dance studio. I need a big dance studio. Just like Suzanne's. Big windows, the whole thing. Then I have a piano and organ. The whole works. Be pretty good.

I not move away from this place. With my family. Someday, when my parents dead, I stay here. I look after the animals. The farm. I stay here. Maybe a girl will live here. With me. Who knows? A couple of things. I got my own horse, Lana. I would like my own dog. We got a dog, Rex. I would like a poodle.

I drive. I pick up right away. I drive truck. I can't go to town. I need license first before I go to Victoria. Not scary to drive.

I had girlfriend. We broke up. We are not friends. Maybe some day, who knows. Me and her argue each time. I try to think of good stuff. I try to remember good stuff. She was blonde, blue eyes. She help me through school. I want to

Brad Magnus
Salt Spring Island, British Columbia

*get marry someday. I ask my girlfriend. She said no. A lot of times. She diffuse
me each times. I feel sad and mad. I courage. Stomach feel not good.*

*When I dance, I feel if I in the mood. I not think, not really. I just do it.
Sometimes I just get it. Most of the time, I listen to the music. First. Then I said
to myself please try it. I did. Feels right each time. I sometimes, I look back at it
and I listen to words. I have a lot of my favorites. I like* You Needed Me. *I
dance to that one in school. School make me mad sometimes. Teachers didn't see
with me. Some do. They let me dance, first time, in school.*

*I am a good guy. Sometimes I like myself. Or maybe I love myself. When I
dance. I am handsome, I think. I got a lot of lines. Funny lines. People say,
"What a funny guy." When I dance, they say, "Look at that guy. He is so flexi-
ble." And there are people who say, "What a hunk!" Girls say that. A lot of
girls. Sometimes I go to the Red Lion, that is a bar. Sometimes I go to Monty's.
That's fun. I know a girl there. Was in dance class. She's good dancer.*

*I find a girl myself. Someday. I don't know which one. I'm not too sure.
I'm not caring age, height. I'm not care. Any height. Maybe a big fat girl. I am
muscular, so why not? I pick up anyone! I do work out. I let my wife choose.
Hair, doesn't matter. I not fussy. I like red hair. My second is blonde. Any color,
it not matter. She would be very nice. We will live here. Maybe Victoria. Or
Vancouver. Maybe the States or something. Maybe Hollywood.*

*I have kids. When I get married. Yeah, I do like kids. Kids are not too
much work. I let my wife change diapers. I be doing my carpentry. I would not
give her a choice! Lots of kids.*

*My dream is be a dance teacher. I teach ballet. I teach anyone. To me, is
important. I feel good, the best. I teach, I say, try with me. Just do it. Just try.
We do it and tape it and watch it. I will say I know you can do it. Be patient. I
say, if you wanna be good at something, you try it. You feel so good.*

I got a sister. I never know it. She live in Edmonton. I always ask for it. I said, "I want a sister, Mom and Dad." Then I got it. She look like Mom. I still can't believe it. Sister, brother-in-law, nieces, one nephew. We are uncles. Mom and Dad is gramma and grandfather! She come out to see me. I keep asking Mom and Dad, "I want a sister! I want a sister!" Then I have one. I coax Dad along to do the S word so I have a sister. I mean the X word!

I will have a new girlfriend. Sometime. Not too sure yet. I will ask her what do you want to do? I cannot take her to Monty's, I can't. Just guys go there to watch the girls dancing. Maybe we go to a movie. My favorite sport, wrestling. They are very big guys. Fat. Too much grease.

Healthy Mind and Spirit

This bridge-building to adulthood is sometimes difficult; it involves helping your son or daughter develop greater independence while keeping the lines of support open. Part of this is accomplished by keeping an eye on your child, learning his or her moods, and allowing him or her enough space and independence to figure out some problems for him- or herself. Those early days of talking with your child, establishing a dialogue, and making him or her feel comfortable in telling you anything will really start to pay off now. Encouraging your child from an early age to participate more fully in conversations rather than merely to respond to questions can support his or her communication skills. As children grow older, they will be more likely to express their opinions about more complex ideas and emotions. DeAnna Horstmeier (1990) suggested ways parents can help children learn to carry on a conversation:

- Don't let others speak for them.
- Don't help them as quickly when you see what is needed. Let them ask.
- Pay attention when they do initiate a conversation.
- Set up some unusual situations and wait for them to comment. For example, put your shoe on your head (in the spirit of fun), and continue with your activities until your child initiates conversation.

What we don't think about for Jim often enough are lifelong interests. We think of skill development and life skills and does he make his bed properly and brush his teeth. But what about making sure Jim has the confidence to make his life interesting? We do; that's how we create our lives. How do we open up enough avenues so that he can have a full life? For most people, it would be clever to have a fetish about the Beatles, to collect the memorabilia; it's a valued activity. It's that fascinating person who knows all about the Beatles. But when someone with a disability does it, it's [considered] obsessive compulsive and we better put the brakes on that. We think we know what Jim likes, but only because of what he's chosen from what's been available so far. Part of the excitement of life is becoming a person who's more than just one dimensional.

—Richard Schwier

Sometimes growing up and away can lead teenagers into a time when they'll need those communication skills to ask for your help to understand their changing moods and emotions. Imagine yourself feeling a little blue or out of sorts. If you're like most people, you'll have family support, a spouse, a therapist, or even a co-worker to sit down with over coffee to talk about feeling crummy or stressed or sad. If you have a bad day at work with too many demands and not enough time to accomplish everything, you can talk about it when you get home. Most of us have buffers against a world that sometimes seems like it's just too much to take. But if you have a disability, those buffers may not exist, or you might not know how to ask for help. Your sadness or anxiety or "blues" may not be recognized, especially if you're compliant or withdrawn. A doctor, for example, may assume your symptoms are "just a part of the disability." You just might close in, close down, and isolate yourself from the bad feelings. The trouble is, those feelings get trapped in there with you.

A while ago, Mike went through a depression and I took him to Dr. Freeman. The doctor said, "Mom, Mike and I are going to have a talk, so you leave for a while." Later, he told me how impressed he was that Michael was so knowledgeable sexually and has a very good understanding of his own sexuality. The doctor asked me if there was a chance Michael would have sex. I took a breath and didn't really know what to say. I came from Newport, Kentucky, where years ago they had a house on the corner where people took their sons and said, "Here. Educate him." But you don't do that nowadays. The doctor wanted to give Michael some protection, but I told him Michael has always been a very religious person and doesn't feel right about being with a girl before marriage. I know people will think that's just me talking, but Michael sort of quashed the idea of marriage for himself. I asked him why not, and he says he just can't. He says he wants to stay here with us.
—Peggy Creamer

Robert Fletcher of the National Association for the Dually Diagnosed (NADD, an association concerned with people who have both an intellectual disability and a mental illness diagnosis) said there are a few things to ask yourself if you think your son or daughter may be anxious or depressed beyond the usual teenage emotional changes.

1. Is there a change in activities of daily living?
2. Is there a change in doing things that the person found fun or pleasurable in the past?
3. Is there a change in eating habits? Has there been a weight gain or weight loss?
4. Have there been any changes in sleep patterns, either difficulty falling asleep or waking up in the middle of the night? Sleeping excessively (beyond normal teenage habits)?
5. Does the person withdraw and become socially isolated, a change from their normal level of interaction?
6. Is there a change in cheerfulness? Do they cry easily?
7. Is there some aggression or self-abusive behavior that is not part of the person's usual personality?
8. How are they feeling? If the person talks, ask! If they do not talk, there are ways to help the person identify how they are feeling. A simple chart of

facial expressions can be shown to the person with a request that they indicate which image is close to what they feel. (personal communication, 1995)

Helping your child identify how he is feeling may take some practice. One
mom began early with her daughter to help her learn to recognize and describe
the major emotions of *happy, mad,* and *scared.* There are, of course, overlaps and
many shades of each. But this mom wanted her daughter to have the skills to
identify and talk about how she was feeling. Mom would have her daughter
make faces in the mirror, first to copy Mom's example and then to label the
"look" of the emotion. As the child grew older, she and her mother would find
"emotion pictures" in magazines, cut them out, and make separate collages for
feelings. Sometimes they would sit in the mall and whisper about people, trying
to guess what emotion a person was feeling by the way they looked and acted.
The daughter soon began pointing out and describing more complex emotions
like *nervous, shy, silly,* and *worried.*

For parents whose children don't speak, visual clues are important. Perhaps
the parent could draw a circle for a face on a small chalkboard so the child could
draw in the features of *happy, sad, mad* or *scared* to identify his own mood.
Alternately, the parent could draw several different faces so that the child could
point to the one that identifies his mood.

> *I had an apartment over the river, and Bob had something to do, so I took
> Katherine with me, not really knowing anything about Katherine yet because
> this was very early on in the relationship. Katherine and I walked over to my
> apartment, and I made meatballs for dinner. Bob was living elsewhere, so I
> thought I'd make these things and then Katherine and I would walk back to
> Bob's and we'd all have supper. So later that afternoon, we started out, me lug-
> ging this great roaster full of meatballs. It was summer and very hot; we got to
> the Osborne Street Bridge, which is very long. We get halfway over the bridge,
> and Katherine decides she's not going any further. She sits down. You think I
> can get her to move? No. And I have these damn meatballs that are getting
> heavier and heavier. I thought I'd try walking, ignoring her, not looking back,
> thinking she'd get scared and run after me. I get way past A & W and finally
> look back. There's this little blot, still sitting there on the horizon. I walk all the
> way back with my meatballs, begging her to come this time. She doesn't move. I
> told her I was going to A & W, thinking she'd like to go there and get a drink.
> Well, I get all the way back to A & W, look back; no, she's not coming. I walk
> back again. I finally tried bribing her with ice cream, and that worked. When
> we finally got to Bob's, I was exhausted and she was quite happy and refreshed.
> My first parenting experience, now referred to as "the Meatball Episode."*
> —Darryl Davey

All people have emotions and feelings whether they have a disability,
whether they speak, and whatever their age. There is no cookbook on teaching
how to talk about feelings. Getting your children to talk with you about how he
feels and what he is doing is a continual game of trial and error. If parents suspect
something more than just a temporary upset, sadness, or swing of hormones,
they may want to find a professional who is experienced in the mental health as-

sessment of people with an intellectual disability. If your answer is "yes" to many of Robert Fletcher's eight questions listed earlier, there may be a larger problem.

If the individual does have a major psychiatric disorder, such as major depression, bipolar disorder, mania, a psychotic disorder, or an anxiety disorder, there may be appropriate treatments that would help (Fletcher, personal communication, 1995). NADD provides resource materials and information about recognized and experienced professionals throughout North America.

> *I can see how people with disabilities could lead a very isolated life if other people didn't get involved. Katherine would be quite happy to sit in her room and watch TV all day and maybe for the rest of her life. Bob and Joyce really encourage her to get out there and do things. I can see if a parent didn't have the energy or the time or had their own problems to deal with, it would be easy just to let the child sit alone and watch TV.*
> —Darryl Davey

If medication is prescribed, parents and caregivers need to know what the medication is, why it's prescribed, what it's intended to do, what outcomes can be expected, and what specific side effects may be involved. Drugs should never be used simply for behavioral management as historically happened in institutions and other facilities. Drugs should be diagnosis specific—they are not a magic bullet, and most mental health professionals agree that a drug should be used as adjunct to a range of other services like support for the individual and the family and support and education of the school, workplace, or residential staff. Drugs may deal with the biology of the problem, but we have to look at the person socially and environmentally. Perhaps the person needs a referral for counseling or psychotherapy. All of the pieces need to be put together and wrapped around the individual according to what he needs (Fletcher, personal communication, 1995).

As your son or daughter grows up, you want to balance your own parental influence with the benefits of connections with other people. Common sense and reason suggest that we maintain close relationships without "taking over" someone's life, especially when they're an adult. If your son or daughter is having some problems, make yourself part of a team to help solve them. If your adult child is living on his or her own with supports, you will need to remember that your child is an adult. Adults without disabilities have a right to privacy about medical appointments, medication, and counseling. Give your child this same respect, but make your willingness to help known to your son or daughter and the people around him or her. Common sense and gut feelings are wonderful tools, especially if they're not used as clubs!

There isn't anyone alive who sailed through adolescence, puberty, and adulthood without hitting a few emotional speed bumps. Part of the ups and downs of the teenage years is a healthy stretching of the independence muscles, a sorting out of the question, "Who am I?" Adults, too, go through periods of upset, sadness, contentment, and joy. Be in tune with your child. Really listen when she wants to talk—to tell her that she is stubborn or silly or that she should "be nice" when she is angry or confused gives the message that her feelings are not legitimate. Keep the lines of communication open. Remind your child that she is loved and is welcome in your family.

> *It's important to really listen to Jim and to have real conversations with him. There are some days when his stutter and his hearing impairments make it pretty rough, but we remind each other every day to talk with him. Not just talk at* him, *but* with *him. It builds his confidence, and it constantly reminds us that he thinks about things and has a lot to say.*
> —*Karin Melberg Schwier*

Being Female

> *She's grown up in a household of four women, so it's been a pretty open envi- ronment. She models everything. Krista went through a silly stage, so Karen models that. We'll say something, and she'll burst into giggles. "Don't say that word! Don't talk about that!" She's got a good sense of humor about sexuality.*
> —*Peggy Hutchison*

Medical and Self-Care

As we discussed in Chapter 4, a knowledgeable, sensitive doctor is a tremendous asset. Generally, most women (with or without disabilities) should have an gy- necological exam, including an internal pelvic exam, a Pap smear, and a breast exam, by their late teens. Young women with intellectual disabilities should be treated no differently. Some doctors suggest that any woman who is not sexual- ly active and has a normal first Pap smear may not require an annual gyneco- logical exam. There are situations, however, in which the parents or caregivers may not be aware of sexual activity.

Dr. Thomas Elkins (1995) suggested that counseling for a young woman prior to her internal examination will help to ease any anxiety that she may have. Parents can request counseling and education using lifelike dolls, pictures, or slide presentations to help the young woman understand the procedure and that it is done so she stays healthy. Check the "Recommended Resources" section at the end of this book for materials. There may still be some apprehension, so a few visits may be necessary. Thomas Elkins advised, "Ask the gynecologist about using newer techniques that can make the pelvic exam much more relaxed....It is possible to use Q-tip Pap smears that avoid placement of vaginal speculums, and to assess uterine and ovarian size painlessly (using high frequency sound waves) (1995, p. 255).

Karin's Story

I remember my first period. My mom had talked to me well in advance; we'd gone to the library for books. Even though my friend Suzanne tried to convince me I was getting rid of all the excess blood in my body so I wouldn't explode, I trusted Mom's explanation. It was almost old hat before it even began. The thrill of this womanly milestone came later when my brother's girlfriend thought

I should use tampons instead of pads. I was game; the commercials looked pretty promising. Expert on these matters, Wendy and her four sisters and I went to the drugstore; we bought large quantities of candy, magazines, and even Elmer's glue, as I recall, to disguise the purchase of tampons. It was all very thrilling, and there was such peer camaraderie as all five sisters later shouted suggestions and encouragement through the bathroom door and I tried to follow the diagrams that came in the box. Mission accomplished! To celebrate, we ate all of the candy, marveled at this ingenious invention and at the fact that we were all *women*.

Menstruation

Your daughter will look to you not only for information but also for the mood around this new phase of womanhood. This information should come well before her first period so that she is not confused or frightened by what will happen. Reassure your daughter that all women have periods when they grow up and that it's normal. Nothing is "wrong" with her because she is—or will be—menstruating, and it will stop in a few days. Make sure she has information about pads and tampons, what they're for, and how they're used. Buy some and take them out of the wrappers to show her; perhaps demonstrate on a doll.

Let your daughter know that although menstruation is normal and every woman has a period once a month, other people are not able to "tell" when it is happening to a woman. It is also a private thing, and she should not talk to everyone about it. Let her know she can talk to you, her teacher, the school nurse, or a girlfriend (identify the appropriate people) but that it would be a private conversation.

Your daughter will watch you carefully for clues about how to act. If you treat menstruation as a "sickness" or a "curse," the chances are good she will, too. Her mother or another trusted adult woman can model the use of pads or tampons, proper hygiene, how to throw away soiled items, what to do if her underwear is spotted, and how to manage cramps or discomfort.

Here's another a passage written by parent Claire Canning:

Martha needed lots of repetition and very practical examples. When she was 9 years old, I began to take her into the bathroom with me whenever I menstruated. At first I was much more embarrassed than she was. "See, Mom is a woman, and all women have periods. Someday when you are bigger, you'll have periods, too, and we'll celebrate that you are growing up and your body is changing and getting ready for womanhood." We named her sisters, and all the women close to her, and said that they too have periods. I stressed that menstruation is private, but that it was okay to talk to Mom or Dad, or anyone really close about it. As months passed, we continued our discussions, and Martha accepted them very matter-of-factly. She began to position napkins in place for me. Once again, it was a good time to stress personal hygiene and cleanliness. When Martha began to menstruate at barely 11 years old, she accepted this happily as part of the celebration of her coming womanhood. She helps me mark an M on the calendar at the onset of each period, and takes care of herself and napkin changes conscientiously and without fanfare. I have explained that, before her period, due to increased hormonal activity in her body, she may feel sad or tired, but that with new medications available, this can usually be remedied simply. Martha herself has solved a problem that was a major concern in my life. (1990, p. 272)

Teenage girls should be taught to do a monthly breast self-exam, in addition to the exam provided annually by their doctor. Ask your doctor or public health nurse to teach your daughter how to do her own breast exam and what changes she should watch for. Monthly breast exams by parents or caregivers are controversial. They should only be done when there is continuing education about sexuality issues, including protective behaviors (Schwab, 1995). Your daughter needs to augment her self-care education with information about sexual abuse and self-protection.

> *She's very aware, and I'm surprised with how much she does know about reproduction. She does try very hard to learn, and she's patient, but she gets frustrated that she has to be patient with herself. She'll often ask me what words mean. We've always asked her to explain to us when we don't understand her, so she has learned to ask us to explain things she doesn't understand.*
> —Lou Shaw

Being Male

> *He has a very good feeling about his own body. He doesn't do it in front of anyone else, but he'll come out in the living room with just a towel wrapped around after a shower and, to make us laugh, he'll give us a little woohoo! George has always been very modest, and he'll say, "Why does he do that?" I say it's because he thinks his body is beautiful and he's proud of it. I don't want to kill that.*
> —Peggy Creamer

Medical and Self-Care

Most young men with intellectual disabilities go through adolescence and puberty at about the same time as anyone else. Your son's voice will change; he'll sprout facial, pubic, and body hair; his moods will swing; and the stereo in his bedroom just might reach new volume levels! Even if a boy with intellectual disabilities has been identified as infertile, Elkins explained that "the primary sexual characteristics that develop during puberty include hormone changes, the ability to manufacture sperm, and several physical changes to the sexual organs (Elkins, 1995, p. 264).

In puberty, young men need to know that "wet dreams" sometimes happen when they are asleep and that ejaculation can also happen when their penis is rubbed during masturbation. Boys are sometimes embarrassed or worried, so the reassurance that this is a normal and healthy part of growing up can be a welcome relief. Boys need to know that this is also a private thing and that the semen should be wiped up with a tissue, which is then thrown away. This responsibility, too, is part of growing up.

As with young women, young men should be taught that there are self-care tasks they can manage. Again, ask your doctor or public health nurse to provide some education about testicular self-exams to supplement annual checkups, how to do it, and what to look for. Professor Yvonne Brown, Dean of the College of Nursing at the University of Saskatchewan in Canada, said that an individualized approach by a health care professional is the main objective (personal communication, 1999). "They should stress the importance of doing the exam, explaining it as well as can be understood, including information about where and when it's appropriate to do the exam," said Brown. "The first time, they can assist the individual so they can teach what feels normal, what the normal contour of the testicle feels like. The discussion...can include staying healthy and what to do if they find something that doesn't feel right." The American Cancer Society has easy-to-read brochures with simple instructions for testicular self-exams.

Staying Healthy

For girls and boys, simple line drawings kept in a drawer in their bedroom or in the bathroom (private places) can serve as a visual guide once they've received some instruction on breast or testicular self-exams. Medical and self-care, along with proper hygiene, exercise, good eating, and lifestyle habits, are all taught in the context of staying healthy. This is an important responsibility as we grow up: remembering to look after our own bodies so we don't get sick.

Parents need to provide the information about and strategies to handle issues like personal hygiene, menstrual care, and evolving sexual feelings. Part of that teaching involves equipping your son or daughter with the competence needed to be private about this. In order for your son or daughter to masturbate privately, for example, he or she needs to know how to be private! Your son needs to know not only that rubbing his penis is private but also that lotion helps it feel better, that ejaculation is normal and feels good, and that he must use a tissue or a washcloth to clean up, which is then thrown in the wastebasket or laundry. And he needs to know that a description of this activity isn't the appropriate response when someone at the dinner table asks, "So, what did you do today?"

All of this stuff is wrapped up in feelings and emotions. When your son or daughter is still a *child,* encourage him or her to tell you about what and why he feels a particular way. For people who are less verbal or talkative, try the *happy, sad, mad,* or *scared* drawings so they can point out how they feel. And think back to the time when you were your son or daughter's age. Try to remember how it felt.

Peer Pressure

We've all been through it to varying degrees. We still go through it as adults. As parents of sons and daughters with intellectual disabilities, we need to be deliberate in our teaching so that our kids become independent thinkers. As a teenager, your child is making the difficult transition to becoming an adult, and his or her need to "fit in" is felt even more keenly. The good news is that the same kind of assertiveness training that we talked about in Chapter 5 can be used to help kids combat unhealthy peer pressure. Ultimately, you want your child to be able to think, choose, and make his or her decisions known instead of to just let something happen. That's being assertive.

Karin's Story

Jim and I had just finished his speech practice one evening on the back deck. Over a glass of wine, I asked him, "What if someone tried to give you a cigarette?"

Without hesitation, he said, "That's gross. I keep my mouth clean. No way."

I upped the ante. "What do you do if someone says, 'Jim, drink this beer'?"

Again, he gave a definite response. "No thanks, I drink red wine at home."

"Okay, what about pills?" I asked. Well, that got a little fuzzier. Jim's been given a lot of medication in his life by a lot of people, so he pantomimed just popping them into his mouth. We'll work on that.

I asked, "What would you do if someone said, 'Jim, see that girl? Go pull her pants down.'"

"No, keep pants up! Private. Not very nice. I tell my dad, my teacher."

I was very pleased with his responses and thought after this exhaustive research that Jim was demonstrating a solid sense of boundaries. Role playing and practice, practice, practice helps Jim prepare for situations he may find himself in. Your child needs a solid grasp on the difference between being pushed and persuaded to do something. The trusty "No, Go, Tell" strategies can help a lot here.

Emily Kingsley, a parent, agrees that one of the best gifts to give a child is helping her to think for herself. Once at a conference, I sat with Emily and her son, Jason. We talked about peer pressure, and I asked Jason what he does when people try to get him to do things that make him uncomfortable.

"If I am at a party," he explained, "and someone tries to get me to do drugs or smoke or do alcohol, I just say, 'No, thanks.' I tell them health is very important. I don't get mad. I just use humor, and they give up." This sounds like good advice.

Homosexuality

Recently at a rights workshop, a group of people with disabilities were discussing the right to relationships. You could see parents and staff turning green at the content of the discussion. This was a group of people with disabilities who live in a facility in which the parent board, supported by staff, had decided that sexuality education was just not going to happen. Then when self-advocates had the opportunity to talk with an "outsider" about their life within the facility, the first thing that came out of their mouths was the desire to form relationships, be intimate, and even marry. Throughout the discussion, a young man, maybe 18, sat quietly. Just before the group left the subject of relationships for other issues, he spoke up. He had difficulty with speech and had a nervous habit of grimacing when uncomfortable. With much effort and much grimacing, he said, "I think I should be allowed to have a boyfriend if I want one." There was silence in the room. Other folks with disabilities just nodded, having no difficulty with what he said, but the faces of parents and staff hardened. They had clearly had enough of this kind of thing.

That young man showed tremendous courage. He knew that what he was saying was going to be received badly. He knew that others would find his desire to love another man disgusting/abominable/horrifying. But he also knew who he was. The irony was that the meeting was happening in the basement of a United Church of Christ, a denomination that has accepted that gay people can be full members of the body of Christ. His courage echoed the courage of the denomination.

Homosexuality and intellectual disability is a difficult issue, but not because there should be any surprise that some people with disabilities are gay. Clearly as members of the human community, they will experience sex, sexuality, and loving in the same way as others. What makes it difficult is that so many people with disabilities have been congregated into same-sex environments or have not been allowed to form heterosexual attachments. How then do parents *tell* whether their child's homosexual behavior is because of circumstance rather than because of affectional attachment? This question is not as difficult to answer as one might think.

First, parents of young teens should remember that homosexual play is entirely natural and is not a forerunner of adult homosexuality. If childhood homosexual play led to adult homosexual orientation, then there would only be six or seven heterosexuals out there! Finding your child engaged in homosexual play with another shouldn't lead to harsh punishment, recriminations, or damning lectures. Like all children, they may need to hear from their parents that what they were doing was natural. This show of sexual interest may be a signal to you to ensure that your child is getting a lot of options to meet with people of both genders in social circumstances. Remember, if you don't allow your child options to form relationships with both genders, then they will have no option but to engage in homosexual behavior.

Homosexual behavior is quite different from homosexuality. One is simply a *behavior;* the other is a way of being. Adults who lived in institutions that were segregated by sex may have formed consenting homosexual relationships. The concept of *situational homosexuality* is widely known and just refers to the fact that in prolonged same-sex situations, people perform homosexual behaviors. But when they return to both-sex situations, they return to heterosexuality. For people who have been in institutions, the same has been found. If they return to places that allow heterosexual contact, they return to heterosexuality if that is who they are. But there are, of course, gay people with intellectual disabilities.

Most parents report that they had some inkling that their child may be gay. A friend in his twenties told me that his Dad sat him down and said, "I hope this doesn't upset you, but your mother and I think you may be gay and that you might find it hard to tell us. Well, just know we love you just the way you are and if you happen to want to date other guys, please let us meet them and keep us involved in your life." He said that he never loved his Dad more than he did at that moment. That father may have been more forward than you might want to be, but if you think your child is gay and you need to deal with it, there are organizations to help you. Parents and Friends of Lesbians and Gays (PFLAG) is a huge organization that was formed to help parents accept their children. It provides an opportunity for concerned parents to get together and support each other. They will help you on your journey through the issues of homosexuality.

Katherine Manwaring

My mom is Joyce. There is apartments. You know, apartments? Across the street. I get apartment some day. I make dinner. I can cook. I make salad. I can make dinner. I like pork and beans. I love it.

My husband will go to the bar. His name is Charles. He is working for his job. He working with files. A secretary. That's his job, so.

One time I saw this man and his wife in that apartment. They have sex. I saw it across the street. I tell Vanessa no smoking, no thank you. I tell her smoke outside. I not smoke. Vanessa have apartment, and she can't move in yet. At my house, we saw Bart Simpson on TV, and Vanessa got up and slam the door and she is gone.

Darryl is so cute. He snores, and I wake up. I snore, too. My dad snores. He says he doesn't. We have flowers and garden. We have rhubarb. Rhubarb crisp. I love it. It's good. I like bacon, eggs, and bread and juice. Orange juice. It's good. I like hotels. They have dinner. Dinner's good. They have chicken. They have potatoes and gravy and carrots. Darryl cooks. He is good. He makes dinner. We have bread and pork and beans. I set the table. And I wash the dishes, too, so.

I like jazz dancing. And I have Guides. Day care, I work there. I do dishes. Make lunch. I have macaroni and cheese. We have snacks. Cheese and crackers. They like me. I go to camp. That's fun. I love it. I like boys. Angie is my friend. She's nice. There are boys, at the apartment. By my dad's house. That's cool. I like parties. I am not crabby. Sometimes, I am.

My mom is Joyce, she working hard. She is tall. I like her a lot. She is old. My dad is old. And Darryl. I am not old. Darryl is handsome. We watch TV. My mom and dad play the organ, songs, on the organ. I watch Power Rangers, but not for little kids. Scary.

I wash my hair, very shiny. I shampoo front and back and front and squeeze it. Lots of shampoo and squeeze your hair. Conditioner. Then dry it. I like showers. Darryl likes a shower. Dad likes a shower. Darryl has shampoo, and Dad has shampoo. Then I comb my hair. I look nice.

Someday I live in my own apartment, make my own food. Maybe I live with Liz. Or my girlfriend. My boyfriend is handsome. We get married. Three years. The lady at the apartment, she's gonna move out. She will move out, so I can move in. Babies grow inside. Then you take him out, and you have a baby. I like a baby. I have a girl baby. When I am older. You're welcome.

Sex Education

You have to set goals and expectations. Let's not aim down here by our ankles. I think that doctors thought they were doing us a favor by trying to not get our hopes up. But parents have to have dreams for their children. Why should a child's disability change all that? For him, personally, emotionally, I want him to have his own experiences and relationships, to move away from home, to have a job, to have sex!

—Elizabeth Popowich

The topic of sex education does appear on its own now, late in this book, but realize that you've really been teaching the foundation of sex (and sexuality) education to your child all along. It is obvious that given that people with intellectual disabilities are capable of love, marriage, and parenting, there needs to be some work done to ensure that they get all the information necessary in order to make adequate decisions. At this point you will be very glad you did all of that teaching regarding privacy, relationships, self-esteem, and decision making. All of these form the basis of any kind of sex education.

Once, when talking to a mother about doing sex education with her son, she said, "How dare you teach my son about sex when he doesn't have friends." This one simple statement has forever changed our view of doing sex education. It is better to conceive the process as *relationship training* rather than *sex education*.

This is not just a mere playing with words. It takes about 6 minutes to do "sex education." The basic facts are pretty simple and can be put into a simple equation:

$$\frac{\text{Slot B}}{\text{Tab A}} + \text{Squirt} (-\text{Protection}) = \text{Baby (or Disease)}$$

For those not comfortable with math, the equation above reads, "Put Tab A into Slot B plus a squirt equals a baby." Okay, okay. There is that other stuff about sexually transmitted diseases (STDs) and such, but it is really pretty basic stuff. Once when asked to give a lecture to a group of teens at a high school, Dave told them that they had been "lied to" by those who taught them about sex. He told them that he knew they believed that they understood about sex when they knew the Tab A/Slot B formula. "You don't understand sex when you know what the genitals do. You understand sex when you know what the heart does." This got a decidedly chilly response from those teenagers who wanted to see a fat guy talk about penile thrusting and vaginal clamping. Oooo, new ideas for the washroom wall.

Let's look at a logical order for doing all of this teaching about sex education. First things first:

- Your child needs to have a language about the body.
- She needs to know the right words for the right things.

This education should have already happened in toddlerhood in natural ways; if you haven't, don't worry. It's never too late. The child sitting in a tub or getting dressed asks questions that should be given answers. As she learns names for body parts, she should also learn about the names for genitalia. This is *so* important. One young woman with an intellectual disability tried to report that she had been sexually victimized. Because she did not know the name for her genitals, she told everybody that she felt sick in her stomach. The doctor pronounced her as "making it up." She never, ever felt sick in her stomach. The problem was that she knew the words *stomach* and *leg* but not the words for other body parts. The closest she could come to talking about what happened was to say that there was something wrong in her stomach.

We have a lot of social-sexual training materials where I work. I wanted Jim to have some exposure to this stuff, so I hauled home some slides during his summer visit. We sat down and reviewed the names of body parts, really just the basics. The next day, we went shopping, and Jim saw a female mannequin in the store window display. It was in the process of being dressed, so he proudly named all the private body parts in a loud voice. He got them all, a few of them twice.
    —Karin Melberg Schwier

While you are teaching the words, please use the right words for female genitalia. The name for the visible female genitalia is *vulva*, not *vagina*. The vagina is *inside* the body. As these words are used, it is important that your child get comfortable saying these words in front of you. Your child needs to know both that you know the words and that you can hear the words. Like it or not, you need to prepare your children (*all* of your children) to feel comfortable talking to you about victimization, and the only way to do this is to let them know that you won't fall dead at the mention of the word *penis* or *breasts*.

As a matter of fact, *penis* just may be the blandest word you're going to hear! Depending on your child's age, you need to be prepared to teach your child the correct words for parts and acts, and explain the slang versions so your child understands the language other people may use.

Rest Stop:

To help you get comfortable, take a piece of paper and write down as many slang words as you can think of that are used for parts of the human body. We suggest using a separate piece of paper because we were all told never to write nasty words in our school books, but if you can buck authority, here's a space. Then write the correct term next to the slang. C'mon, you can do it! If you're really brave, read your list out loud. It'll help you say the words out loud to your child.

Slang words for body parts:	The Queen's English version

We just heard a loud sigh. We know, this is difficult stuff, and we know that you probably didn't have to go through this with your other children. True enough. We know that typical kids seldom get sex education at home. We know that they get it from school, from peers, or from sneaking peeks at "medical books" (a euphemism for *Playboy*). Norm and Emma, friends of ours, decided that talking to their kids about sex would have sent the kids into an adolescent tizzy. So, they took one of Norm's books from a class he took at university. The book was "subtly" entitled *Sex*, and they left it in the home library and never mentioned it. As each child got old enough to be interested, the book would disappear, reappear, disappear, and so forth. When one of the kids was old enough, she told Norm and Emma, smirk spreading, that *she* had taken the *Sex* book when she was younger. They responded, "Why do you think we left it in the library?" They had tricked her into sex education.

This is a funny story, but your kid isn't likely to do that. Although typical kids get sex education elsewhere, kids with disabilities who don't get sex education from their parents get it from television. The idea that some soap opera diva, Madonna, or Steve Urkel might be the primary sex educator for your child should motivate you to you ensure that your child gets adequate sex education. If your child goes to school, check whether they have a sex education program and see whether your child can attend. Although integration of kids with and without disabilities in school is a wonderful thing most of the time, the sex education class may not be geared toward your child's level of understanding. Some school systems have adapted their programs for typical kids to the learning styles of kids with intellectual disabilities. Seattle Public Schools and the Seattle–King County Department of Public Health have a program called *FLASH* (*Family Life and Sexual Health;* Stangle, 1991) that they have adapted for kids with disabilities. It is a nice program with emphasis on all of the right things, like relationships, self-esteem, assertion, feelings, and all of that good stuff that can be forgotten in a rush to teach about sperm, eggs, and fertilization. Make sure that your school at least takes a look at it or develops a program from which your child can learn. Here are some questions to ask about a sex education curriculum:

1. Does it teach about sexuality in context of relationships and consent?
2. What values does the program promote? (There is no such thing as a sex education curriculum that doesn't teach values.)
3. How will I know that my child learned the concepts taught?
4. Does it teach the following: abuse prevention, disease protection, and avoiding unwanted pregnancy?
5. Does it teach about sexual pleasure and ensure my child learns that his body is okay?
6. Does it encourage my child to talk to me if he has questions or fears?
7. What provisions does it make to teach to my child's learning capabilities?
8. Does it teach general social skills? Does it teach about making friends and reciprocity?
9. Does it teach about other ways of being intimate and showing affection besides sexual intercourse?
10. Does it teach about the heart or just about the body?

If your child is not in school, it is good to know that the curricula for teaching adults with intellectual disabilities are among the best available. They are clear, graphic, and well thought out. The problem is that they are expensive and set up for group teaching. This means that you need to see whether your local agency that serves people with intellectual disabilities has a sex education class. If they do not, get on the board of directors or go to the board and force them to. (Oops, we got a little political there.) A sex education group can be one of the best things that your child attends. This will allow him or her to meet others and learn at a rate that makes sense while being in a supportive environment. Your child is just as curious about his or her body as you were and has all of the fears that you did. Sex education allows your son or daughter to relax about his or her body and how it is changing.

If neither school nor the agency will educate your child, then try your local Department of Public Health or Planned Parenthood; they both can offer that service. If they don't, then you need to do it. This isn't as harrowing as you might think.

 ## Rest Stop:

Sit down and make a list of the facts that you want your child, depending on his or her age, to learn. Think about the "two Ps" of sex education: prevention and pleasure.

Facts my child should know and understand:

Once you have written these facts down, you need to get materials. *Being Sexual: An Illustrated Series on Sexuality and Relationships* (Ludwig & Hingsburger, 1993) is a cheap series that is aimed at teaching people with disabilities one to one. This series gives you several booklets that you can go through with your children.

They are written in both English and Blissymbolics (a system of icon-like symbols used by some people who do not speak) and are laid out logically. There may be things in the books that are too abstract for your child, so just use what is needed.

Again, you know your child best and can adapt the information and the age level to suit your child's ability to understand. You may be surprised as you explore these issues that your relationship with your child deepens in a way that you didn't think possible. You may find that your child's feelings are much more profound and much more adult than you may ever have guessed. There is a population of people who already know what love is but have somehow come to believe that love is not for them. You will hear fears and experience tears as your child talks about a future that she desperately hopes includes love, marriage, and partnership.

It's scary sometimes. How am I going to bring her up? How am I going to make her self-sufficient and strong? It's almost too scary to think about sometimes, but we have to do it. I feel a lot of responsibility, but she needs us to be thinking about these things, even though she's just a baby now.
  —Shelly Garner

You can't just single out sex and teach your child in isolation. All of this stuff is tied in so tightly. Learning how to treat other people, what's appropriate in different situations in your life, liking yourself. On his date with Sarah, Chris was wonderful. He opened the door for her, pulled out a chair for her to sit. He was a perfect gentleman. He held her hand, spoke to her, and on the way home, she asked if he might like to be her date for the prom. He thought that would be nice. I think proper dating behavior, with practice, spills over into the job and other areas of life as he interacts with all kinds of people. We make sure that every couple of weeks, at least once a month, he goes out on a date. I insist that he call someone; usually it's Sarah or Ellen. The first time, he asked Sarah to go to The Wizard of Oz. She said yes. He held the phone out to me and said, "What do I say now, Mom?" Her mom and I confirmed the details later, but he has to do it himself.
  —Gayle Foy

The emotional tone of your teaching needs to communicate a sense of acceptance and the willingness to talk about future relationships. When your child talks about marriage, as much as your heart may drop in your chest, you need to realize that this is a *normal* hope and is now a *real* possibility. You may want to tell your child that you would be proud to walk down the aisle on his arm. Your son needs to hear that you think that he is lovable and that someone else will find him equally lovable. Again, this isn't so very different from other parents with typical kids who go through pity-fests when they have a pimple or have just gotten dumped.

What is different, though, is that people with intellectual disabilities find themselves living in situations where there is fear or misconceptions on the part of parents and professionals. Although this is changing in a much more healthy way, people with intellectual disabilities don't often have a way to express interests and desires because they may live in a segregated residential program or may live at home longer than their siblings. Television soap operas and fantasy may be the only tolerated outlet of emotion. Educator Jean Edwards said,

> Without an appropriate sexual outlet, these young people often express their normal needs by touching strangers, standing 'too close for comfort,' or confusing relationships, perhaps calling a staffperson a girlfriend or a boyfriend—in effect, presenting themselves as socially and sexually immature. This inappropriate behavior occurs because [they] have not had the opportunity for normal expression of real and present needs...A life shared with another person, a caring relationship, is a need that shows no bias, regardless of the presence of...or degree of [intellectual disability]. (1988, p. 196)

Sex Can Make You Sick

The idea that sex can make you sick sounds simple. Years ago, our parents warned us with messages like "Don't get/make anyone pregnant." Today, the message is literally deadlier. STDs like gonorrhea and herpes are not new, but since HIV and AIDS have reared their ugly heads, there is more reason to worry than ever before. In fact, STDs are now often referred to as sexually transmitted infections (STIs) because HIV is a virus and AIDS itself is a syndrome, not a disease. Your son or daughter needs a good foundation of information and must be aware that taking sexual risks could kill him or her. Kids need information about proper hygiene and what can make people sick. By the way, *HIV* stands for *human immunodeficiency virus* and *AIDS* stands for *acquired immunodeficiency syndrome*.

This grounding in the dangers of sex and disease begins when your child is very young: We cover our mouths when we cough. We wash our hands after using the bathroom and before meals. We don't use someone else's utensils or toothbrush. We use a tissue when we sneeze.

When your child understands the concepts of *germs, diseases,* and *viruses* and how they can be spread, teaching about STIs in conjunction with more explicit sex education will make more sense. People can pass germs to each other in different ways. Jane Stangle explained, "Some [STIs] are very serious, others more of a nuisance; some have symptoms, others don't. It is important for [your child] to know it is possible to avoid or reduce the risk of exposure to STIs (1991, p. 236).

There are different kinds of STIs. Some are harder to get than others, but sexual contact with an infected person isn't the only way to get infected yourself (although no sexual contact is a pretty good guarantee of avoiding infection). Touching a cold sore, then your own genitals without first washing your hands can spread germs. Pubic lice can be passed from one person to another through infested towels, clothing, and bedding. One of the best ways to reduce the risk of infection is to use a condom properly during sexual intercourse. You can't get an STI from a toilet seat, doorknob, or water fountain. Check with your local public health department or Planned Parenthood office for booklets or pamphlets about STIs. *An Easy Guide to Loving Carefully: For Men and Women* (Kempton & Stigall-Muccigrosso, 1996) has some excellent information for "easy readers and people who need things read to them. There are lots of pictures that explain the reproductive systems of men and women, birth control, lifestyles and infectious diseases," said Kempton (personal communication, 1998).

Talk to your child about the importance of telling someone when he or she doesn't feel well. This is another reason for all of the work you've done: to create a comfortable and easy line of communication between you and your son or daughter. Children need to feel that they should talk their parents, a doctor, or nurse when they notice something "unusual happening in their bodies that might make them wonder if something is wrong, if they might have an STI" (Stangle, 1991, p. 237). Symptoms of some STIs include

- Discharge (something unusual, like a liquid, coming out of the body)
- Sores
- Pain or burning when urinating
- Rash or itching
- Lumps or bumps
- Fever
- Unexplained weight loss (Stangle, 1991, p. 237)

If there is a chance—or a confirmation—that your son or daughter has an STI, the doctor is not the only person who must be contacted. It may be embarrassing, but your son or daughter's sexual partner(s) must be told immediately and encouraged to also get tested and treatment, if necessary. Embarrassment now is better than the spread of the disease or even death later.

Abuse and Exploitation

It couldn't happen. It just couldn't. But it did. There is guilt and shame in the mother's eyes as she talks about discovering that her son had been sexually victimized by another teenager at the summer camp. She had prepared him well, she thought, for the world. He knew how to stand up for his rights. Good touch, bad touch: He had it down pat. He knew that adults other than his family weren't supposed to sit close and hug him. But she never thought for a second that one of his peers might take advantage of him. Now, here he is, a 13-year-old boy with Williams syndrome, and he's quiet. Kids with Williams syndrome are never quiet. And he's crying. But he doesn't cry alone. His dad has left the room, but his sobs can be heard through the thin walls. His mother is standing looking out the front window. It's odd, but you can feel blame being passed back and forth between the two parents, a phantom hot potato that lands first in his hands, then hers, then his. One of them has to be responsible for this, has to be.

One of the hardest things for *all* parents of *all* kids to realize is that the world has so many hidden dangers that there really are few safe places for children. Heck, there aren't many safe places for adults either. Parents of kids with disabilities realize that they have to prepare their child for a world in which there is bigotry, hurt, and purposeful meanness. Of all the concerns, the one that brings the most worry to a parent lying awake in the middle of the night is that of sexual victimization. "How do we as parents protect our kids from sexual victimization?" is one of the first questions asked at any parent training seminar on sexuality. It's tempting, isn't it, to just take control, reduce the risk, and keep your child safe. Well, there are three basic temptations to avoid along the path to creating a safe world for your child:

1.   Denial of risk
2.   Denial of relationships
3.   Denial of rights

The First Temptation: Denial of Risk

One temptation while your child is becoming an adult is to deny: to deny that your child is sexual, to deny that your child could be victimized, or to deny that there are those out there who would hurt your child. This leads to a set of parenting practices that don't acknowledge danger or risk. Parents who deny that danger exists won't ask the questions they need to of babysitters, of teachers, or of social workers. They won't provide the kind of supervision that allows both freedom and protection. They won't think that abuse is a possible explanation for their kid's sudden change in mood, in temper, or in skills. Denial of risk is, well, risky.

   Your child depends on you to help identify risky situations:

•   New babysitter
•   New teacher or teacher's aide
•   Overnight at a friend's place

And your child depends on you to check out these risks. This doesn't mean living with paranoia. It simply means that parents need to be alert to those times when their kid may be exposed to new people in unsupervised settings or to situations where their kid may lack the assertive skills to avoid hurt. All a parent needs to do is recognize risk and make concerns public. With a new babysitter, after checking references, ask questions about boundaries. Ensure that the babysitter knows what is acceptable touch and what is not. This checking informs the babysitter about your rules. But it does something else: It alerts any potential abuser that you are a parent who is watching. With a teacher's aide, pop by the classroom, show the aide how any personal care is done, and alert them to the child's boundaries. Let them know that the child has been trained to identify inappropriate actions. These can be done in friendly, informative tones that alert the new person in your child's life without accusation. (Good care providers appreciate information like this—beware of those who get defensive.)

Another Temptation: Denial of Relationships

Equally problematic are those parents who accept that there is risk in the world and have imposed a "jail sentence" on their child. Their child is allowed no free access to the world, every moment is supervised, and they would never—God forbid—be allowed to make a friend, go on a date, or take a walk to the store. The idea that you can protect your child from risk by acting as a jail keeper is a tempting one, but you expose your son or daughter to something often more damaging—toxic levels of anxiety that can lead to a lethal life of loneliness. There are *good* risks too! Here's an example: A young man became besotted with affection for a young woman. Yes they both had disabilities, and yes they both liked each other. But their parents had laid down the law before the first date! The parents decided that the relationship would be allowed ("allowed"!) to continue. But... the kids would only ever be able to hold hands. No kissing. No petting. No quiet, shared conversation. They would be forced to sit in separate chairs, but they could hold hands while seated. This situation is absurd to the point of being almost abusive in and of itself. Where is the "hurrah" that these two found each other? Where are the flower petals that will fall as they walk to the altar? The parents all stated that they don't want their children in a position to get hurt. Well, you can get pretty squashed under a tyrannical thumb!

Being aware that there is risk means that you are *mobilized* not *immobilized*. You are mobilized to ensure that your child have sex education, assertiveness training, streetproofing, and a heck of a lot of opportunities for healthy socialization. Understanding real risk means knowing that when your child goes out of the door on a date with a girlfriend or boyfriend, he is much less likely to be hurt than a child who is denied all forms of relationships and all forms of risk. Being exposed to little bits of risk at a time (with supervision and teaching) is almost like inoculation. Your child is getting used to handling social situations without you but while he is still safe. Denial of children's right to lives of love, friendship, and intimacy leads directly to a situation in which adult children with disabilities are so starved for affection that they are easily victimized.

The Final Temptation: Denial of Rights

There are many rights that people with disabilities are routinely denied. Parents have fought hard for the right for their children to attend typical schools with typical children. Equally, parents have been at the forefront of the fight for everything from good medical care to access to employment. Without question, parents have been a driving force in the community living movement. But there is one right, one that occurs within the context of the family, and of the parenting relationship that is so subtle it's often not acknowledged. Gaining *the right to grow up* is one of the most important rites of passage that people with disabilities need to go through. Your child must grow up. He needs to understand rights, responsibility, risk, and self-respect. A lifetime of passing responsibility from parent, to staff, to sibling, and back to staff is flat out dangerous. Your child needs to grow into taking responsibility for himself. Individuals with disabilities do not need to be parented throughout their lives. In fact, keeping them "forever young" will keep them "forever victimizable."

Your child needs to learn things from you, such as decision making, consequences, and assertiveness. It's odd that parents want children to say no to unwanted touch but would go ballistic if their child said no to them about food, bedtimes, friends, or any other important issue. You can't have one without the other! Remember a simple thing: Your child is growing—and so should your parenting style and technique. If you find yourself treating your 16-year-old like she were 6 years old, call it a big "oops," and start over. And don't beat yourself up over this. All parents make this mistake. Your child may not be able to adequately protest your parenting style. In fact if your child is over the age of 8 and hasn't said "Mom, I'm not a baby!" it ain't normal.

Letting your child grow up will give you enormous pleasure. It will terrify you at times, too. But adults are less victimizable than children. So, it may surprise you, but one of your most important jobs is to help your child grow into a full-fledged adult with adult expectations and adult responsibilities. Who ever thought that the greatest antidote to risk was freedom?

What Your Child Needs to Learn...

If you understand our saying that your child needs to learn how to become an adult who is capable of being her own defense system, you are quite right. Let's face some facts. First, people with intellectual disabilities are one of the most victimized groups in our society. Research tells us that if a child has an intellectual disability, she is three to five times more likely to be sexually victimized than any other member of any other group. The exact statistics aren't important here, but you need to be aware that almost all of this abuse has happened in supposedly safe places for people with disabilities, done by those people who are supposed to be safe people. The very places where you expect protection have been the places where abuse has occurred, and the very people who you expect to be protectors have been the people who have done the abuse. *Don't start thinking that this is a hopeless situation; it isn't.* All it means is that the "old" approach of "us" protecting "them" hasn't worked. *But* there is growing evidence that people with disabilities are quite able to be their own first line of defense and that with a certain set of skills and abilities, they will be able to repel abuse and if that fails, report abuse. That's our goal. But it means that your child needs to learn some basic concepts.

Sex Education and Privacy Awareness

Although many people think that sex education belongs in the home, the fact is that sex education for people with disabilities involves a lot of rigorous (but fun) teaching, often in a class or group setting. Beyond that, most sex education packages or curricula include a lot of group exercises and practice at social skills. Learning manners, dating skills, discriminating and choosing appropriate greetings, and social distance...these are all things that are best learned and practiced with others.

But don't breathe a sigh of relief just yet. You aren't off the hook. Teaching begins at home, and the most important thing your child needs to learn from you is broken down into one category and two concepts—body parts, public and private. Learning that her body is her own is vitally important for your child. In Chapter 5, we brought up the concepts of public and private. These concepts are relevant to the topics of abuse and exploitation and your child's safety because too many people with disabilities learn that their body is very public. All sorts of people touch them, usually while providing some kind of support or service. Begin at the beginning, and ensure that your child knows that there are parts of the body that no one sees or touches without permission. Don't worry about upsetting some service provider in the future. If the provider hasn't learned to ask permission, let it be your child who teaches her through protests that permission is necessary. This means that you yourself need to learn to knock before entering your child's room and asking when helping him. This can be gently done and practiced.

Someone to Talk To   To be effective, sex education needs to teach a person the language with which to report abuse and then give the ability to use it. While your child is learning language about the body or participating in a class to learn about sexuality, set yourself up as a "talk-to-able" person. This may feel highly unnatural for both you and your child. (Dave thinks that he would shrivel in embarrassment if he had to talk to his mom about his "pee-pee" and as far as he's concerned, she doesn't have a vagina!) It's kind of natural and healthy for us to desexualize our parents and for them to refuse to see us as sexual beings. But you need to realize that you may be the only person whom your child can trust who provides support but is outside of the "system." Therefore, in case something happens and your child needs to talk, she needs to know that it's okay to say words like *penis, vagina, vulva,* and *rectum* directly to you and that you won't get upset with her. Many times people with disabilities have suffered abuse and have wanted to report it, but everyone they see around them is connected socially or professionally with everyone else. "How can I tell my favorite staffperson, who would never hurt me, that I was abused if I see her going out for a beer after work with my abuser?" Being external to the system and being talk-to-able is of vital importance.

Self-Esteem

We've talked a lot about self-esteem in the book, but we'll only add here that pride begins with honest self-evaluation. Help your child to become proud of who she is, including the disability. There is definitely a growth in the "disability pride" movement as is reflected in everything from self-advocate organizations like People First and magazines like *Mouth: The Voice of the Disability Nation* and *Ragged Edge.* Helping your child become involved with these organizations can be the best thing you do for your child. Coming to understand that the label "retard" is like "nigger," "queer," "spic," or "broad"—words used by hateful bigots— is important. Too many people with disabilities hang their head with shame, absolute shame, when they hear disability discussed. This is changing.

  Get involved yourself. Subscribe to *Mouth* and *Ragged Edge,* and check out disability pride World Wide Web sites on your computer. These will help revolutionize you. Read the following story, and see how you react.

Dave's Story

My friend Judy has cerebral palsy, and she and I often go out for drinks together. On one occasion, as the night wore on, her speech improved and mine deteriorated. At one point she said that she didn't think I understood what it was both to have a disability and to be proud. I said that I thought that I did, and then she said...

  (Drum roll...watch your response to this) "If God came down here right now and said, 'Judy, I will give you the ability to walk,' I would say, 'No thanks, I'm happy with who you made the first time.'"

Now honestly, is that hard to believe? Can you even really hear what she is saying? Doesn't it seem almost impossible for someone to say that they are happy being in a wheelchair or having a disability? Why is it that when a woman is proud of herself as a woman, we think it's cool, but when a person with a disability is proud of themselves as a person with a disability, we think they are brave (deluded but brave)? Why is it that we think this attitude doesn't fit with those poignant stories about overcoming a disability. Isn't that a bit of prejudice right there? Your child needs to feel the self-confidence of knowing exactly who he is and the self-esteem of being proud of exactly that person.

Victimizers look for victims. The first thing taught in a streetproofing course is "Walk with pride." Well, you can't walk with pride if you haven't felt it in the first place.

  ## Rest Stop:

Set a goal for you and your child: that your child will be able to describe herself in a positive way as simply or in as much detail as possible. Most parents teach their children to recite their address and telephone number in case they get lost. How about helping your child learn to recite a list of her strengths and positive qualities? Make a Pride Poster for your child's room. Put your child's photograph on it. Add to the list over time. Help your child understand that she is wonderful!

Pride Poster

[My child's photograph here]

This is me.

Who am I?

What can I do?

Remember that there's a difference between who your child is and what she can do. Both lists are important.

What Else Your Child Needs

Beyond the basic skills of understanding public and private, being able to say no, and having self-pride, your child needs two things: someone to talk to and access to healthy relationships. We looked at the first in Chapter 5. Unfortunately a lot of folks with disabilities have neither. Fortunately you can be that someone to talk to, and you can facilitate the second: access to relationships.

Go back to Chapter 4. Read again the list developed by families in British Columbia who wanted to nurture friendships and connections for their children. Keep in mind changes that you might incorporate for an older son or daughter. Think of the ways most of us meet people who have similar interests, passions, and talents. We join clubs, take classes, try new things, or walk the dog.

Parents throughout the world know that some of the most successful strategies are discovered by talking with other people. If you want to create rich and interesting connections for your teenage or adult child, then speak up. Ask around. Talk to your own family. If you bemoan the fact that your daughter has never had a movie night and sleepover at your brother and sister-in-law's home, suggest it. Maybe they think that you've never considered them capable of taking on the responsibility. Keep stirring the waters for your child while you keep helping your daughter learn the skills to take advantage of what floats along.

Yes, we're saying it a thousand times in this book: Being in healthy relationships makes people with disabilities less likely to be manipulated into abusive situations. By establishing healthy relationships and by feeling loved and valued in friendships, in families, and in couples, a person with a disability will no longer be that lonely man or woman who would spread his or her legs for a bit of attention and praise. Don't shake your head at that last sentence as though it's an exaggeration. It's not. Tragically, it's not.

Dick Sobsey, a parent of a son with disabilities, is a published author and lecturer about abuse and disability issues. He explained that parents, advocates, and people with disabilities need to raise the priority within the police force of addressing abuse involving people with disabilities: "Police have to choose between competing priorities....Without [strong] advocacy, it's very easy for police to lay aside investigations that may take a great deal of time and resources" (1997, pp. 18–19). Sobsey has lobbied the Canadian Department of Justice to support a 1995 report called *Amendments to the Criminal Code and the Canada Evidence Act with Respect to Persons with Disabilities*. In it are recommendations for changes to laws that would allow for stiffer sentences for some crimes when the victim is a vulnerable person. The report proposed changes in the courtroom that would allow people with disabilities to give evidence by alternative methods, like giving testimony via videotape, using nonverbal communication strategies when identifying perpetrators, or giving testimony behind a screen so that they don't have to be intimidated by looking at the accused.

Citing research studies, Sobsey said,

When looking at 320 cases of sexual abuse of kids or sexual assault of adults with disabilities (about half have an intellectual disability), and wherein the abuse was severe and chronic and the victimizer was known to the individual, there is an eight percent conviction rate overall....Interestingly enough, of those cases which make it to the courtroom, the conviction rate is 33 percent. The biggest impediment is getting the information to the police. The two primary reasons that the abuse is not reported outside the system are a fear of consequences and a lack of trust in the justice system. (1997, pp. 18–19)

Teaching "No, Go, Tell"

Almost all of the training regarding risk reduction of sexual victimization for kids includes a simple formula: "No, Go, Tell." These seem like three simple words. Yet is this concept so simple? We don't think so. Each of the words requires a different assertion skill.

To say no to a powerful adult is a difficult thing to do. The child has to be able to determine that she has a right to body privacy and a right to protect that privacy. The concept of body privacy, born in bedrooms and bathrooms while learning basic skills, is only a valid one if the person *understands that privacy means control.* Saying no to unwanted touch is an exercise in control.

"Go" requires the person to break a direct rule. In abusive situations, the child is often told what to do, how to do it, and to stay put. For a person to escape or attempt to run when she has been told not to requires her to *understand that not all demands have to be complied with.*

Finally, "Tell" requires that a person break a promise or defy a threat. Abusers are using their power and trying to exercise that power from a distance by making the person promise silence or by threatening retribution. For a person to defy a direct threat or break a promise, that person has to *understand that she decides what is a secret and that she decides what is safe.*

Once, after a workshop with people with disabilities on how to say no and avoid abuse, a young woman came up to the podium. She was agitated and upset, and when she finally spoke, she said that the trouble with the word *no* was that it didn't work; the trouble with "Go" was that people won't let you, and the trouble with "Tell" was that no one would listen. She had been badly victimized by a family member who forced her into submission, and even though she had said no clearly, he hadn't stopped. Even though she wanted to run, he held her down, and even though she told her mother, she wasn't believed. This was a difficult conversation. It would be easy in the face of such overwhelming evidence from this one, frail young woman that "No, Go, Tell" doesn't work and simply give up on this as a means of teaching. But that would be abandoning an approach that is very easy to teach and has important components.

We need to first recognize that "No, Go, Tell" is a process and that although the individual components may not magically work to stop the abuse, the process of "No, Go, Tell" is one that is both healing and helpful. Let's look at the steps again more closely to examine what is important in each and how to possibly teach them and create an atmosphere wherein they may just work.

The young woman was right. Saying no will probably not stop abuse. In fact, the likelihood is that the abuser has the person in a situation wherein it doesn't matter what the person does or says or how loudly he or she does or says no: It won't work. Then why is this important? Saying no is important legally: When asked if nonconsent was clearly indicated, it is good for the person to be able to say that he, without question, communicated the word or the meaning *no* to the abuser. Saying no is important therapeutically because as much as we don't like it, society still somewhat mistrusts people who have been victimized and because it gives people a strong place to start healing if they know that they have been really clear about the fact that they didn't accept what was going on. Finally, saying no is important as a means of demonstrating *strength* in the face of tyranny. As more people (including abusers) come to see people with disabilities as individuals of strength and conviction, their vulnerability to assault will ultimately diminish. Again, *no* is not a magic word that will immediately stop abuse. It may, though, lead to a conviction, enhance the personal healing of the victim, and ultimately stop a general perception of people with disabilities as willing and easy victims. This makes it worth the effort to teach "No."

How do you teach this? *Role plays* are a wonderful way to teach "No." It is important that everyone around you know what you are doing. One mom was teaching her son to say the word no when his boundaries were violated, and then another caregiver, who did not know that this was being done, punished him for using his new strategy. The caregiver interpreted his assertiveness as rudeness. Here are 10 role plays in which your child can practice saying "No!"

1. A stranger wants you to get into the car.
2. Mom wants you to eat fried snake.
3. One of the kids at the school wants you to go into the bathroom stall with him.
4. Dad wants you to listen to Barry Manilow.
5. A friend dares you to put your hand down a neighbor girl's panties.
6. The waitress gives you the wrong order.
7. Someone asks you to take some pills.
8. A friend asks you to eat worms with spaghetti sauce.
9. A stranger wants you to let her into the house.
10. Uncle Harry asks you to play a game that scares you.

The danger in even putting a list like this into a book is that sometimes only these 10 examples will actually be used! But we know that people with intellectual disabilities learn best when the things they are learning are related to what is going on in their lives.

 Rest Stop:

Think of the people who are in your child's life, and then come up with role plays with circumstances that are really pertinent to your child. Make your own list here using people and places known to your child. Remember, the point is not to trick your child, but to help reinforce his confidence about saying yes and no.

Circumstances in which my child should say no:

You will notice, too, that not all of the items are extremely dangerous situations and that the way your child says no will vary. In fact, some examples are just plain silly. This turns it into a game that is fun and funny. The sillier some things are, the better. All people learn better when they're laughing.

Be a role model. Believe it or not, your kids look up to you. We know, we know, it doesn't seem that way, but they really do. And they need you to demonstrate how to appropriately say no to things. A friend said that she found it difficult to teach her son to say no to people, and she realized that it was because she couldn't do it herself. She said that he had spent the first 10 years of his life watching her say yes to people when she wanted to say no. She wondered if she was teaching him the wrong thing when she said yes to a friend asking for a ride, then hung up the telephone and said, 'I just don't know why she always calls me whenever she needs something. Does she ever do things for me? Ha! I don't think so. No, as far as she's concerned, she is the only one with needs, but me, I always have to be there for her! Just one time, one time, I would like to just tell her what I think.' Is this teaching her son the wrong thing about saying no? Well, yes, we think so.

Saying no is much more difficult that you can imagine. Just how many times this week did you say yes to something that you really wanted to say no to? Do you think your kids were watching? Well, yes. So they need to hear you say no to others. They need to see that saying no doesn't mean people won't like you anymore. It doesn't mean you will get into trouble. It doesn't mean you are a bad person. It doesn't mean that in every instance you yell "No!" at the other person. It does, however, mean that you are a person who is clear about your boundaries, your expectations and your limits. This is a good lesson for children.

> *You feel like such an ogre sometimes, too. We're standing in line at the store, and Hillary gives a woman a hug, someone she's been talking to for 10 minutes because she likes her. And I say, "Hillary, that's not appropriate," and, of course, the woman says, "That's okay." I say, "Well, thank you, but it's not okay." I've learned to add, "No, it's not okay because we don't want her hugging people who might not be as nice as you are." Then people seem to understand.*
> *—Michele Shaw*

Next, you need to help your child out in difficult situations. For example, if someone your child doesn't know is reaching out and grabbing at her and saying (as someone actually did), "Oh, what a cute little Downie! They have just the cutest faces!" you need to see your child's discomfort and say no for your child. Kneel down and say, "No, please don't touch me. I don't know you." If this person continues, you need to then be firm and say, "No! My child is learning to keep herself safe." Do not allow this person to grab your child.

One of the biggest difficulties parenting a child with an intellectual disability is that many strangers (and some friends) can be overenthusiastic in their greetings both as a means of expressing a legitimate reaction of finding your child

Lou and Michele Shaw
Woodland Hills, California

adorable and as an eager message of acceptance. These are important moments for your child. In the past, parents have often encouraged their
children to respond with warmth and openness to these kinds of interchanges.
For example, one of the reasons there is the stereotype that kids with Down
syndrome are so "loving" is that some of them have been taught to be compliant
to boundary invasion by perfect strangers. We're not suggesting that
you make your child into a cold fish who stiffens up at any display of kind-
ness or affection. Although someone may be really put off by your insistence that
your child be respected as a human being rather than be treated like a
cute puppy, it is worth the effort in two ways. First, your child will see you
using the word no forcefully, and second, she will be learning a whole lot
about boundaries.

> *It's tricky. It's unfortunate, because you find yourself telling your child that
> something warm and affectionate and decent and nice isn't the right thing to do,
> that it's inappropriate. It's something that's sweet and warm and maybe if that
> behavior was appropriate, we'd have a much warmer world. But it does lead to
> misunderstandings, and our children are very vulnerable.*
>   —Michele Shaw

> *There's one woman I often see at the conventions we go to. For a long time, she
> would see me and run right up and hug me. It wasn't a quick hug, a greeting;
> it was really quite a womanly hug, sexual almost. I didn't want to offend her,
> but I started say, "I think when you see someone you like a lot, it's good to
> shake hands with that person." She was able to understand, and now we shake
> hands. I didn't want to push her away, but by explaining what was more ap-
> propriate, she understood and we still like each other.*
>   —Lou Shaw

Try role reversal. This is fun! All this means is that your child acts out the role
of the stranger trying to get you into the car or the parent trying to make you eat
fried snake. You get to get up and say no. This often leads to lots of laughter and
allows your child to really see how they are to respond.

Rest Stop:

Think up some scenarios that you and your child can act out, in which your child can be assertive.

Situations in which my child can be assertive:

A child may well become assertive enough to say no. In order to reduce the risk further, your child also needs to learn to get away from the problem. The most important thing about teaching "Go" is getting the child to look for an avenue of escape. Believe it or not, fire drills in the home are a wonderful way of teaching your child to think when afraid. Get a bucket, and paint it red. This will be the fire. Have your children—all of your children—run through fire drills, but each time put the fire in a different place. When the children see where the fire is, they need to come up with another way of getting out of the house or protecting themselves while waiting for help. This will have children become aware of their surroundings; they'll learn to look for doors, windows, and other means of getting out of the situation. The nice thing about this is that you are teaching your child observation skills and strategy without talking directly about sexual victimization. Constant emphasis on abuse can scare a child about the world. The important thing here is that your child becomes aware of both danger and escape.

To teach "Go" about abuse, just add it to your role plays. Pick a number of examples—a stranger offering candy, schoolmates in the schoolyard, an aunt or uncle visiting—and get the child to tell or show you how he or she would get out of the situation. The best thing going for your child is that the perpetrator will not be prepared for a child with a disability who knows how to escape. Ability always takes them by surprise. This is the best defense.

Teaching "Go" also means teaching "Destination." Be careful not to teach the child just to run away from a situation. This could spell really big trouble, and you may end up with a lost child. When doing the fire drill, make sure that the kids know not just how to get out of the house but also where to go when they leave. There needs to be a rendezvous point. The same is true about escaping abusive situations. They need to recognize the importance of going to the school, a friendly neighbor, a convenience store, a pay phone, or the police station. Strategy involves knowing how to get out of a situation and then where to go afterwards.

Finally, "Tell" is the most important of the three components. "No" may not work. "Go" may not be possible. But "Tell" is always possible and can always work. Just the fact that you are reading this book means that as a parent you are thinking about issues regarding sexuality and abuse. This means you are open to hearing about the issues. That openness needs to be translated to your child. Your child needs to learn early on that you are a person to whom they can talk.

The "Tell" part of this is really difficult. Abuse is almost always accompanied by threats ("If you tell, I'll hurt your mom"; "If you tell, I'll kill your dog"). Children may want to become the protectors of their home environments. Knowing that making threats is an abuser's strategy gives you an advantage. Tell your child the truth: "If someone threatens you, that means that he or she isn't a very nice person. You need to tell Mom and Dad when someone makes threats. Threats are meant to make you scared of talking to us. We love each other, and that means we never have to be scared of talking to each other.

I think Hillary understands very well there are private parts to her body, that her body is her own and that anyone who makes you uncomfortable is wrong. You are not wrong. If someone tries to do something you don't like, you get away. She needs to go and tell somebody. The thing about that, however, is that the person you tell has to be receptive. There are plenty of people who will say, "Oh, no, you must have misunderstood." When Hillary was first bothered by a boy at school, the first person she told didn't do anything. She needs to know that she has to keep on telling until someone believes her.
—Michele Shaw

Remember that your child will "tell" you things without saying a word. Many books print lists of behaviors that are possible indicators of abuse. These lists can be quite dangerous in that a lot of children who have never been abused engage in the listed behaviors, and this can terrify a parent. Also, children who have been abused may act in ways that have never been listed, and a parent can be tricked into believing that nothing is wrong because the child didn't do "Item 3" on the abuse behavior list. Given these concerns, we believe it is counterproductive to list these behaviors. What *is* important to realize is that if your child's behavior changes quickly, without explanation, you need to investigate. *Behavior change* or *affect (emotional) change* without explanation is the greatest worry. The behavior change can be anything from loss of skills to acting out; the affect change can be anything from obvious depression to lack of affect. So, look for *unexplained change* as something that needs to be investigated.

Your child may not be able to "tell" you with words, even if you are the most open parent alive. The shame may be overwhelming, the fear may be crushing and the words may be lacking. Fear not. Your child will find a way of bringing these things to your attention. Listen with your eyes!

I spent a lot of time getting Brad to focus. If I was speaking to him, I made eye contact and made sure he knew I was talking to him. I didn't let him just walk off and ignore if he didn't understand. I tried to always wait for an answer. I still find it hard to avoid speaking for Brad, especially if he gets stuck. His speaking fluctuates and motivation plays a part in how well he can get others to un-

derstand him. There are times he can call me from town and he's clear as a bell.
Then I can be face to face with him, and I haven't got a clue what he's saying. If
that happens, I always try to say, "I didn't get that. Can you tell me another
way?" or "I can't remember that. Can you tell me some more?" Sometimes I'll
ask him to show me. It's very clear to him, but I just can't get it, so I try to help
him make the story more specific. I think that's very important.
—Ethel Magnus

Assertion Begins with "No" and Continues with Choices

Self-protection requires an assertive child. Many children with disabilities are
taught to comply. They know that the quickest way to approval and favor is to
just do what they are told. A very frightening study showed that people with disabilities would do what they were told even if they knew it was wrong and even
if they knew it was dangerous (Flynn, Reeves, Whelan, & Speak, 1985). Why
would they do it? This comes from a lifetime of being told what to do and being
expected just to do it. They had lost the discrimination skills about how and
when to comply or not comply.

 Think about it. How often do you comply to requests or demands made at
home? Probably, if you are like us, about 20% of the time, you just won't do
what's asked of you. Or, you will say you will do it but just won't get around to
it. This is normal. But, for a person with a disability, compliance is often expected at a 100% level.

Dave's Story

I was asked to do some behavioral programming with a family who had a child
with an intellectual disability whom they said was noncompliant. I met a fairly
typical kid, and when we did our "baseline measurement" (counting the behaviors to see the rate at which they were occurring to start with), I was not surprised to find that the kid was complying 95% of the time. That means out of 100
requests, she refused or balked only 5 times!

When I talked about this with the family, they said that they didn't want her
to "grow up and be a bother to other people." They also said that when they left
her with family members or babysitters, they wanted her to be liked. They felt
that the best way to do this was to teach her to do what people ask so that they
wouldn't be frustrated with her. I asked them about their other kids. They told
me that they were pretty typical. I asked if their friends or family *liked* their other
kids. They laughed and said, "It depends on the day." We worked through to the
understanding that they expected family members to love their typical kids regardless of their behavior but that they thought that their daughter with a disability had *earn* love by good behavior on her part. It was a difficult conversation
because we had to dig down to an understanding of what their child needed and
why the problem was exactly the opposite of the reason for the original referral.
She complied too much!

 I asked them this question, which I now ask you: What do you want your
child with a disability to do when a strange person wants her (or him) to get in
a car? They said with outrage, "We'd want her to tell the stranger where to get

off and then come tell us." I asked them if this behavior would be a "bother" to the person in the car. "Well, of course it would be," they replied.

So, the point really is that you want your child to learn when to do reasonable things in response to reasonable requests to get along with reasonable people. But you also want your child to become a "problem" and a "bother" and to stand up for himself when the requests, situations, and people are unreasonable. This goes all the way from the stranger in the car to your son Gerry, for example, who expects his younger sister to do all of the dishes and clean up the entire kitchen because she is a girl or because he and his friends want time to play on their own.

Learning as a child to say no and to be heard plants the seeds of legitimate self-protection in adolescence and adulthood. A child who can't choose to say no to peas grows into an adult who can't choose to say no to a penis. So beginning in toddlerhood, children need to be offered choices, and their choices need to be respected. It's actually fairly easy to teach making choices. Imagine asking your child if he wants corn or peas. If he says, "Corn, please," you say, "Okay, we'll do it your way. Peas it is." If you child doesn't kick up a fuss, you have some work to do. You want your child to say, in some form, "Hey, I said I wanted corn." There are a million opportunities for your child to make sure that his wishes have been heard and to make sure that they are respected.

Because of Jim's disability, his choices are ultimately going to be limited. The question is how are we, as parents, helping him nurture and experience as much as he can so that he can make reasoned choices about what is open to him? How do we keep challenging those limits for ourselves?
—*Richard Schwier*

 Rest Stop:

Think of a few examples, even just two or three, in your daily family routine when your child can have the opportunity to think, consider, and make a decision about something. Practice **and carry through** on the choice that's made, even if it does mean going to the video store to rent **Ernest Goes to Camp** again!

Opportunities for my child to think about something and make a decision:

As a parent, you can be aware of your daily conversations with your child and how your responses may influence her decision-making and self-assertion skills. Respond to your child in a way that respects her feelings and recognizes the effort to communicate. If your child expresses a fear of the dark closet in the bedroom or is frightened to go down to the basement freezer for a package of hamburger, how do you respond? Try not to brush off the expression of fear by saying, "Don't be silly, just go down and get it. There's nothing to be afraid of" or, "You're not afraid of the dark." If your daughter tells you she is worried that the neighbor's dog doesn't look well, how do you respond? Avoid saying something like "The dog is fine. Hurry up and get dressed or you'll miss the bus." Over time, your child's confidence in self-expression will be eroded, certainly not intentionally, but it will ebb away nevertheless. A more supportive and respectful response about the neighbor's dog might be "Do you think so? I didn't see the dog today, but maybe he's not feeling well. If I see Mr. Brown, I'll tell him that you would like to know." In a simple exchange, you acknowledge your daughter's feelings as genuine and you add another small building block to her self-confidence.

Now, we aren't saying that children don't have to learn to follow through on requests and expectations. Children need to learn to do their chores and follow some basic familial rules. We are just saying that they also have to learn to speak up, make themselves heard, and become Mighty People.

We don't recommend that parents tell their children to not talk to strangers. We do suggest that parents tell their children to keep their distance from strangers and not to get into anybody's car unless it's a parent or a teacher and only then if you know and trust them. Telling your child not to talk to strangers simply doesn't make any sense. The chance your child will get lost and will need to ask somebody for help or directions is a lot greater than the chance that talking to a stranger will result in a problem (Sobsey, personal communication, 1995).

Chris used to wrestle at school, like his brothers. The year he was a junior in high school, he did a summer program while his brother went to wrestling class. I'm thinking I have to pick him up at 5:30, but practice was apparently cancelled and he missed the bus. His problem-solving skills are very good, so he just figured, "I walked here. I can surely walk home." Well, he got turned around and ended up walking out of the city instead of turning toward home. He was walking up a major highway when a classmate drove by with her mom and yelled, "Hey, that's Chris!" They brought him home, and although my first reaction was terror, the answer was that we'd better teach him a better way to remember how to get home. We got in the car and went to the place where he'd made the mistake. I didn't say, "I'll never again let Chris take that risk!" We went through it, and he learned. The worst thing I could have done when he got lost was to deny him any chance to learn anything new. Now he can cross four lanes of busy traffic because he believes he can. You cannot make your child afraid to try.
    —Gayle Foy

Community and integration make a huge difference. Dave teaches a class to people with disabilities regarding protection from sexual assault. In this class, people with disabilities may attend, but staff, parents, and other care providers may not. This is to be an experience of learning how and when to say no and an opportunity to freely talk about what concerns they have about saying no. Teaching this class always leaves him feeling in awe of the untapped strength of the minority called "people with disabilities."

Dave's Story

The first time I taught "No" was in Dawson Creek and in Courtney, British Columbia. It was exciting to walk into the hall and realize that I was going to teach 70 people with disabilities how to say "No." While this was going on, another facilitator was going to teach their care providers and parents how to hear "No." My group ranged in age from 7 to 70, and it was incredible to see the group dynamics and watch the group work together. At one point, the parent of a little girl with a disability, perhaps the youngest attendee, snuck in to see what was going on while we were talking about feelings. The little girl's hand flew into the air. I picked her out for discussing feelings, and she said, "Can we talk about embarrassed?" I said sure, and asked her what embarrassed her. She said, "My mom. She is in here watching me, and she is supposed to be in the other room." Mom got up and slunk silently out of the room.

At break, Mom came and apologized and said that she was just concerned that her daughter was okay. After all, she was so much younger than everyone else there. I told her that she should be very proud of her daughter. This little girl, and indeed all of the young teenagers in attendance, had more assertion and more pride than those who were adults. I guess that these kids had never been caged, had never been locked away, and had never known a day of forced segregation in their lives has made an incredible difference. Tell me that community living and community integration aren't worth the heartaches along the journey to full emancipation.

Still, when the mother was asked why she chose to bring her daughter to this session, she said that she was concerned that because her daughter was the only person with a disability at her school, her daughter would pick up the attitude that others with disabilities were unacceptable. She said that she makes an effort to have her child have all sorts of friends and that in that range of friends will be other people with disabilities and other kids with disabilities her own age. She wants her daughter to realize that friendship is what is important; what the person *has* is not. Who the person *is* is the most important issue in friendship.

If you, as a parent or family member, suspect abuse, ask questions. If a person's behavior changes markedly, make sure that he is safe and is not being hurt. Document your concerns in a private record, using as many specific dates, times, and names as you can. Make the system respond: Your child needs protection from further abuse, an opportunity to file a complaint, and support from family, friends, and advocates. Check with your local police department's sexual assault personnel. In many areas, you have not only a moral and ethical responsibility to report suspected abuse, but a legal obligation as well. Remember that abuse, exploitation, intimidation, and sexual victimization are all abuses of power.

Abusers think that no one will believe your child. You need to empower your child to say no, to speak up, and feel a sense of self-control. Your child needs to know that you believe him.

The police department can give you advice about what steps to take both now and in the long term that will help you provide support. You need to convey the message that your child is believed, that what happened to him was wrong, and although traumatic, that it should not be a life-defining experience that must overshadow future happiness.

 ## Rest Stop:

By being armed with information, you've already won half the battle (hopefully before the battle ever begins). In all likelihood, you'll never need this information, but go ahead and list the telephone numbers of local support people, agencies and police departments in the space below. Your child may never need you to know whom to call, but maybe someone else's child will. You'll be the one who knows what to do.

Names of people or groups my child can contact:	Telephone numbers

The past approach of protecting people has not worked. We need to see people with disabilities as their own first line of defense. That means that they have skills to recognize and report abuse, that they have lives of emotional fulfillment, and that they have parents or others to whom they can talk about whatever happens to them. Abuse of people with disabilities will end only when we are brave enough to face it down side by side with people with disabilities who have discovered their own sense of power and control.

I don't want to talk about my biggest fear, abuse, because I don't want it to become a self-fulfilling prophecy. But Brad is very vulnerable. He's becoming more responsible, and he does fit in well in the community. He's not one to go around and say hi to everyone, but it seems people light up when they see him. They usually respond to him first, and many times I don't know who they are. People have been following his dancing career in the paper, so a lot of people know him through that. He likes Salt Spring and says he wants to stay here forever.

—Ethel Magnus

Ideally, there will be enough independence, friends, income and connections for all our kids. There are many fears that parents have for all their children that have nothing to do with disability. A University of Guelph study showed that 20% of the women there claim they've been date raped. What kind of a culture have we got here? I hope that all the girls, including Karen, have a life rich in networks of people. Whether Karen lives alone or with other people, whether she gets married, all of those should be possibilities within reach.

—John Lord

Francis Schaan

The best thing about me? Me? That's a hard one. Well. Ah. I think I can make new friends. I get along with the Eighth Street guys at McDonald's. They took me along to a Blades hockey game on Sunday.

I don't know what mom and dad should teach a baby. Ah. Table manners? That's one thing. One more thing. If you're in trouble, call 911. If someone does something you don't like, tell somebody. Sometimes I can tell Bev or Helen. I can tell someone to stop. I can call my social worker, and we go for coffee. We talk about it. He sometimes says he will look into it.

I get along with my sisters, for one. I can talk to them about stuff. I got four sisters. Two brothers. There are two babies in the family. I am the boy, and Doreen is the baby of the girls.

Those things I do, like reading and cooking and swimming for one, I like to do it. I would like to get another Crew Member of the Month. To get that one, I have to work and be nice to customers. If I would be grouchy, then I wouldn't get it. Some of those new managers are good, and we get along good.

Wrestling is my all time favorite, the WWF especially. But it's not quite my favorite thing. Easter is. I don't want to think about wrestling when Easter is around. Because Lent starts. That's for Catholics. That means you believe in God. When it's Lent, you don't have to eat meat until Easter Monday and then you can. It's because of Jesus. God died for us. 'Cause he loved us. It means we should be nicer to the customers at work.

For one thing, I'm going to try to get that Crew Member thing. Darrel is helping me to read, and that will help. When I can read, then I'll get the Crew Member. When I learn to read, I can read the wrestling magazines. I can read a kid's book. Maybe I can read one to my goddaughter. I can read some of it. I know it. Learning to read is easy if you go slow.

I met this girl, Margie. It's going. We went to school together. She came back into my life. Oh, um. She's the same way, like me. She's handicapped, too. She has Down syndrome. I can tell. That don't matter. I still want her as a friend. She takes part in dances, too, like sock hop dances at Walter Murray. That was the best year in school. We just went out to a dance last week. Her sister drove us. I got her phone number, and she got mine. We talk about Walter Murray school. She lives with her folks. I don't think I did met them. I met her, Margie's sister. Margie is about 35. And my friend Roy is the same age.

The worst thing in my life. When they picked on me. In school. That made me feel bad. I don't know why they do, they just don't like my kind of guy. The best thing is just walk away from them. Ignore them. Just walk away. I would never hit them. I just don't want to do it. People don't pick on people as much anymore, I don't think so. Sometimes people think I'm a boy. But I am 35. A man. I just ignore it. People should treat you like a human being. My family does. They treat me like I'm a adult.

Maybe I will ask Margie to go for hot chocolate someday. I plan on going to the People First conference again this year. I went to last year in Regina. I went on the bus. It was good. I would like to go to it again if I can.

The most important thing in my whole life, I have to think about that one. I think one of them is my work and 15 years at my work. Crew Member of the Month again, that would be the best. When I saw Dad in that bed when he got his stroke, I got very scared. I would be happy if they would move up to the city. Then I could look after him. I could work 7 days a week to pay the rent for them. I would give them my money.

I am an uncle, too, that's one thing. I'm a uncle to Adam, Daniel, Michael, and one more person, she's my goddaughter, Emily. I'm an uncle 20 times already. Well, I would tell them if they want something, they come to me. For some advice. I tell them don't run. Sit down and play nice. Be nice to each other. If they are fighting, I say stop and they stop, too.

When I was 7, Mom sent me to the Moose Jaw Training School. I didn't like it there. They picked on me, and I turned black and blue. I was there for a little while. I tell parents to keep the baby. Raise the child. Maybe that child can be like me and have the same job and get the Crew Member of the Month. Maybe the Customer Service award. If they say they want to do something, then

Francis Schaan
Saskatoon, Saskatchewan

let them. Try it. Try stuff until you learn more things. Like me. Even my dad can learn new things.

Q

Our son has had a couple of favorite toys since he was little. He's now 12, and it's very inappropriate for him to take them out in public. But we don't want to strip him of his prized possessions.

A

Don't! It's just fine to have prized possessions and for those possessions to be *age inappropriate*. Dave was in a near–plane crash and was quite shaken up by the ordeal. The steward, recognizing his anxiety, came up to him at the end of the *very harrowing* journey and handed him a small plastic lamb, a baby's teething toy, and said, "Take this, and remember lambies never crash." To this day he carries that lamb in his briefcase and will not fly without it.

He keeps the lamb in a place that gives him security but that no one else can see. If your child likes something that he wants to take on a journey, how about putting it in a knapsack? Teach him that he is to keep it in the knapsack and that he can take it out when he gets where he is going. Why not teach him that these toys are to be kept in bedrooms where he can play with them whenever he wants? If you have other children, as they grow up, let them help guide your child with a disability about what possessions are "cool" for different ages. If you don't have other children or if they've already left home, pay attention to other people around your son or daughter's age. Sometimes people still have the possessions they had as children because they haven't had an opportunity to acquire new ones.

Q

This year, our oldest daughter went away to college. Our other daughter, who has an intellectual disability, still lives at home. Lately, she's been very moody and grouchy. What can we do to cheer her up?

A

There's always been a general myth that people with an intellectual disability, particularly Down syndrome, are perpetually jolly. You've heard it, or you will: "They're always so happy and affectionate." This is an unfair misconception. People with Down syndrome and other intellectual disabilities have the same ups and downs as anyone else. They can have feelings of sadness, depression, anxiety, confusion, aloneness, despair, and joy; they experience the same full range of emotions that anyone else has, regardless of disability. People with disabilities can go through life with mental health problems that are never recognized. Things that happen in any family will affect the family members. When a close sibling leaves for college, her departure is bound to have consequences for the sibling left behind. As parents, encourage your daughter to express her emotions and feelings. Think of ways to help your daughter keep in touch with her sister, whether it's a weekly telephone call, letter writing, or an exchange of photos. You'll need to talk with your older daughter about the important role she plays in her sister's life and to make sure she responds to letters and calls. It's important that you don't "make a huge deal" out of the emotions your daughter is feeling, but you also should not dismiss them as silliness. Keep the communication open. If you think there is a more serious problem rather than just a temporary upset or sadness, you should consider finding a professional in your area who is experienced in the mental health of people with intellectual disabilities.

Q

We think our son, who has a disability, might be gay. This is all very new ground; how do we cope with this?

A

Well, it's difficult for all parents. There is a sense that when a child is gay, he or she will live an entirely different life path. But yes, gay people live lives of value and form relationships that last for long periods of time. But you probably aren't ready to hear this yet; you are wondering if your child's sexuality can be changed. The short answer to that is *no*. The long answer is: You can try, but everyone will end up disappointed and damaged by the process. Get in touch with PFLAG for support and information. Check your telephone book for other support and advocacy groups near you.

Q

Our son is 37 and lives in another city. This summer when he came to visit us, his personality seemed quite different. We hadn't seen him for several months, and we were alarmed by his loss of speech, his diminished comprehension, and his quietness. Our first thought was abuse, so we called the people he lives with and they agreed he seems much quieter and withdrawn lately. But they didn't think anything bad had happened. We believe them, but we still wonder if something happened they don't know about. Our son can't tell us. What should we do?

A

You are right to be concerned. But be careful about your assumptions. You can be fairly sure that something did happen. But what happened? There are all sorts of things that your son could find traumatizing, from being teased to being sexually victimized. You may never know what happened. We'd love to tell you that there is some trick, some technique that you can use to determine what happened, but there isn't. What you need to think about now is the future.

How can you develop a means for your son to communicate with you better about his life? Picture boards, sign language, adaptive communication strategies—all of these need to be investigated. If he can even learn to accurately tell you how he is feeling, this is a great start. Look at a feelings education curriculum. The trouble is that so much time has passed that you may learn about how he is feeling, but you might not be able to determine what caused it. By ensuring that he can accurately communicate his emotions, right when he has them, you will be better able to find out what happened immediately. Imagine for a second that your son was struck at school by a bully. Now imagine that the moment when he came home, he pointed to emotion pictures of mad and scared. What would be the first thing you would do? You'd telephone the school and ask what went on. We would too. If the school said nothing, I'd ask for an immediate meeting. Letting everyone know that you listen to what your child says (or gestures or signs) makes him more powerful and less likely to be hurt.

If you are genuinely concerned that he has been sexually abused, you may want to consider tests for STIs. Don't let your fear get in the way of your child's receiving good care. This may be upsetting, but the tests are fairly routine and shouldn't overly concern your child. Try not to let your anxiety transfer to your child. If he has an STI, then you need to inform those who care for him, the people who supervise his school or program, and demand an investigation. If he doesn't, sit down, thank God, and get busy ensuring that he has a better way of talking to you. Oh, by the way, it's possible to teach abuse prevention, even to those with significant disabilities. Let's make sure it never happens...or never happens again.

Q

I don't want to be suspicious of everybody, but what do I do if I think my daughter has been or is being abused? What should we be on the lookout for?

A

Although there are no easy answers to your questions, there are some general rules. First, whenever there is a radical change in your child's behavior, skill level, or temperament that seems unexplained, investigate carefully. For example, if your child does not have temper tantrums regularly but seems to be throwing a lot of tantrums and there are no discernible differences in how the day runs or the expectations made of the child, investigate. Call around. See if you can discover anything that would cause the behavior change. Behaviors do not occur in a vacuum. Ask questions. If your child loses skills that she has had for a long time, such as toileting skills or the ability to tie shoes, look for stressors that might be interfering with her learning. Ask questions. If your child, who is normally happy, seems to be spending time looking sad and wanting to be away from people, *ask questions.*

You need to do some detective work. Don't put thoughts into your child's head by asking, "Did Uncle Ralph touch your breast?" Rather, reflect on the present. Steer the conversation to how your daughter is feeling: "It looks as if you've been awfully sad. Are you okay?" or "You don't seem to play with your trucks any more. Do you want to talk to me about it?" Beyond talking with your child, start asking questions of other people who interact with him. Have they noticed changes in behavior, mood, or actions? Start collecting information.

Often, the probability is that you will find another explanation for the behavior change. But you will become known to others as a parent who takes their child's behavior as a means of communication. Sometimes the best defense a person has against abuse is the fact that there are people around the person who ask questions.

If you suspect your child is being abused, call for help. Call Children's Aid and talk to them about what you should be doing or whom you should call. This will be an emotional time for you and having someone there on your side and who knows the process will be very helpful for you. If you know your child is being abused, including if your child tells you so, then you must report the abuse to the police.

Q

I'm a staffperson in a residential program as well as a parent of someone with a disability. For some people I work with, I'm their only friend. What's wrong with a little hug and kiss if everyone feels good about it? There's nothing sexual in it; it's just affection.

A

It ain't affection. It's a violation of boundaries. If you are their only friend, then get to work! Why should they have to rely on you for the rest of their lives for affection? This is too dangerous a position for them to be in. Our job is to teach people the skills or put them in situations where they can get those needs met in healthy and safe ways. *You* may be a safe person, but every time you give them a hug and a kiss, you are setting the boundaries for the next person to come along. Realize that there are people lined up into this person's future waiting to work with them. Are you willing to bet that *every one of them* will be a safe person? If not, as the statistics say, then set healthy boundaries. You can be affectionate without violating boundaries; learn how. You will never forgive yourself should someone you work with get raped because your actions made them a good target for a victimizer. As someone who works in human services, you must remember that the abuse of people with disabilities is commonplace. Don't think that all people who choose such a career are trustworthy humanitarians. And don't add to the vulnerability of the individuals you serve by perpetuating behaviors that can lead to abuse or, at best, misinterpretation.

Q

I have a friend whose son has disabilities. She is very afraid that a family member has been sexually abusing him, and she wants to stop it. On the other hand, she's scared to death that if she's wrong, the consequences for the family will be terrible. What should she do? What should I do?

A

This is an impossible question to answer because we don't know *why* she thinks that a family member has been abusing him. Is it because of a change in behavior? Is it because she has always been concerned about the family member? Is it because she herself was victimized by this person? Each scenario will give different answers. But you need to know when you need help. This is the time to seek help from a professional in the area. Find someone to talk to, call the local agency that supports people with disabilities, and they will direct you to someone who will be able to listen to the concerns and give direction. If they aren't able, then talk to the local children's aid or family care agency or children's advocate—find someone! What can you do? The mother has enough on her plate with the fear that her boy is being hurt. So why not pick up the telephone and make the calls yourself? Remember, if someone reports to you that abuse *is* happening or *has* happened, you are obligated to contact the police. If you *suspect* abuse may have occurred, you are not required to report it, and you can make calls and get advice and information without informing police of the particulars. Be discrete. Don't give out the family name. Leave your name as a contact. This will make the mom much more comfortable because, as your question stated, she doesn't want to go public with her concerns. Once you have found a person willing to help, get the mother to that person. You may be surprised to meet resistance; Mom may want help and fear it at the same time. Good friends know when to insist!

Lucky Smith and Tim Feser
Whitehorse, Yukon

Chapter 7

Let Me Go

Marriage and Companionship

By now you will have noticed that in the list of facts and our discussions so far, the issue of marriage, pregnancy, and parenting has only briefly been touched on. That is because these things are the stuff of adulthood.

"She was just beautiful."

The woman who said this is a mother of a young woman with an intellectual disability. This time, however, she said this at a reception following her daughter's wedding. Dave was at the wedding and cried great big tears as he watched two people whom he had known for years walk up the aisle. They had decided, all on their own, that they wouldn't be walked up the aisle by others. They would walk to the altar of God together. Family members were taken aback at this decision. And they were even more taken aback that no amount of "friendly pressure" could change their minds. The wedding happened as was designed by two people with disabilities.

First, their parents walked together up the aisle. This group of four was followed by several friends of the bride and groom, who were followed by a young woman who worked with bride and groom and helped them fight system, family, and church for their right to marry. Last, in came the couple. They were holding hands, grinning, and waving to all of their friends and family. They stopped several times to talk with people along the aisle. They posed for pictures and made faces at some of the children.

The minister was looking quite uncomfortable, not with the wedding but with the indecorous entrance of the couple. They arrived at the altar and fell silent. The minister began to speak, and the bride "shhhed" him because she hadn't finished saying a prayer. He looked a bit miffed, but he waited. On her signal, the ceremony began. The room, once noisy at the couple's entrance, fell silent. The vows were simple; the intent was complex. They promised to love each other forever. Dave believed that they would.

At the moment when the groom kissed the bride, Dave saw (maybe for the first time) what the groom saw when he looked at her face.

She was just beautiful.

Dave's Story

I cry at every wedding of people with disabilities that I go to. I never cry at the weddings of my friends, although that is primarily because they are on their third or fourth try. Why the tears? Well, I recognize the journey that they have traveled to get to that altar. It has been a long journey, through prejudices, antiquated laws, smirking relatives, and disbelieving systems. There is no question that the triumph of love between people with disabilities is a significant one.

One of my first jobs was working at an institution, one of the largest in the country. On Sundays, we rounded up a bunch of folks for their "community integration" program and took them off to church. We sat at the back, filling up a significant number of pews in a congregation that was shrinking drastically. The first Sunday I was there, I was shocked to note that my companions, the people from the institution, were not invited to take communion. Why? Well, I found out later that the church felt that people with disabilities were not whole in the eyes of God and therefore could not take communion. I left outraged. No wonder the church was dying from lack of attendance. How dare they say that God could only differentially love people? So the march to the altar to marry is a march full of more than just symbolic importance.

Studies on the marriages of people with intellectual disabilities have shown that people with intellectual disabilities find gratification from marriage and that they often marry people with complementary skills so that they function better as a married unit than as separate individuals. Surprise, surprise! (Don't we all strive to do this?) People with disabilities do better at choosing partners and get more out of marriage than do people without disabilities. Oh, and their divorce rate is much lower as well.

Research shows that the lives of people with intellectual disabilities are typified by loneliness and depression. In fact, loneliness and a sense of isolation may be the biggest problem that people with intellectual disabilities face. Many parents get a growing awareness of this as they see their child grow from a child, who is semi-accepted in a school, into a young adult with limited social contacts. After attending a yearly planning meeting for a young man, I walked out with his mother and we chatted. She said, "I don't want you all to think I am ungrateful or critical, but when I leave these meetings now, I think we have all missed the point of what we should be doing." As we talked, she said that as she got older, her perspective regarding her son had changed. For a long time, she "bought" the idea that we needed to "normalize" him and give him "independence" skills. Now, she said, she is not so sure.

She looked at me and said sadly, "You just don't know what it is like to be the one light." I asked her what she meant and she said, "Go home tonight, sit down in a dark room, close your eyes, and picture above you a dark night sky. Then, for every person who is in your life, voluntarily providing you with support, put a star in the sky. The more important they are to you, the brighter the star. When you are done, you will find a constellation of lights up there. But for me, for my son, I am his one light. When I die, he will live in darkness, and that terrifies me." We both cried.

Loneliness is a crushing experience. What have we done wrong so that people with disabilities have such a sense of aloneness? Well, part of it is the time in which we live. If you are an older parent, you understand this. We are in transition. This generation of adults with disabilities is the generation that traveled the distance from being labeled "idiot" and "moron" to being called *neighbor* and *friend*. It has been a hard journey, and it is not complete. This generation has been cut away from families with surgical precision by professionals who knew better. This generation has been deprived of a community by systems that could care better. This generation has been oppressed by those who mean to do good. And it is no surprise that there are little in the way of social contacts, familial relationships, and community involvement.

Although this chapter is called "Let Me Go," parents never really do let go— of any of their children. If you have any doubts, ask your own kids! But letting go is something we all need to understand. We need to understand that everything we do with and for our children prepares them for the time in their lives when they take flight on their own. We can, though, still worry and can still give advice.

Our fear is that we haven't anticipated what things might be like in the year 2000 and beyond. Imagine, in 2050, Jim will be at an age where he could live another 15 years. We want to make sure his life is full and rich and full of family and friends and choices. There are a thousand things I want Jim to be able to decide for himself. I really want him to make the decisions on as many things as he can. Can I be strong enough to step back?

　　—Richard Schwier

Michael's been learning about taking care of other people. Since George had his stroke and I had heart surgery, Mike's been taking over more responsibilities. At night, he gets the coffee in the coffeemaker and pours the water in for the next morning. He helps a lot more around the house. In the future, whichever one of us goes, he'll be able to do a lot of the caretaking for the other. The house is set up so nothing much really needs to be done. He can continue to live here and not worry too much. He dreams of winning the lottery and buying himself and everyone in the family a new house.

　　—Peggy Creamer

You worry about things. That's what moms do. He was cooking one morning, making himself instant oatmeal for breakfast. As he reached for the pot, he dragged the sleeve of his bathrobe across the burner, and it caught on fire. He hit it out right away and wasn't hurt, but I said, "Chris, what did you learn?" He said, "Fire, Mom!" So we learned how you don't reach over the burner, you reach around the side. He learned a very good lesson, and it scared him. But he knows what to do now and is very careful. It's all a matter of survival.

　　—Gayle Foy

One of the things we put in our wills was that Jim and a companion should get enough money to go visit a relative at least once a year. Family is so important to him. He loves his grandparents and misses them so much. If they're still living when we're not, we want to make sure he can get to Florida to see them. Or

Christopher and Gayle Foy
Indianapolis, Indiana

to his relatives in Indiana or California. He should be able to say, "I want to go see these people," and have that wish happen. We can't direct things from the grave, but we are including a letter that asks whomever is left behind to listen to Jim. Sit down with him, and learn how important family and friends are to him. Ask him what he wants.

—Richard Schwier

Cathy and David Conrad

Cathy: Well, when we met was at Goodwill and bowling and dances was when we met. And I look at him, and I think that's what I want. And then, then David told me he had feelings for me because he told me, "You are the lady that I want." We did date for 5 years. And then, David ask me for a date. We went to King's Island, and then David got down on his knee and he proposed.

David: I do love her.

Cathy: I was hard when people said no, we can't kiss or hold hands. I finally say I can't take it any more. In the cafeteria at work, I didn't want to, but I smoked. David looked over, and he said "If you wanna die, that's fine. But I want you to live." He doesn't want me to smoke because he doesn't want me to die or anything. But instead, I went back to work, and I didn't smoke after that. I felt bad.

David: I am in love with her lot more, lot more, lot more. She is my darling.

Cathy: I kept following him around.

David: After that, I was getting mad. I meet somebody, and I not wait for her. Her scared. Her definitely scared. Then I say "Honey, what's wrong?"

Cathy: I wasn't really scared. Just a little chicken. I think he was drinkin' too much beer.

David: I didn't drink beer! I drink pop! There was this girl there, and Cathy was there, too.

Cathy: I finally got serious, and I said to her, "I'm sorry, lady, but he's mine." She didn't say nothing. She walk away.

David: I think she's the one, my darling. She is in love with me. Now we are together. That was the beginning. We got wedding rings but we got to get them fix so they fit. The ring is too small now for me, and her.

Cathy: David ask me to marry him. It was at my apartment. David's mom was outside waiting on him, and she didn't know what was going on! I didn't know what was going on either.

David: *I said yes. I will show you how I ask her to marry me. I said to her "Honey, I give to you a ring because we get married, darling." Then I give her a big kiss. I ask her if she be my wife.*

Cathy: *I never thought it was gonna happen. I always wish for a nice husband, but I didn't know it would happen so quick! My cousin John was getting married, and I said to my mom, "I wish a man would ask me to marry him." And then it was so quick. My parents and I started making plans. We looked at flowers and gowns. My dad was getting the invitations, and we had to buy a wedding book. A friend of mine, she made my dress. I have a big family. Three sisters and three brothers. I am 34. I have a wedding book.*

David: *I am...*

Cathy: *38.*

David: *38. And June 12 comes, then I be 39.*

Cathy: *I was very nervous before the wedding.*

David: *My mom went on the honeymoon. It was great!*

Cathy: *We went to the Ozarks on our honeymoon. His mom sleep in a different room. She had to sleep in a different room because I was makin' out.*

David's mother, Eda, interjects: *When we got to the hotel, I wanted a room kind of apart from them but still close enough they could get to me if they needed something. It was either an adjoining room or another building, and I didn't want to be that far away, so I opted for an adjoining room. I said to them "Okay, I'll leave my door unlocked, but you lock yours." I turned the fans on high and the TV up in my room; I didn't want to listen! Cathy stuck her head in after a while, and she said, "You want to come over for a party?" and I said, "No, that's okay," and she says "Well, we're having a naked party," and I said, "No, really! You go ahead! I'll pass!" Then she opened the door again after a while, and she said, "Mom, David wants to do all kinds of things to me." I said, "Well, you're married now, and if both of you like it, then anything's okay." Her eyes got really, really big, and she said, "Oh...Okay!" and slammed the door shut. I didn't hear from them for 12 hours! They didn't even want to eat breakfast the next day!*

David: *I would like a baby, but we have tubes tied.*

Eda: *When David first moved into a group home, before he even met Cathy, I had looked into possibility that he might become a father. I spoke to a urologist, but we didn't really pursue it at the time. When he and Cathy started dating se-*

riously, we talked about whether they would want children. After a while, Cathy told me she wanted just to look after David, and David wanted to look after Cathy. It made a lot more sense to me than the discussions a lot of other couples have. He went ahead and had a vasectomy.

David: I want one bad, a baby. It's so quiet in the house.

Cathy: Since David had his tubes tied, he talks all the time about it, having a baby. I would like one once in a while. When my mom took me to this one doctor, she said, "Do you think my teenage young people like my daughter, but do they get pregnant by getting babies?" And the doctor told my mother, "Yes." And now we are married for 3 years and David still keeps on talkin' about having babies again. Our life would change a lot if we had a baby. You have to get up with it all the time...

David: Rock it...

Cathy: Walk it. Bath it. Change it. And stuff like that. It costs a lot of money for things for the baby. We have nieces and nephews. Some of them have their own babies. The only way to make a baby is with a husband and wife, a man and woman. Together. That's how you make a baby that way. At Goodwill they showed us a slide presentation. It was at Goodwill. On sex. Oh, we could ask questions. On sex. David was in the same group also. So he knows, too.

David: Yeah, we are married. And her like it. And my penis, you know, my penis? Her kiss my penis, and I feel good all over!

Eda: Honey, that's called oral sex. That's okay when you're in private and you're married. I told you, everything's okay when you're married, and you both enjoy it.

David: I do enjoy it. A lot, I do. I like my house to live with her. We like it here, our house. One neighbor, she is very nice. One neighbor is not nice. His dog is barking, barking, barking. I say to his dog, "Be quiet, dog," and the neighbor man, he call me, "Shut up, you retard." He is not very nice man.

Cathy: Some of the kids around we don't know, they do bad things. Spray paint on our house. We don't like it. They do it because they are mean. It is not very nice. David try to talk to him, but it do no good. They were phoning us on the phone. Now we have unlisted. It makes me sad. But it is all worth it. Because my feeling is we are married, and this is our house where we live together. By havin' him around, havin' our own house is better.

David: There is a nice lady next door, not the man, the other lady. She is a nice lady, and she say hi to us. But she is movin' out because the dog barking, barking. Why? Why her move *and not him? She is the nice lady, and he is not. When I take the trash out, here come the dog, growlin', barkin'. He yell at the dog, too. Some people never learn. I work at Carpentry Plus store, and I make my money. I talk nice to the ladies who are shopping. I talk to the babies and make them laugh. Happy. Joy. I tell the ladies they have cute babies. You have to be nice to them. I like my mom. She helps us out. I call her and tell her when it's time to change her clock ahead or back. We call her on the phone. She is really great. Because I want to be free with her, my wife, if I want to. That is married. My wife said no, don't take my tie off after work. She say I look nice with my tie.*

Cathy: *We are grown up, and we start our lives, and we don't want to hang around with our parents all the time. If you do find a hunk, and if he wants you to marry him, and if you say yes and everything, then you should let your daughter get married and go off to her honeymoon and sex and babies if she wants one. I would say yes if I was a mother. I would say yes to my daughter. It makes me feel wonderful to get married. We decide together to do things. We talk about it. We love each other and like each other, but we just do that at night. For other things, one time when David was having some problems, I call, and they took him to the hospital. People say it cost too much money, and my brother said I shouldn't do it.*

Eda: *Well, I live way on the other side of town, and I was thrilled that Cathy knew to call the Lifesquad. So she did make the decision on her own to do that, and I think it was responsible. We've talked about it, and there are times when they'll ask advice of others, but they're very good at working out things on their own. When everyone else makes decisions for you, you can get out of practice!*

Cathy: *When we get our marriage license, we tell them we want to be I am his guardian and he is my guardian. We got married at All Saints. I know the priest there because I was baptized by him and I had my first communion there. I know him a long time.*

David: *We talk about our decisions. Like with our groceries, like we get one steak. Just one. And chips. We get two. We talk about it at home. But when we get to the store, she don't want that what I want! I like beef. Beef. Because it's my favorite meal. My favorite drink is beer! Sometimes we make a spaghetti dinner.*

Cathy: *I am adorable to him, but I buy low-fat at the grocery store. I love low-fat; I buy tons of it! I think my favorite thing at the grocery store is the whole place!*

David: *I think she is adorable to me, my sweetheart. I give all my love with her. I got some money to support my wife. I take care of her. I call her adorable. 'Cause I like to be married. I have fun with her every day and in bed and, you know, because I like it. If people don't want me to get married, I say too late now because I am married. I can get married if I want to. I don't care if they get married if they want to. Why should they not let me if I want to?*

 ## Rest Stop:

In Chapter 2, we said we're big advocates of dreams: of having your own dreams and encouraging your sons and daughters, other family members, friends, and co-workers to have them. Dreams keep life sweet, hopeful, and fun.

Try this exercise. Pick a time when you're relaxed and unhurried. If you and your spouse or partner do this, by all means compare notes afterward, but do this as a solo exercise. On a single sheet of paper, write these words at the top: *My Dream for My Child.* Sit back, close your eyes, and relax.

Picture your son or daughter 10 years from now. Make it a positive picture; do not allow negatives, rationalizations, "yes, buts," or "if onlys" to enter this dream. How do you see your child living each day? Be specific. Describe the routine and rhythm of their day. Describe the ideal life you would create if you had a magic wand. Write this down—phrases instead of sentences or even doodles are fine, if they capture your dream. Remember, no one is looking over your shoulder, telling you to "be realistic."

Keep this dream map. Look at it from time to time.

Parents of young kids: Say a great big thanks to the parents who came before you who fought diligently for their children to have services here in the community. Say an even bigger thanks to those people with disabilities who came home from the back wards of institutions and showed that they could, should, and would succeed if only given a chance. You are lucky to be where you are in time and space. You may not feel this at times, but the many battles you fight—and there will be many—are quite different fights from those that have gone on before. Your vision and dreams for your child will sustain you.

Parents now in their seventies shake their heads in wonder when they hear younger parents fighting for their children to be in general education classrooms, to have typical experiences in their day, and to learn about relationships. To them, these were the "impossible dreams" of parents who were blamed for having the child ("What sin did you commit?"), blamed for wanting the child ("If you love your child, you will put it with its own kind"), and blamed for their anger at the system ("They are so difficult to work with"). There is still a fight. But it is a different one.

Michele and I'll give each other a peck on the lips sometimes, but mostly it's a kiss on the cheek. One time, I gave Hillary a peck on the lips, and she said,

"That's for when you're married!" So she has some particular ideas about what marriage means and what you should do or not do if you're married.
　—Lou Shaw

Financial and Legal Implications

Love conquers all...usually. Marriage for people with intellectual disabilities is a new frontier. Not too long ago, it was a new frontier for people with physical disabilities, too. In fact, people with physical disabilities have paved the way with loud and insistent voices about human rights. Today, more marriages are beginning to join couples with intellectual disabilities, their families, and friends. Intimate relationships and marriage are one of the best hedges against one of humankind's most devastating experiences: loneliness. This is not to suggest that people with intellectual disabilities are somehow exempt from imperfect unions and divorce, but perhaps an advantage to marriage is the circle of support that can exist when families, friends, advocates, and service providers come together.

What love sometimes has difficulty with, however, is the social assistance machine. Although marriage offers emotional well-being, such a union often brings with it financial uncertainty. In 1977, the U.S. Supreme Court ruled that termination of financial benefits to people with disabilities upon marriage was constitutional (Russell, 1994). It's not clearly understood why the government set up marriage disincentives for couples with disabilities. In her article, "The Cost of Saying I Do: How Social Security Policies Can Silence Wedding Bells for People with Disabilities," writer Marta Russell suggested that "some say the law was a simple attempt to curb government spending. Others say it resulted from paternalistic ideas about disabled people; still others suspect it was a part of a more malevolent eugenic social policy....Regardless of the source, it is clear that these policies continue to have profound implications" (1994, p. 38).

The disability matters only in that it influences his life by threatening his opportunities. He might have rights taken away from him just by virtue of an extra chromosome. For instance, there will be people out there who say he shouldn't have a job; he should be at the workshop. That he shouldn't think about marriage. My beliefs about integration and community life are threatened all the time. But I think I've lost enough fights that I'm willing to listen to other opinions. I may reject them, but there may be things I can learn, too.
　—Richard Schwier

Michael Hartzog, District Manager with the Social Security Administration (SSA) in Charleston, South Carolina, has a particular personal interest in how the rules apply to someone with a disability who wants to marry. His 17-year-old son Dave has an intellectual disability. Hartzog encourages people planning to marry to contact their local SSA office to see what the implications of their marriage will be depending on the type of assistance one or both partners might is receiving.

"If the person married receives SSI [Supplemental Security Income] benefits, the total amount of the SSI benefit paid to the couple will be based on the *couple rate* versus the *individual rate,"* said Hartzog (personal communication, 1999). The income and resource limits for an eligible couple are higher than for an individual but less than twice the individual's limit. According to SSA information, generally if unearned income exceeds $520 per month for an eligible individual or $771 per month for an eligible couple, then the individual or couple would not be eligible for SSI benefits. Any countable income received, such as Social Security benefits (e.g., Social Security Disability Income [SSDI], survivor benefits, retirement benefits), pensions, wages, and so forth, would reduce the SSI amounts. Unearned income reduces the SSI payment amount dollar for dollar after a $20 exclusion each month. Some unearned income (like Veterans' Administration pensions) does not get the $20 exclusion. Earned income, on the other hand, has a more liberal exclusion: It gets a $65 exclusion from the dollar-for-dollar reduction (if there is no unearned income, the $20 unearned exclusion can also be used), then one half of the remainder is excluded from the reduction. The individual resource limit at any one time is $2,000; the couple resource limit at any one time is $3,000. There are many different rules as to what will count as a resource; in general, resources are things that a person owns or has access to at any time, such as bank accounts, stocks, bonds, certificates of deposit, real property, personal property, and vehicles. The house someone owns and lives in, however, in does not count. Generally, the value of one automobile can be excluded. Up to $1,500 can be set aside for burial expenses. Of course, Hartzog added, if the income or the value of resources is too high, the eligibility for SSI would end.

"Since there are so many exclusions to both income and resources," Hartzog said, "it is always advisable for someone to check with Social Security about individual circumstances" (personal communication, 1999). SSA offices have pamphlets and booklets about several types of benefits. In addition to the federal SSI payment, individual states may provide additional benefits to their own recipients in recognition of the variations in living costs from one state to another and for the special needs of some people. Hartzog again suggested that people contact the particular state's Department of Social Services to get specific information. In Canada and other countries, Social Services and similar departments will have relevant information about the impact of marriage on financial benefits.

For people with intellectual disabilities, it isn't always a financial barrier that makes relationships and marriage difficult. In 1995, Anna and Matthew Russell, a couple with Down syndrome in Chelmsford, England, successfully fought a High Court attempt by the Anna's father to nullify their 15-month marriage (Davies, 1995). The father sought to prove that his daughter was incapable of making rational decisions. But Anna, age 20, made a very rational move when she went, on her own, to a solicitor to make a very clear statement about whom she wanted to live with and whom she wanted as her husband: Matthew Russell, age 21. The couple had met at school in Essex. It was a relationship that had survived for 4 years, despite Matthew's being moved to a different residential training center. Anna's father eventually dropped the action and, when they heard the news, the couple collapsed in each other's arms, cried, and hugged. Anna handed her husband a hand-made card on which she had written "Anna loves Matthew" (Davies, 1995).

I would love her to have a relationship with a man, another gentle spirit to share her life with. I would love to see her married. Children, well, I think we've talked to her a lot about people we know who don't have children and who are very happy. I want her to understand that just because you're married, you don't have to have children to be happy. We're beginning to talk to her in more detail now about the responsibility of looking after each other in a relationship and how it may take longer to look after each other if you have disabilities.
—Michele Shaw

Still, in most parts of North America, a first glance at the laws would make you think it's very difficult, if not impossible, to get married if you have a disability. Lawyer Orville Endicott said there are three types of restrictions on the right of people with intellectual disabilities to enter into marriage in Canada:

The first restriction is that no one is permitted to issue a marriage license or solemnize a marriage if the marriage would be invalid because at least one of the parties lacks the "capacity" to marry. Capacity to marry means that you need some basic understanding of what you are doing when you get married and what your responsibilities will be as a married person....You are not in fact married if you had no real awareness of what you were doing when you went through the marriage ceremony....Ontario and the Northwest Territories have provisions of this type in their Marriage Acts....In the second type of limitation imposed by some provinces, if you have been declared incapable of things such as managing your money, then it is presumed that you are also incapable of marrying....To get around this presumption, you have to produce a letter from a doctor ([from] a psychiatrist, in Manitoba) certifying that you are capable of understanding what marriage is and the obligations married people have. In Quebec, if you have a "tutor" appointed by the court (i.e., a partial or temporary guardian), you have to go back to court to get permission to marry.... If [in Quebec you have] a permanent guardian for all decision making, known as a curator, then [you] are prohibited from marrying. A third restriction is found in British Columbia and Prince Edward Island. Their laws say a person with an [intellectual disability] simply cannot marry under any circumstances. Saskatchewan, New Brunswick, Nova Scotia, Newfoundland, and the Yukon have no statute law standing in the way of marriage for men and women with intellectual disabilities....You still have to have the "capacity" to marry. But there are no statutory requirements to enforce the rule about capacity to marry or to extend it beyond the scope of common law. (1992, p. 9, reprinted by permission of the Roeher Institute)

Endicott believes that all three of these restrictions seem to violate the Canadian Charter of Rights and Freedoms and could be open to a legal challenge. Endicott suggested checking into the picture today; since 1992, at least British Columbia has since done away with its archaic provision barring marriage altogether on the basis of "mental disability" labels. Nunavut became Canada's newest territory in April 1999 and is still organizing itself and its legislation. The issue of "capacity," too, is not clear. Who could honestly say they fully understand what marriage is all about before getting into it? Usually, love is the primary motivator for marriage; an understanding of legal rights and obligations of each partner are secondary.

Ultimately, no matter where you live, if the laws do not support relation-ships and marriage for people with disabilities, those laws should be chal-lenged. This is where advocacy comes in. If marriage is a right not to be denied to people with disabilities and if they are to have the same inalienable rights as anyone in the human family, as the United Nations (1948) has declared, then fight those barriers.

My older daughter Sheena has said to me, "Mom, do you think Becca will get married and have kids some day?" My response is always, "Well, you never know." I won't put any restrictions on her, any more than I would my other two girls. Everyone grows up different, and 20 years from now, the world will be a different place. So who knows?
—Shelly Garner

So, love can triumph. But for many, growing old hand in hand with a part-ner still seems an elusive dream. Beyond the financial and legal obstacles, the mere inconvenience and logistical problems of simple social contact can seem overwhelming, To form relationships of any kinds, people with developmental disabilities need support in just being "social beings."

Understanding the "Two" Communities

Hey, wait a minute. *Two* communities? Isn't the word *two* wrong? Aren't people with disabilities supposed to be fully integrated? Isn't there supposed to be just one community?

Dave's Story

I had been attending the United Church in Magog for about a year when I first heard of Joan. She had been coming to the church for a couple of hours a week for more than a year. Her job was to fold the church bulletin and place any in-serts into the fold. She has a severe disability, so it took her teacher much time and patience to teach her the skills. When I learned that a woman with a dis-ability helped to make worship possible, I suggested that she be invited to hand out the bulletins one Sunday so that she could see the importance of her work and so that the congregation could meet our most faithful volunteer.

She came on Anniversary Sunday. This is one of the days that the church is especially full. Joan stood beside her instructor at the back of the church, ready to hand out bulletins. She seemed a bit confused, and I watched her watch her in-structor, looking for a cue as to why she was standing at the back of an empty church. I settled myself down into a pew and watched. I didn't have to pass by Joan and her instructor because I had dropped off some baking for the lunch after service and had come in through the door in the hall at the front of the sanctuary.

When the first person came in, the instructor gave Joan a bulletin and indi-cated that she was to give it to the person standing in front of her. Joan took the bulletin and held on to it with all her might. Her face darkened. You could see her thoughts on her face. She had worked hard to fold these. She had piled them carefully and stacked them with pride. There was simply no way that she was going to just give one of them to this stranger in front of her. Her instructor nudged her gently and again indicated that she was to give it to the woman in front of her. This Joan did, begrudgingly thrusting it out in defiance. The woman took it, smiled, and said something I could not hear. Joan paused, looked closely at the woman, and then tentatively returned her smile.

The next person came in, and Joan only had to be instructed once to give the bulletin. Again, there was a smile and a couple of words, but this time Joan brightened and smiled right back with a big, bold, beautiful grin. She understood now. Person after person came in, and Joan was given a bulletin each time. Her hand now anticipated that next bulletin, and she would reach for it often before the instructor had a chance to get one out. Bulletins flew out of her hand, and the smile never had a chance to leave her face as people were coming in a steady stream.

I looked hard at the instructor and tried to will her into just giving Joan the pile. This did not work, and because I was in church, I thought maybe I could do a "bank shot" by bouncing a prayer off heaven's floor back down to the instructor. "Give Joan the pile. Give Joan the pile. Give Joan the pile." Prayer after prayer soared upwards. My aim was poor. The prayer went up, hit heaven's floor, bounced down, and hit Joan. She grabbed the pile from the instructor and quite independently handed out bulletins to people as they came in. The instructor quietly stepped back a bit and let the limelight shine completely on Joan's accomplishment and participation.

When people were in their seats and only latecomers were arriving, Joan began to look around and see all of the people in the church looking at the bulletins for the order of service. Then a straggler arrived. Joan took a bulletin and handed it to him. He stood for a minute and said something to her. Joan doesn't speak using traditional messages, but she desperately wanted to answer the man. She took the bulletins, held them to her chest with one hand and tapped her chest. This is a woman who had given up on communication, and the word I saw her communicate was "Me!" The sentence I saw her convey was, "Me, I did this!" The sentiment I saw her say was, "*Me...*I'm proud of me!"

During the service—and many more to come—Joan was pretty much like every other Christian. She spent most of her time looking around at others, ignoring what the minister was saying. But every time people picked up the bulletins to find the order of the service, she smiled. By the final hymn, she had settled back into her pew and relaxed into our church community. She was home.

Over the next several weeks, Joan became more animated and more interested in what she was doing. The community responded by recognizing her and making sure that she was invited to participate in church activities. Joan is working hard at making the community more accepting.

And it takes work. One man who runs an agency serving people with intellectual disabilities has a disability himself. He said that the thing wrong with the "community living" movement is that we don't seem to realize that the "community" of which we speak does not exist. He says that every time he hears someone wax poetic about community, he is reminded of the naive belief that there ever was a Norman Rockwell world. It seems, he believes, that Mr. Rockwell chose to paint pictures of the perfect society. Pretty, white, and able-bodied. No pictures of white people spitting hatred at people of other races or abilities painted in pretty hues would ever swirl from his paintbrush.

As children are integrated into the larger community, one needs to expect pain, frustration, and grievous hurt. This is true for all children with any difference. They do not build special schools for fat children so that they can be *protected* from teasing or tyrannical gym instructors affectionately dubbed "The Whipper." Undoubtedly, you will read horror stories regarding how people with disabilities can be treated. You may have heard about a young man with a disability who was coaxed into an area where a bunch of youths used him as target practice for martial arts. They beat him to death. Did they go to jail? No. They performed community service. Community service—that's it.

As a parent, you may be recoiling in horror from what you just read. It may cross your mind that maybe people with disabilities would be better off in protected environments. Wait. If the person being beaten had been black, or gay, or Jewish, would you suggest that he be put in a special place for protection? No. You would demand more severe sentences for the victimizers, and you would work to educate the community about the dangers of hatred and violence. The same action needs to be taken with people with disabilities.

Even so, it just isn't likely to happen, though there have been many "It'll never happen" predictions about people with disabilities that have been summarily broken and buried. But if your child marries, he or she is not very likely to marry a community member without a disability. Good heavens, there are employers who don't want anything to do with hiring people with disabilities; able or not isn't the issue. The issue is prejudice. We are still working hard at creating friendships that are real friendships in community settings. This is hard. Norman Kunc (personal communication, 1999), who works toward the day when the community will be welcoming, said that he was growing wary of the *friendship circles* we were creating for people with disabilities. He wondered if we were failing at creating friendships and succeeding at creating a new generation of charity and charity recipients. A *buddy* or *pal* is, by definition, directly opposed to a *volunteer*.

We can't be afraid to ask the community to include our children. I think that's hard for parents to be asking all the time. Families have to create the alternatives with their families and friends and communities. You can't just assume that the service system will provide what you want. At some point, we might need to take some money out of the traditional system to make a new option work well, but you've got to create the alternative you want for your child.
    —John Lord

Sometimes you need to reach out to the community if you want your child exposed to the community. Before Jim began to stay with us for an extended time, we sent a few letters out to some local businesses near our home. Well, people called. Three or four times a week, Jim volunteered a few hours with Jason, the butcher on Broadway Avenue. On Thursday afternoons, he worked at the tote desk at the YMCA with Ian. Both of those turned into long-term experiences for

Jim. Chris was the manager at the Broadway Theater; he called and said to bring Jim over and we could figure out what could be done. It takes some juggling, but people want him. He's busy, and it takes effort, but he isn't buying into a disability-driven system. We're building something unique around Jim.
        —Richard Schwier

Again, there is hope. Relationships, real relationships are developing. Some of the stories from schools are truly inspiring as children play together, regardless of race, creed, or disability. The Glide Church in San Francisco convinces us not only that community is possible but also that it can be as beautiful as the prophets of integration say it is.

Another man told a very similar story. He was absolutely determined that his daughter would not be "corralled" with other people with disabilities and that the fact she had an intellectual disability would not be a consideration for anything, ever. Well, he said that he was really challenged when he took her for the first time to a conference on Down syndrome and saw her eyes light up when she saw other young teens who looked like herself. She quickly made friends and did so more readily than ever occurred in the classroom or natural community. His daughter, he said, shy of attention and scrutiny, took a modeling class and just loved being up in front of her peers. She basked in the attention. He was shaken by the experience.

We talked about how his daughter may just need opportunities to experience *sameness* rather than always *difference*. We talked about how there is a need to balance integration with separation and to make sure that people with disabilities are not "trained" to hate people with disabilities by the messages we give them. The tragedy of community integration, if there is one, is that we have met people with disabilities who now dislike people with disabilities with the same vehemence as some of the most bigoted people in our society. Self-hatred leads to future pain and loneliness.

We used to worry a bit when she was around other people with disabilities because she acted strange. I suppose that's one of the good things about integration; she's met lots of people now, so she realizes that people are all different. She was almost afraid. The first time our friend who uses a wheelchair was over, she was very afraid. But she got to know him, and she's used to it.
        —Peggy Hutchison

Jim was involved with a group of self-advocates for awhile. At first I thought, man, another segregated group. Where are his opportunities for connections outside that community? It made me uncomfortable. Now I think I've mellowed a bit, and I'd like to see him have a couple of friends here he could get together with. I used to be very critical because he didn't have any other options. By the same token, if we exclude any involvement with people who have disabilities, there's a whole segment of the community we're denying Jim access to in the name of integration. I think we have to continue to be unrealistic in our expectations for him, and that means a life beyond the disability system. But he needs real choice, and sometimes he may choose friends who have disabilities.
        —Richard Schwier

What is a parent to do then? How to strike the balance? Well, there are a number of issues when considering segregated activities. At the Special Olympics World Games in Connecticut, there was the usual rah-rah and razzle-dazzle of opening ceremonies. There was music. There was dancing. There were skydivers dropping from the sky. It was quite the show. The final speaker rose, before the lighting of the flame, and Eunice Kennedy Shriver looked out over the thousands of athletes and told all of the participants that now they could go home and say that they had represented their countries as world-class athletes. She said that they should now demand to be trained in a job that they could be proud of, demand good health care, demand a sense of community, and so forth. It was a powerful speech.

It strikes us that segregated activities, when done by other minorities, are done for respite from the struggle and used as a harbor from the storm. When women left consciousness raising groups, they left stronger and more committed to change. When blacks left black caucuses with the idea of black pride, they left stronger. When gay people march on Gay Pride Day, they gather and celebrate the unity of the cause and the development of a community. The same measure must be used when considering segregated groups for people with disabilities.

It is, however, not the same experience when physically unfit people are forced out into a segregated Special Olympics event to run tiredly around a gym, are hugged quite inappropriately by volunteers, some of them even strangers, and then sent home. They do not go home stronger. They have not experienced respite or the joy of community. They have experienced force, and they return home weakened by the experience. This must be avoided at all costs.

My greatest fear for her is that she'll be isolated, not part of the community. I really want her to have friends and not just in a segregated group. One older parent said to me, "You can have her on the bowling team, just like our older children." Who were all disabled. It's hard sometimes to make older parents understand we don't want that. If she chooses a friend with a disability, that's fine, but why should she have no other choice? Why should she associate only with other disabled kids?

   —Shelly Garner

I remember when People First was getting off the ground and the real integration purists were saying it was a segregated approach. We had to be careful that we weren't creating just another isolated group. I think as Karen gets older, it's a real benefit to her to be able to talk with other people who've had similar experiences. They discuss how you get a job, how you handle other people's views, how you overcome segregation. Right now, Karen doesn't have any peer models who have Down syndrome. There are very articulate people who speak at conferences, and I think it would be good for Karen to meet people like that and talk with them.

   —John Lord

She does like comfort. At lunchtime at school, she'll choose to hang around with the students from the resource room rather than go into the big cafeteria full of students. That's a bit intimidating. She knows when she's comfortable; we all

do. But she does need to be challenged, and she needs to challenge herself.
Meeting new people is intimidating for all of us, but we need to do it.
  —Peggy Hutchison

If your daughter is going to a dance held by an Association for Community Living and spends hours on makeup and excitedly wants to meet a girlfriend at the dance to cruise for guys, this is a good thing. If she comes home talking about a guy she met and how *"Wow!* he's cute," this is a good thing. If she goes back to her school or job in the community the next day feeling more confident and more beautiful than the day before, this is a *good* thing. Yes, good things can come out of segregated activities. People First is an organization of self-advocates that works toward social change and discusses the politics of oppression. We know of more marriages that have come out of People First than out of any other organization. People have a chance to meet people, discuss commonalities, and work for change. There is nothing wrong with this.

The key to community is participation and inclusion in *every* aspect. People with intellectual disabilities need to revel and bask in all the community can offer, and like Joan in church, they need the opportunity to give back and help build community for others. Perhaps we need to agree that a little flag should pop up when we, as parents, are considering getting our child involved in a segregated group. Is this the only choice? Or, is it to be part of a colorful array of experiences and opportunities the child will have in the community? Is it set up by people who do not believe people with disabilities need to be with anyone but other people with disabilities ("their own kind")? We believe that people with disabilities, as well as the rest of us, deserve to know and interact with a variety of people in the community. That some of those people have disabilities should not be taken as permission by service providers to offer only segregated opportunities to "the disabled" or for parents to isolate their child from chances to become involved with other people.

Tim Feser and Lucky Smith

Tim: *I work at Career Industries. I make stakes. December 19, my birthday.*
       I am 35. Old man!

Lucky: *I 28.*

Mona Sullivan-Curtis, support worker, interjects:
       Remember, Lucky, the party? The big sign that said Lordy, Lordy, look
       who's 40?

Lucky: *[Giggling] Forty! Yeah, 40. Balloons, cake. Yes.*

Tim: *I cook. Me. Macaroni. Macaroni and cheese. Our apartment. Lucky*
       and me. Walk to work, Career Industries. I like her. At Headway
       House, I like her. Wonderful. She is wonderful.

Lucky: *Tim nice, cute. My brother has his cat. I not want one.*

Tim: *My dad has dog. Aggie. Girl dog, big. My apartment. Lucky has bed-*
       room. I have one.

Lucky: He snore! Yes! He has cold. Me, too.

Tim: Mona, she's great! She help us. Sometime I say "Go home, Mona!" Karen, Nick, Peter, John from Headway House. Old friends. Allan has apartment. His kids, nieces, nephews, they come visit. I don't know, I not have kids. Name is Jake. My nephew. Just one, my brother Terry. He's is old man. He lives in Calgary. I like summertime, not cold. We have Halloween party. I am a cowboy. Lucky, she is ghostbuster. I have a hat, I am rodeo cowboy. We go to show, sometimes. I like Coach on TV. That's me! I be coach. Mona, she's great. She is hound dog. I go to work, I not be late. We walk downtown.

Lucky: Go swimming. I like it. Supper, I make noodle soup. Yeah. Noodle soup. And corn. Tea.

Tim: Ice tea. No beer. Mona not drink beer. Dan, he does! Dan her husband. I like Lucky. We can get married. August 1. We can talk about it. I want to. Cause I like her. Her smile. I wear white suit.

Lucky: Wedding? Dress. Red dress. My hair, flowers. I wear angel shoes. Angel shoes, yeah.

Tim: I say "I do" for her. I give ring. Like Mona's ring. How about that, Lucky? That be all right?

Lucky: Hawaii? Yeah. I go Hawaii. My wedding, buy ring. Janet Stick come to wedding. My dad wear tux.

Tim: August 1. That's the one. We have to. I wear black tie. White suit. I look good. I like dance. Me and Lucky dance.

Lucky: My dad, brothers, sisters Teslin. Clara, my sister.

Tim: Her dad, he like me. I like them.

Lucky: Tuesday night, McDonald's. I like it. And chicken. Fries.

Tim: I not fight with Lucky. Nope. We friends. She wonderful. I tickle her, she giggle. I want to get married. I think so, August 1. I just love her.

Pregnancy and Parenting—the Facts

We don't want to arbitrarily tell her, "No, you can't have children." We want her to think about what having a baby means and to understand the responsibility.
—Lou Shaw

All of this talk about meeting people, dating, and marriage brings us to a really tough subject. Pregnancy and parenting. Whenever these issues come up, we cringe inside because one of the questions that is always asked is, "Well, won't their babies have a disability, too?" The question is always asked as if the obvious sentiment is that they should not be allowed to "breed more of their own." Before looking at the facts regarding the child, everyone needs to really think about the question and the assumption. Personally, we despair in thinking of the world without people with disabilities in it. Some of the finest people we've met have intellectual disabilities, and the world would be significantly diminished if they were not here. We need to challenge the attitude, even though the facts are quite different:

1. Women with Down syndrome, for example, have a higher chance than do women without Down syndrome of having a child with Down syndrome; the chance ranges between 35% and 50%. One review of more than 30 pregnant women with Down syndrome found that 10 of their babies had Down syndrome, 18 had normal chromosomes (there was a set of twins), and three pregnancies miscarried. Ninety-five percent of all people with Down syndrome have the trisomy 21 variety. In a person with trisomy 21, half of their egg or sperm cells have the extra 21st chromosome and half contain only one 21st chromosome. So, theoretically, that person would have a 50% chance of having a baby with trisomy 21 and a 50% chance of having a baby with the normal number of chromosomes. In reality, however, these figures are modified somewhat by the natural miscarriage rate for conceptions with trisomy 21 (approximately 80% are lost). Therefore, the odds are greatest for having a baby with normal chromosomes (Knutson Brasington, 1995). This, however, is all based on very little research.

2. As we mentioned in Chapter 3, there is even less research on males with Down syndrome and their likelihood of fathering a child with Down syndrome. There has been one documented case (in England), confirmed by paternity testing, of a man with Down syndrome and a young woman who became pregnant. The couple was told there was a great risk that the baby would have severe disabilities. They agreed to a chorionic villus sampling procedure (a medical procedure conducted when a woman is only a few weeks pregnant to find out whether the fetus has a genetic disorder that may cause a disability). Within 2 weeks, the woman lost the pregnancy. An examination showed that the fetus had had no apparent abnormalities.

3. We also mentioned in Chapter 3 that the old information on the fertility of men and women with intellectual disabilities comes largely from people who were institutionalized. Some doctors believe that *any* group of men or women who were institutionalized since birth and who had institutional diets and lack of exercise, stimulation, and education would be infertile!

4. People with disabilities can successfully parent. There are self-help organizations of parents with intellectual disabilities who support one another, and researchers show that parents with intellectual disabilities can learn how to parent their child. See the "Recommended Resources" section of this book for more information.

5. Many couples with intellectual disabilities choose not to have children for financial reasons. Others decide not to have children because of the hard work, responsibility, and personal sacrifice that child rearing can mean. As one young engaged woman with an intellectual disability said, "You gotta change, you know, the diapers, and keep feeding them all the time. They cry. It's just a hassle!" Counseling for couples (or individuals) can put the pros

and cons of parenting into comprehensible perspective. Many schools offer family life courses which describe the rigors of parenting. There is even a life-like computerized infant, complete with a "crying" response that can only be satisfied (usually) by the student who has been assigned to act as parent for a "reality weekend." The infant is appropriately named "Baby Think It Over." Perhaps some volunteer work in a child care center or a kindergarten or babysitting for friends or relatives could provide some basic awareness about the responsibilities involved in looking after infants and children.

Birth Control

I have to tell you I've planted the seed about not planting the seed, if you know what I mean! That basic sex education is part of her education is very impor- tant. I've gone through things with her. We've used the book Where Did I Come From? *with her. That's a good book with real but simple explanations along with more complex issues.*
   —Michele Shaw

One parent of a young man told us that "it would be foolhardy for us to pro- ceed in this life as if [being a father] were not possible; he assumes that he will be a parent some day and I haven't told him he can't because we don't know! For that reason, and also for disease prevention, of course, he has had many practice sessions with his father on when and how to use condoms. Like most other red-blooded young men, there is one in his wallet at all times!"
   There are many methods of birth control, and a person with an intellectual disability can learn how each is designed to prevent pregnancy and/or reduce the risk of disease. Your son or daughter needs to know that a pregnancy can hap- pen because a sperm from the penis gets to the egg inside a woman. If they do get together, a baby can start to grow. A contraceptive is a way to stop that sperm and egg from getting together, and some birth control methods don't work as well as others.
   In the *FLASH* curriculum, it's recommended that you check with your local health department or Planned Parenthood for the most current and accurate in- formation on birth control methods. Sit down with your child and go through the pamphlets and booklets. The methods include

- *Abstinence:* The only sure thing people can do if they want to be sure they don't start a pregnancy is to not put the penis in the vagina. This is called "ab- stinence." Many people think it is best to wait until you are an adult (or mar- ried] to have sexual intercourse.
- *Condoms and diaphragms:* Put something in between the sperm and egg to keep them from reaching each other. Barrier: Some things that people use to block the egg and sperm are a) condoms, which cover the penis and keep the sperm from getting near the egg, or b) diaphragms [and sponges], which cover the opening to the uterus and keep sperm away from the egg.
- *Spermicides:* Kill the sperm as they come out of the penis, or make it very hard for them to swim up to the egg. A couple might use creams, jellies or foams, films, or suppositories. They use them before the penis goes into the vagina. [Some couples use spermicides with a condom or a diaphragm].

- *Birth control pills, Depo-Provera, [and Norplant]:* Tell the ovaries not to let any eggs out. This is done by taking a birth control pill every day or getting a Depo-Provera shot. [There has been considerable controversy around Depo-Provera because of the potential side effects, such as extreme weight gain.] If no egg comes out, the sperm cannot meet it. [Norplant consists of six small tubules placed under the skin on the upper arm. It lasts for 5 years.]
- *Intrauterine device:* An intrauterine device, or an IUD, makes the sperm less likely to find an egg and makes the egg less likely to nest in the uterus. It is a little piece of plastic or plastic and metal that a doctor puts inside the woman's uterus [which, in most cases, the woman can't feel once it's in place] that makes the uterus an "unfriendly" place for a sperm and egg combination.
- *Sterilization:* A process called *sterilization* changes the man's body so no sperm come out or changes the woman's body so the eggs stay where no sperm can get in. This must be done by a doctor. It is a small operation for a man [called a *vasectomy*], and a bigger operation for a woman [called a *tubal ligation* or "getting your tubes tied"]. Once sterilization is done, it is very hard to change. So the decision to sterilize must be made very carefully, with a lot of thought about feelings and beliefs. (Stangle, 1991, pp. 221–222)

In addition, *emergency contraception* is an option. If a woman has unprotected sex (without using any birth control), she can take a special combination of birth control pills. This can be taken up to 3 days after sex. This should only be for emergencies.

When you are explaining the various forms of birth control, it is helpful to have samples of the various kinds to show your son or daughter. By actually seeing and touching a condom, for example, your son or daughter will become more familiar and comfortable with it. A health nurse or sexuality educator may be available to show and explain each of these to you and your son or daughter.

Women with intellectual disabilities require the same kind of medical attention as women without disabilities when considering appropriate birth control measures. Contraceptive methods that rely on a barrier, such as a diaphragm, require motivation and physical skills. IUDs usually increase menstrual flow and hygiene problems (Elkins, 1995). Both young men and women with intellectual disabilities need plain language information on a variety of birth control methods, including various side effects and effectiveness in preventing both disease and pregnancy. Women with intellectual disabilities are generally able to use any kind of contraceptive available and may experience side effects just like any other woman.

Men with intellectual disabilities, fertile or not, need to learn to use a condom. The chance of transmitting STIs is not related to sperm counts. And it is the *couple's* responsibility, not just the woman's responsibility, to avoid pregnancy should a child not be desired. It is also the couple's responsibility to avoid giving each other STIs. Part of a responsible, loving relationship for a couple is to help each other stay healthy.

Although there are various laws about marriage and sterilization, it needs to be recognized that these laws were written because of a long, oppressive history of segregation (people with disabilities were separated not only from the general public but also from the opposite gender) and the forced sterilization of people (usually women) with disabilities. It is a bleak legacy.

According to Yvonne Brown, Dean of the College of Nursing at the University of Saskatchewan in Canada, a hysterectomy for the sole purpose of sterilization is "a very extreme solution and would not be done unless other problems warranted such extensive surgery." The American College of Obstetricians and Gynecologists Ethics Committee agrees that sterilization is only a last resort; alternatives should be sought in every instance (Elkins, 1995). Generally speaking, each state has its own statutes with respect to sterilization, said Marcie Roth with The Association for Persons with Severe Handicaps. "There are states where this procedure will be a last resort, or outlawed entirely. There are others where I wouldn't be surprised if it was commonplace" (personal communication, 1999). Individuals and families should check the statutes in their particular state. In Canada, the "Eve" decision by the Supreme Court in 1986 brought a legal end to sterilization without informed consent (G. Allan Roeher Institute, 1987). As in the United States, the practice may vary across the country.

A process that leads to informed consent (no coercion) regarding sterilization, however, should be considered a viable option only if the individual decides to terminate any possibility of parenthood. If people without disabilities can make this decision, so, too, can people with disabilities.

Sexuality educator Jean Edwards said that too frequently, parents and professionals construe sexuality as being inexorably tied to childbearing; furthermore, they may believe that performing a hysterectomy or tubal ligation will decrease sexual vulnerability or sexual activity. Sterilization *does not*

1. Decrease sexual desire
2. Remove the possibility of vulnerability
3. Remove the risk of sexual abuse...
4. Remove the risk of venereal disease (1988, p. 199)

Instead of rushing to tie tubes and remove uteruses, Edwards suggested that parents, caregivers, advocates, and professionals look at the removal of fears and the provision of current information on alternatives to sterilization. With this approach, people with intellectual disabilities will be viewed with raised expectations and will be more assured of their dignity and right to be involved in decision making about their own bodies.

Today, some past wrongs are being righted. In Canada, a 1996 landmark ruling held that the government must pay nearly $750,000 (approximately $465,000 in U.S. currency) to Leilani Muir, age 51, for forcing her to be sterilized when she was 14 (she was told she needed her appendix removed) while she lived in an institution. Madame Justice Joanne Veit of the Court of Queen's Bench in Alberta said that a travesty was done to Muir, one of nearly 3,000 people sterilized under Alberta's Sexual Sterilization Act of 1928–1972. She said that the sterilization was "undertaken in an atmosphere that so little respected Ms. Muir's human dignity that the community's and the court's sense of decency is offended" ("Eugenics Decision," 1996, p. 19).

Years ago, a Phil Donahue show had as guests Patty and Tony Cecere, a young woman and her husband, who both have disabilities. The couple had fought through the courts for the right to parent their child. They had won the fight and proved that they could adequately care for their child. One of the questions always asked of parents who have disabilities is, "Well, won't those kids grow up and become ashamed of their parents?" Excuse us, but what kid *doesn't* go through a period of being ashamed of their parents? It's a rite of passage to adulthood! In one of these discussions, a woman spoke quite eloquently of her mother...who has Down syndrome. The woman said that when she was growing up, she was unaware that her mother was different and that when she went to school, she would always win the "Yeah, but *my* Mom..." stories. But she also said that she always, down deep, felt a little luckier than the other kids she knew. What her family lacked in money was made up in love. She said that she never has gone a day in her life feeling that her mother did not love her and was not proud of her. She wakes up knowing that somewhere in the world there is a woman who is praying for her and on whose love she can always depend.

When she was asked her to describe her mother, guess what she said. "She is just beautiful."

Nannie Sanchez

It hasn't been easy sometimes. One of my teachers in high school called me a re-tard and an asshole. She didn't want me to take my purse to my P.E. class. She should just say a better way to say is "Nannie, don't take your purse to P.E." Then I can say, "But I have to take my purse because it has my key for my lock." The teacher pull my hair. She don't want me to be in that class because my writing is difficult. They want me to do cursive, and that is very hard for me. They didn't listen to me. Sometimes I want to quit, but I didn't quit, I keep going because I want to go to CPA someday. That is to college, and they just laugh at me when I say that. CPA is for Career Preparation Academy. They just laugh at me, right in my face. But I didn't quit.

I graduated in 1993 and went to CPA, but they didn't want me to go there. They still don't want me. They think I can't do the work. I was very upset be-cause that was my dream. The counselor want me to sign something but I said no. They demanded me to sign in, and I was scared, but I said no. I was ner-vous, and I sign it finally. It was something to say my classes at CPA don't count if I go. I went to Santa Fe Legislature and make a civil rights complaint.

I am very strong because of my mother. Her and me walk every night, and we talk about things. I am very smart and...articulate. One time I take a test for college, and they laugh at me and told me I would fail it. I said no, I'm not. I prove them wrong. They want me to fail. That makes me very angry because they don't like to give me a chance.

I talk to people at a big conference in New Mexico. I was not nervous be-cause when my mother and me walk, I practice saying my speech. I talk about my disability, how people treat me at APS, that's Albuquerque Public Schools, and how I go to CPA and different stuff. That people treat me and I was a little nervous before my speech but before it was my turn, my mother said to me, "Nan, this is your chance to kick some butt!" The governor was there, too, and that was the first time I speak. They did a documentary on CPA, and they did a video of my speech. There were 300 people there, and I talk about that I want to go to CPA and I have a right to go there to college, and the president was there so I say in my speech, "So...that means I'm going." He was there. Everybody clapped. When I start making speeches, I practice at home and they get a little bit better and better. I like doing good speeches because it brings up stuff for peo-

ple and it really tell all the parents and students how to get along in high school and how to treat people. I speak at YDI, that is for Youth Development Incorporated. They treat me nice and give me a scholarship for CPA.

One time this person was staring at me, and I finally ask him, "What are you staring at?" because I don't like that. I don't like when they stare at me. Because I am somebody. I am adult and independent. I cook, too! I make bread, one time I did. I make good spaghetti with pasta and tomato sauce, and it is a step-by-step process for me to make it, and it is excellent have to be patient and controlled of yourself. Take it easy, and take it very slow. Inside, you out of control, then you get mad. It's better to walk and be careful. In school, I deal people staring at me. I do get upset, and then I walk away, but sometimes I ask them what are they staring at. One day a kid was staring so long at me that he walked into a wall. Then we all laughed. He did, too.

Sometimes I get nervous, and sometimes I not get nervous because I know what I'm doing. I think. My mother, she tells me when I am ready to speak, and I am looking out at everybody. She says, "Don't get nervous. Close your eyes. Think positive." So I do it. When I was 7, I make a speech in Texas. One time at CPA, I speak to a representative from Washington, D.C. He's a representative, a senator, for New Mexico. His name is Pete Domenici. I told my mother I wanted to talk to him, so we practice. I went up to them and ask if I could speak, and he said okay, you can have 3 minutes. My mother says I bring the house down. I tell them some people need SSI, but I don't want have SSI forever, but some people with disability need it forever. I tell them they should start giving people some good jobs and good education so they can make their own money.

I love college. I am doing Word Perfect 5.1. I'm taking Microsoft Word. Word Perfect 6.0a and Human Relations, Job Skills, you know, how you get a job. I take typing. It's a lot of classes, and it is hard work. Computers are amazing to me. I love computers. I have one that is IBM. I don't have a Mac, I have IBM. This summer I take my Internet course. I got all information about Down syndrome on the Internet! There is tons of it! I put Downsydrome.com and it all comes up! At the airport, I love my job. It's fun. I wear professional clothes because that's important. I work at the City of Albuquerque Aviation Department on the second floor. If you go there, you have to ask the person sitting there if you can speak to Nannie Sanchez, and she will get me. Her name is Debra Saine. D-E-B-R-A. S-A-I-N-E.

I don't have a boyfriend anymore. I had one, but he wants to get married with me, but I said no, I don't want to get married yet. Let's just be friends, I tell him. I had another boyfriend. It's hard for me to talk to him now. He proposed to me, and I said no, let's wait. But he don't want me to finish school, and I say let's wait for a while and I get a good job or something. He not listen. He's 22 now, and he dumped me. I stick to my guns, but it is hard. You have to respect, you have to trust them. Like common sense is important. You need a good relationship to trust. You need that. Trust and respect, you can't lose respect for a girl or a boy. You have to have right feelings or you can get hurt. I like to be friends with him first, and he can make me laugh.

My boyfriend wants to have a baby, and I said, no, a baby is very, very hard. It was a very hard decision, and my mother and I talk a lot about it, and I finally make a decision to not have babies. My mother said it was up to me, but I don't want to have a baby. I like my nephew and niece, and I think I don't want to have a baby. I work too hard at college. I want someone to respect and trust. To start with to be friends. Friends move on and then maybe think marriage. You have to think the process, and I would like to get married one day like with a hunk, or something! I like Patrick Swayze, now he's a hunk! I love Dirty Dancing, that movie. I love Fabio, too. I love his hair and his muscles. He is gorgeous.

I would like to go to Italy, France, Alaska, South Padre Islands, Las Vegas. I feel like living in Italy and France. Maybe I could find information on the Internet. I would like fancy wedding, a dream-come-true wedding. I feel like getting married in that church in Old Town and I wear a fancy white wedding dress with a long tail in the back. A long veil. A bouquet of flowers, maybe tiger lilies and, um, roses. My mom doesn't have a boyfriend. She's very single. I think she is too old for a boyfriend. She has me. No, no, no. No guys for her. I am her role model. If I find a boyfriend, well, that's different! I don't know if I get a boyfriend or what. They are too much trouble. Maybe one like Patrick Swayze, that might be okay.

I love makeup. One time my mother tell me I look like a clown. I put on too much, so she show me how to do it. And I love fashion and designs. I like prom dresses. We walk all the time. That's our talking time. Sometimes we get ice cream. My mother has a treadmill, and I do it for five minutes. I like pizza and spaghetti and lasagna and eggplant. We see a lot of movie, my mother and me. I love Whitney Houston, I love her music. And Celine Dion is very good, too. She is from Canada.

My mother had a heart attack 5 years ago. That was very scary traumatic for me because I love her and I don't like to be alone. That's the scariest part to leave me by myself. I am care for her. I love her to death. I do things for her. We share; I do some of her chores, she do some of my chores. We share clothes together. We walk every night, and sometimes we go out to eat. Only once because you can spend a lot of money if you eat out too much. My brother Mark, he lives with my nephew and my niece. He is pretty good, but sometimes he is a monster with his mom. But I love him, but he treats me good and I like that. I like his wife a lot. They baptize me.

My mom was Hispanic and my dad was Italian from when I was born. This is my mom, but Kathy, she was my mom when I was born. I just saw her four years ago. My mother help me get in touch with her so I know who I am. We find her. It was very hard. I just want to see her one time. I ask her why she had to give me up, and she not listen. I ask about my dad and my half-brother, and she not listen. I don't like it. But I like my mother best of all that I grew up with. She's everything, she's my mentor, she's my friend, she's my hero. Sometime I am mad at her when she forgets to lock the door, and I have to check. I always do. Sometimes I have to get after her to hang up her clothes. Her name is one word: R-O-S-E-M-A-R-I-E S-A-N-C-H-E-Z. Down syndrome is trisomy 21. That means there's a chromosome inside of your body. It is a scary point for me when I know some parents want to give their baby away. I could tell parents don't give up their child. Keep him because it's worth it. The child is very lucky to have lucky parents, and that's it. I would like to try ballroom dancing. I would like to take a class in that. I love music, and I sing along with Celine and Whitney. I speak a little Spanish. Hola, ¿cómo está usted? There is some Spanish music that I like a lot. I like Nelson Martinez. He's from Santa Fe, and he has a mariachi band, and I love mariachi music. My name is from Hawaii. It means beautiful one. *When I came to live with her as a baby, she had a party, and everyone bring a baby gift, and they even brought my name for me.*

One day I want to be famous. One day I want to be on TV. I would love to be on a talk show. I would like to design clothes and make speeches. Sometimes when I make a speech, I see people crying, and I feel funny. But my mother said it is not sad crying, it is happy crying. I would like to be maybe a stage manager, for parties. A fashion designer. I am very creative. I feel like doing different stuff in my life, lots of stuff.

Q

My greatest fear is to be 90 years old, hanging by a thread, still worrying about what might happen to my son when I die.

A

This is why relationships are so important. You need to see your child in relationships that are sustaining and freely given. As your child grows, insist that everyone from teachers, to teacher aides, to group home workers, to social workers, see that the primary goal for your child is that your child learn the social skills necessary to make and keep friends. True, your son needs *functional skills*, but he also needs a life of consequence. This comes from being in healthy relationships. The only thing that will let you rest peacefully is the thing that will also keep you up at night: loving relationships.

Q

My son wants a girlfriend, but every time he tries, he is shot down really badly. What do I do?

A

While discussing the realities of relationships, we have to talk about things that are quite controversial, even to this day in our field. All of the research and all of our observations have shown that if people with disabilities marry, they will likely marry another person with a disability. In order for marriage or a long-term relationship to happen, a number of other things have to happen. First, the person has to be able to love another. (That's easy enough.) Then they have to be comfortable in their own skin and see themselves as worthy of love. (That's a *little* more difficult.) Next, they have to understand relationships. (That's teachable.) And sex. (Gulp, okay, this is still teachable.) Then they have to be able to see others with similar characteristics as lovable.

Q

Our priest says he will not marry our daughter and her boyfriend of 3 years. He says they will not understand the marriage classes. What should they do?

A

It's hard to type with steam whistling out your ears. This is a distressing question. It's hard to know how to answer. Has your priest ever met your daughter?
If she has managed a relationship for 3 years, she is already doing better at relationships than almost 50% of the people that the priest *will* marry. You can
try to educate the priest. Tell him that people with disabilities who marry have
a lower divorce rate than couples without disabilities. They communicate better
between themselves, and their disability doesn't get in the way of learning
about love. The fact is that none of these will probably work—but you still
have choices. You can fight the priest by going above his head. You can bring a
class action suit against the parish for discrimination. You can stomp your feet,
and tell him that he's a bigot. None of these is a particularly good idea. So what
do you do? Well, maybe you should pray. In your prayers, ask God whether
you should stay in the parish or whether you should look for a priest who understands people with disabilities. You may be surprised by God's answer. A
Jewish woman said not long ago that her rabbi wouldn't perform the bat mitz-
vah for her daughter, who has a disability. She ended up going to a synagogue
with a rabbi who had a very different understanding of God, of disability, and
of faith. She said that the move was one that benefited her, separate from any
disability issues. She felt that the new synagogue was more welcoming and loving. Pray. Then decide what action you want to take. But do take action.

Q

*Our son and his girlfriend would like to live together, and we're prepared to support
them. But the residential agency and the girl's parents are blocking it. The agency says
it's not their policy to move people from different programs so they can live together (they
said something about "then we'd have to do it for everybody"), and her parents feel she
is too young to manage such a relationship. They are both in their mid-20s.*

A

The temptation is to get on the white horse and *charge!* It's hard, but you have
to remember this is *your son and his girlfriend's* issue, not *yours*. By going in and
leading the charge, you will subtly (or not so subtly) communicate that your
son and his girlfriend aren't capable of fighting their own battles. Forgive us,
but if they aren't capable of speaking up for themselves on this matter, then
living together or marriage might be a bit of a stretch. Start thinking about self-
advocacy. In many cities and towns, there are People First organizations or
some other form of self-advocacy group. These groups teach people with disabilities to speak up for themselves and to make their needs clearly known.
Your son and his girlfriend would surely benefit from such an organization, and
it might be the first step in this process.

As they learn to speak up for themselves, you can arrange to support them
in their demands to the agency and in the young woman's discussions with her
parents. By being in a supportive and supporting role and by letting the couple
speak up clearly for themselves, you are indicating by your behavior that you
believe in their competence and they are demonstrating it by their behavior. If

the agency still blocks it, you have a couple of options. In Canada, people with intellectual disabilities have their rights enshrined in every provincial human rights code as well as in the federal Charter of Rights and Freedoms—they have a strong case for discrimination based on disability. In the United States, they have rights under the Americans with Disabilities Act of 1990 (PL 101-336), and there are strong disability rights organizations like ADAPT (American Disabled for Attendant Programs Today) that may be able to help place pressure on the organization. Still, it should be your son and his girlfriend who lead the fight.

Q

How do we teach our son to put on a condom?

A

Here is an answer we think you'll like: If at all possible, *you* shouldn't teach your child to put on a condom. Could you imagine your Mom or Dad sitting down with you, a condom and a banana and not just wanting to die of embarrassment? It is important that you teach your child about responsibility, reciprocity, and loving. This way, your son will learn *why* it is important to take care of and be responsible for how his behavior affects another person. As your son gets older, ask him questions about love. Ask him how people who love each other take care of each other. You will probably get answers like, "Be nice to them," or, if your child is a true capitalist, "Buy them something." Get your son to think in terms of "taking care of someone" and "making sure they don't get sick."

When there are programs on television about AIDS, other STIs, or teenage pregnancy, use these as conversation starters about responsibility and loving. Your child needs to know that the condom is a thing that represents love as well as a thing that protects against disease. Who then should teach your child? Well, there are a number of places to look. Try public health, your local AIDS organization, your local school, or your local agency for people with disabilities. In one of these places, you will probably find people who do condom training. They will have the condoms and perhaps the wooden penis that is used during training (Dave has one at the sexuality clinic; he calls it Woody Wood Pecker), the videotapes, and other training materials. These materials can be expensive for you to buy, and the organizations will have the expertise in their use. By the way, girls also should learn how to operate a condom properly—disease prevention and pregnancy control are the responsibility of the couple.

If none of them can or will train your child, then you will have to do the training. Get them to train you and borrow their materials from them. If they don't want to do this, *get obnoxious*. Go to their funding body and *make a lot of noise*. Your child shouldn't get AIDS because some doofus doesn't want to do his or her job. You need to arm yourself with one fact: People with intellectual disabilities are extremely vulnerable to AIDS and, as a result, get AIDS in the same proportion to the *highest* risk group. See Chapter 3 for more information on this issue.

Q

My husband and I hope our daughter will find someone she loves who will love her in return. We mentioned to friends that maybe an arranged marriage might be a good solution, sort of like finding someone for her, if she agrees, of course. Our friends were horrified. What do you think?

A

Well, arranged marriages last longer on average than freely chosen marriages. But that may be because of cultural demands rather than true "domestic bliss." So, unless you come from a culture where arranged marriages are common, this probably would serve to set your child apart rather than include her. But arranged social opportunities, cool! These are a great idea, in fact. Most folks with disabilities could make friends, develop relationships, and fall in love if they had just one thing: opportunity! By working to ensure that your child gets to go to dances and social and sporting events and by ensuring that she has some good social and conversational skills, the marriage will arrange itself!

Rosemarie and Nannie Sanchez
Albuquerque, New Mexico

Chapter 8

A New Future For You
and For Your Child

Strangely enough, one of my specialists in 1947 was named Dr. Fortunato. He looked at me and said, "Florence, I wish you'd stop being so foolish." The opinion at the time was that you just sweep a retarded child under the rug or literally hide them in the attic. Get rid of them. They wound up in the institution...which to me was a pretty horrible place for anybody. I took her home. She had Down syndrome. Let's face it, at the time they weren't quite as generous with the term. In the 1940s, she was called a "mongoloid." I despised it because it was such a horrible, ugly word. To me, Loretta was beautiful.
　　—Florence Schulten

I think Bec should be a fairly independent person. She should be able to go through school fine. I guess I expect the same things out of her that I expect out of Jac, basically, maybe with a little more support. I don't expect Bec to be a brain surgeon, but I don't see why she couldn't be the brain surgeon's secretary.
　　—Dawn Thompson

One of the things I've learned since Brad was born, and it's probably become stronger in recent years, is that it's okay to make mistakes. It's not something I really allowed myself in years past. I still struggle with it, but I know it's one of the best ways to learn.
　　—Ethel Magnus

If your child is young, she has arrived in a much different world than existed even 10 or 15 years ago. People with intellectual disabilities are now living in the community, working, playing, worshipping, shopping, and doing everything else that other people do. Many of us grew up in a world in which there were no people with disabilities living next door, going to our schools, or worshipping with us; or, at least these occurrences weren't commonplace. It was unusual if these things happened at all. This has completely changed.

A young woman with Down syndrome walks with her mother every morning along the neighborhood boardwalk at the nearby lake. A woman with an intellectual disability volunteers at her local church. A man with an intellectual disability works as a janitor's assistant in a large high school nearby. A young woman speaks carefully to a visitor who arrives at her reception desk in a large office building. "Please take a seat," she smiles. "I'll let them know you're here." A 60-year-old man with significant disabilities who spent more than half of his life in a large institution lives in his own apartment and works at a plastics company with some support. A young man walks to the local college of education on the university campus twice a week to meet his literacy tutor. There is a growing recognition that people with disabilities are whole human beings.

The messages of love and acceptance are the beginning of a journey to self-acceptance and self-love. This will help in the building of boundaries. Each of us has to look at our personal journeys. We have to learn, really quickly, that our son or daughter with a disability has a *future*—a very real future, full of potential and exciting variety. When society, and sometimes parents, look at a child with a disability, they sometimes see a "burden" or a "hopeless being." Be really careful here.

When I think about all my boys, I think about Brad in much the same way. I hope that all their dreams can come true. I hope they all find fulfillment in whatever they decide to do. I don't have my mind set that one should be a doctor or a lawyer. I see potential in each one for one thing or another, but only they can determine what course their lives will take. When John and I are gone, the boys will not just care for Bradley but continue to like him and want him around. For Brad, I hope he will live as independently as possible, living with someone he feels comfortable with, knowing there are people he can go to. Families need to pool resources in the community and be resourceful in creating something better than what we alone can provide.

   —Ethel Magnus

When all the kids were born, they got a share of responsibility for each other. That's what family is all about. Part of being a family is sorting out who needs what from time to time. Erin and Ben don't have primary responsibility for Jim, and they're not sitting around worrying, "Oh my God, when Dad and Karin and Mom die, we'll have to take over." But they both know they are a big part of Jim's life, and that carries some responsibility. Prince Charles was born with the responsibility of the Crown, and there are times when he probably feels like he's not up to the task, but that's life! We need to paint for them a very clear picture of our hopes and Jim's own dreams for his life, and we need to share that together as a family all along the way.

   —Richard Schwier

Dick Sobsey does a lot of work regarding the victimization of people with disabilities and likes to challenge assumptions about these people. As a parent of a child with a disability, he has a vested interest that society begin to change its view of those who have disabilities. He told this story to members of the International Coalition on Abuse and Disability:

When Japanese author Kenzaburo Oe won the Nobel Prize for Literature, he made an unusual announcement. At the Stockholm awards ceremony, he informed the world that he would not be writing any more novels, at least not for the foreseeable future. He has no more reason to write.

In an extended April 16, 1995 interview with the Canadian Broadcasting Corporation's *Sunday Morning,* Oe detailed his reasons for writing and why he no longer needs to write. Oe sees his writing as a healing process. Thirty-two years ago, when his son was born, Oe and his wife were told that the child had a herniated brain. The parents were told that surgery could be done but that if the child survived, he would be severely disabled. Doctors tried to convince the parents that they should let their son die, saying the most they could hope for "was a kind of vegetable existence."

Oe, already depressed about his stagnating career as an author, struggled with the decision, thinking he and his wife must escape from the "monster baby." While considering their options, they visited doctors at Hiroshima who were working with atomic blast victims; some of these physicians themselves suffered from the effects of radiation. They told him about their process of growing from despair to hope. They decided to get the operation for their son, Hikiri. Their son survived; he was epileptic, developmentally delayed, visually impaired, with limited physical coordination.

Oe's novels gained new vitality as he attempted to give voice to his son who never learned to speak beyond a few limited words, and as the father spoke of his own challenges. While he says that living with a child with a disability brought suffering to him, he also says that his son taught him invaluable lessons, and gradually the "burden" became a gift. The son gave meaning to the father's life. Kenzaburo Oe went on to reach the pinnacle of his profession and credits his son for this achievement.

But that is not why Oe stopped writing novels. It seems his son has found his own voice. At age six, Kenzaburo Oe's son spoke his first word, identifying the call of a bird. At 32, Hikiri still speaks only a few words, still is severely disabled. Hikiri, however, has learned to express himself through music. Hikiri won his own prize last year. A CD of music composed by Hikiri Oe won Japan's top prize for Classical Japanese music. Not bad for a "vegetable.'"

What if Hikiri Oe's parents had followed their doctor's advice and let their son die?

Life probably would have been a little easier. There might have been less suffering, but also less joy. Neither father or son would have known what they had missed. And if someone tried to tell the parent who made such a choice or the doctor who advocated for it just how rich those lives would have been if they had chosen to keep such a child alive, no one would have believed it anyway. (personal communication, 1995)

Catherine Schaefer
as told by her mother Nicola

We've always seen Catherine as Catherine, rather than as "a person with multiple disabilities." She happens to have some fairly significant inconveniences, but we've tried to work our way around them over the years and we continue to do so. So many people with disabilities don't live their lives; they live programs. *For instance, they don't have swimming; they have hydrotherapy. So much of what we've done for Catherine has been ordinary, unconscious, common sense, and really wasn't much more complicated than that. It's very difficult to analyze how we've helped Catherine create a network, a community. It wasn't until years later that we realized we had been doing integration and inclusion just as a matter of course. We did it because it was the thing to do that was right for her.*

I don't know that early on we did anything consciously to see Catherine, who she really was, *instead of her disabilities. But I remember that when she was 7 months old, my immediate thought was, "Okay, right, she's going to have some big problems, but she's going to have as normal a life as possible." That was my guiding principle.*

We soon realized that her basic problem was that she couldn't go out and discover the world, so we had to bring the world to her. That included inviting all of our sons' friends over as often as they went to their friends' houses. So our house was often full of little kids, and Catherine was always sitting or lying in the middle of all the activity, getting crawled on and run into and having things dropped on her. She loved it. One thing we discovered she enjoyed was being hauled around the house by her feet while she was lying on her back, so the kids would do that with her.

At some point I realized I hadn't talked to *Catherine enough, that I hadn't* explained *things enough to her. It was terribly late when, via friends, I came to that conclusion. I hate having to be this honest, but I suppose she was in her teens. I had always talked about what was going on, but she just didn't seem to get it. I'd say things like, "Okay, Catherine, we're going to the doctor today to see if your brainwaves are still moving," but not much more. My understanding of Catherine was that she didn't understand intellectual processes. And it's jolly difficult to have a philosophical conversation with someone if they're not responding, just staring off into space. I was far from the model mother of a wonky kid; it was other people who really helped me see how to do things better. A big thing I remember making a conscious decision to do was to stop talking* about *her as though she wasn't there when she was. Even if she didn't respond at all or if she was in a different space, I'd include her in the conversation. I found this very important when I was presenting her to doctors, teachers, civil servants particularly. It's so easy when someone is just sitting there with drool hanging out of their mouth and eyes crossed to talk* about *them. That is a huge danger, and I don't think it's worth the risk to assume she's not getting any of the conversation. It's like people in a coma whose relatives are talking with the doctor, "Oh, she's not long for this world," or "I wonder what bits of her jewelry I can get when she shoves off." People have come out of comas who can tell you they've heard those conversations going on over them but they were unable to do anything about it. It was when I heard a story like this that I made the effort not to talk about Catherine in front of her anymore. Some doctors are incredibly recalcitrant. No matter how much I talk* to *Catherine, they just talk to* me. *I was at an appointment with Catherine at her neurologist recently, and he's actually pretty good. But I think he's learned over the years to incorporate her into the conversation instead of just asking me, "Well, how's she been?" And I try to lead by saying, "Oh, hello, I don't think you and Catherine have seen each other for some time, have you?' Then I'd look at her and say, "Well, Catherine and I both think that she's doing incredibly well." I don't do it too obviously, because that's boring and silly. I'm not consciously trying to teach other people; what I am doing is trying to enhance Catherine's image and insist that others treat her with respect. And I still don't know how much she understands. I asked the neurologist about her CAT scan, what her brain actually looks like. Basically, there is very little in the area that deals with intellectual thinking, imagining and all that sort of thing.*

Nicola and
Catherine Schaefer
Winnipeg, Manitoba

Hence the title of my book [Does She Know She's There?, *1988*]*, but also hence the fact the title is a question. She really is a beautiful mystery, but we must assume she understands what's going on and explain things to her.*

It's vital to see her now as Catherine, a 35-year-old woman who lives in her own house with friends. It's a complex thing. I still very much think of her as my daughter who is in need of protecting. It's really been her contemporaries who have quietly shown me the way. I'm not being self-deprecating, it is actually true. A few little stories I remember as I began to see Catherine more as an independent person: I dashed over to her house to drop off some things and popped in the back door. A young man was sitting with her, and he turned and said, "Hi, my name's Hari. This is my friend Catherine and this is her house. And you are?" Another time, I went in and realized Darlene was wearing Catherine's earrings, and I looked at the three women (their friend Leanne was living with them, too), and they were all wearing each other's clothes. It wasn't a spectacular revelation or anything, but in a way it was. Here were three young women sharing an apartment and each others' clothes and jewelry. It made me wonder how many staff in a group home would borrow the pants of someone who lived there. That was indicative to me of how the house works and how it is different from some sort of program for people with disabilities.

When Catherine's brothers were talking about leaving home, I was basically on my knees in gratitude because they were teenagers. Then I started thinking, gosh, maybe Catherine deserves to move out and have her own place, too. We had evolved, you see. In the beginning, it was well, we'll always have Catherine with us and anyway we don't want her to go anywhere else. Then with the boys moving out, I thought, maybe Catherine would like to get away from us. It wasn't a question of her moving so we could have an adult life after children. Maybe it was her right to move, and that was a startling thought. It was a big shift from caretaker to a recognition of her right to be on her own.

It was always important for Catherine to be in contact with people. One of my biggest discoveries was the idea that if you have a child with a disability you should perhaps get a dog. When you're out for a walk and meet another dog owner, the two dogs stop and do this sniffing routine and the two people attached to them inevitably do theirs: they chat. You meet some very interesting people in your neighborhood that way. Our dog had a mad fling with the red setter up the road and had eight puppies. Everyone in the neighborhood then had to stop by and see the result, and all the while, Catherine is there in the middle of the whole thing.

Early on, as young women who lived with Catherine in her house came and went, she started looking like them as far as her dress went. When Darlene was living with her, she wore long flowing things, very pretty, with lots of earrings, that sort of thing. Then Laurie moved in. Laurie's a lady who likes to wear big clothes in earth tones. Suddenly Catherine started wearing these massive brown sweaters and baggy green pants. Then came Rika, who is of the generation that wears only black, so Catherine started appearing in black. Thank God they couldn't find any Doc Martens to fit her. It's not that she looked awful in any of those styles, but the big question was what is Catherine's taste? And even bigger: Is how she's living what's best for Catherine and what she really wants? In the end, however, you make your best guess. I had to be told years ago was that I should be giving Catherine a chance to make choices wherever she could. If I held up two items of clothing, she would sort of look and point. I didn't learn that until she was about 20. I had always just put on her what I thought looked good. An English psychologist type...suggested I do it. So I did. I thought she probably wouldn't react. And then she did. I've had frequent lessons like that over the years.

In terms of Catherine's sexuality, I think we always just saw her as a daughter, as a sister, as female. For instance, it never even occurred to me to do anything but simply help her manage her periods. It wasn't until much later that I heard about people being routinely sterilized, and I was appalled. Some years ago she had a massive nonmalignant tumor on an ovary. They described it as eight oranges strung together. So she had surgery. I spoke to the gynecologist who told me about the surgery, and she said everything else was perfectly healthy. I know that many doctors would have made an executive decision during the surgery and would have whipped out the lot, assuming that Catherine didn't need reproductive organs anyway. I made a point to thank the doctor and tell her I noticed.

Catherine is definitely heterosexual. She likes men and will often shoot out her hand to make a grab. One of the first summer programs she was in, she was with a lovely young man called Tom, who was amazingly hairy. She loved plunging her hand down his chest and grabbing hold. There would be a loud roar now and then. She does flirt. My sense is that she loves being cuddled and hugged and lifted by men. She's always, very definitely, enjoyed being lifted by men much more than by women. She seems very comfortable and content with that level of closeness with men she knows.

She's not as outgoing with people, men or women, whom she doesn't know. In fact, she's quite shy. I'll introduce her to someone new, and she'll look away and give a raspberry. It struck me that people in Catherine's situation have little or no control over people they meet. She doesn't have the capability to just fade out or if she doesn't feel like meeting someone, to just not do it. People who can't move their wheelchairs or speak are very vulnerable that way.

For Catherine to be surrounded by the kind of people who seem to gravitate to her, the co-op housing arrangement is essential. If that wasn't there, she's probably still be stuck with us, the ultimate nightmare for her. At best, she'd be in a group home, but having her in a "facility" is something that makes me very uncomfortable. I went to England one time, and when I came back I went to pick her up from where she was staying at a local institution. When I got there, I walked past a group of about 16 people hanging out of wheelchairs all arranged in a semicircle, not watching a television showing a steamy soap. She wasn't there, so I went to her room. She wasn't there either, so I went to ask where she was. They said, "Oh, she's watching television." I said no, she wasn't, but they insisted, so I went back and stopped to look at each person in that semicircle in front of the telly. There she was, head down, fast asleep. In a sense, she had disappeared literally before my eyes. It was quite frightening. I think it's very important for Catherine to be a presence as much as any of us, so we keep at that all the time.

I hadn't even really thought about Cath's future particularly until a friend asked what my dream for her would be. I decided she'd probably like to live *with people more or less her own age, doing things people of that age liked to do as they lived typical lives. Ted and I donated a Jacuzzi to the house. Catherine not only loves it, but it's been a great attraction for people to come over to the house. Anyone in the house can invite people over, and there are often riproaring parties 'til 1 or 2 in the morning. It's Catherine's version of getting a dog. As a matter of fact, they do have a new puppy in the house, and a baby person is expected at Christmas. There's a 10-year-old living upstairs. She and Catherine have forged an amazing link. One day I had some towels to drop off at the house, so I came in and found Catherine lying on her bed with the cat sleeping on her stomach, and Angel was sitting beside her reading* The Secret Garden. *It was just lovely.*

I did manage to accept fairly early on that I needed help. I'm frankly terribly unimaginative and lazy, but I do have the wit to surround myself with creative people who are doers. I could never in a million years have thought of all the things that have gone into helping Catherine create the kind of life she has now, to help her surround herself with people who see her as a beautiful, worthwhile and interesting person. That's the strength and magic of support networks.

—Nicola Schaefer

My biggest fear is that if something happens to George, it's going to be bad for Michael. But if something happens to me, it's going to be tragic. He's so close to me....I tell him someday I won't be here anymore. At first, I don't think he got it, but he's accepting it now. When he was sick, he asked his sister, "What's going to happen to me when Mom and Daddy are gone?" She told him the family would take care of him and he shouldn't worry. They would all be very sad and...he might even live with her for awhile, but everything would be okay. He thinks about it from time to time.

—Peggy Creamer

Q

What if we simply don't agree that our child will ever be a "sexual" person in the way you've described in this book? We just don't believe it, and we also think any relationships open her up to too much chance of someone taking advantage.

A

Your fears are well founded. You are quite right to worry about sexuality and relationships. The fears are huge: AIDS, unwanted pregnancy, and exploitation. The question you need to ask yourself is *How best do I protect my daughter from a disease that could kill her or a relationship that may exploit her?* Please remember that protection has not worked—and this is an understatement. People have taken a protective approach, yet still see AIDS skyrocketing in people with intellectual disabilities. People with intellectual disabilities are one of the most victimized groups in our society. People with intellectual disabilities face loneliness, isolation, and depression.

Although you may not see your daughter as being sexual, that does not prevent abusers or others who would exploit her from seeing your child as vulnerable. You need to ensure that your child has the knowledge with which she can protect herself. Remember that sex and sexuality education, if anything, is linguistics training. It is giving her a language about her body that she can use. This way, should anything abusive happen, she can tell you or someone else about it. Please also remember that your view of your child is *entirely natural* and *entirely normal.*

Q

My son is 27 and has a lot of disabilities and needs help to do almost everything. He doesn't speak or walk, but he has amazing blue eyes! With all of this talk about sexuality, sex education, and self-esteem, how do I even begin to teach my son any of these things?

A

You already are! Just the way you describe your son tells us you are on the right track. Remember, you can teach self-esteem. People develop positive self-esteem when they see themselves reflected in loving eyes. People start to feel good about themselves when they hear loving things said about them. People come to love themselves when they learn they are worth love. In the words "amazing blue eyes," it is clear that you are doing all of these things. Don't worry. Self-esteem is probably already there.

When you speak of your son, you say he has a lot of disabilities. Let's forget sex education and sexuality for now. We know that the more severe a person's disability, the less likely it is that he or she will form a sexual relationship. That being the case, let's talk about two other things: boundaries and intimacy. Your son requires intimate care. Ensure that all of his care providers know how to perform personal care while respecting boundaries. Take a look at developing a protocol for his personal care; write down how care providers should do everything, and ensure that they follow the procedure. That way your son will become used to respectful care. We hope that the first time someone doesn't follow the procedure exactly, your son will be able to communicate discomfort and upset to others. Even if this doesn't happen, the mere presence of the protocol tells all of the care providers that you have thought about safety issues and that you are watching. A little bit of paranoia can be a good thing.

Now, ensure that your son has intimacy in his life. Remember that the drive and need for intimacy is greater than the drive and need for sex. Look at all of the ways your son can experience intimacy and pleasure, from having a pet snuggle in his lap to experiencing the feel of wind on his skin. By focusing not on sex but on intimacy, you can become very creative in developing a very healthy lifestyle for your son. Beautiful eyes and all.

Believe it or not, all parents of all kids (no matter their age or ability) have difficulty seeing their children as sexual and have difficulty talking to their kids about sex. Most parents can see that their children are beautiful, but mistrust the intentions of those *others* who love their children. What you have to do is allow yourself to grow through these feelings. You also have to be a ready "listener" to your child. When your child develops crushes on others, if you tell her that her feelings are wrong, she will stop talking to you about them. When your child asks questions about sex, if you tell him that him questions are wrong, he will stop asking you. When your child tries to make himself look attractive and asks for your opinion, if you tell him that he is "ugly," he will believe you. The costs are high.

We don't ask that you change your view of your child. We just ask that you make sure that your child gets messages of acceptance and worthiness. We also ask that you ensure that your child has a parent who can listen and answer. If those two things are there, you will have a relationship with your child wherein he learns about love from you and you learn about ability from him.

Last fall, Dave went with some kids to a local fair. They treated him like kids always treat adults at a fair. They asked for money, and as soon as the cash hit their hands, they evaporated. This was fine; he wanted to just walk around the fair, look at displays, and visit some friends who had a couple of cows in competition for some kind of prize.

Then Jill, Tasha, and Beth found him and tried to convince Dave to go on the Gyrator, a ride that whips people through the air at lightening speed and leaves them as green as the prizewinning zucchini. He agreed to watch them defy logic and gravity to fly through the air for pleasure. They stood in line behind a group of young Québecois girls whom Dave only noticed because of a spontaneous burst of laughter. It took a second for him to notice that one of the very fashionably dressed young women had Down syndrome. When it came time to load for their ride, they all scrambled toward the waiting death buckets.

Once the ride began, Dave brought his camera up and clicked some pictures of Jill, Tasha, and Beth as they flew by. Everyone else on the ride were just anonymous blurs. Two weeks later when the pictures came back from the processor, Dave found that one of his shutter clicks was either a second late or a second early. In his hand was a picture of that young woman with Down syndrome, sitting with a friend or a sister, flying by with a look of pure joy on her face.

It was a face that many professionals have never seen before. It was the face of a woman, who clearly had a disability but who in the joy of a moment felt the thrill of friendship, belonging, and incredible, incredible speed. At the moment the shutter clicked, she was nothing more and nothing less than a young teenager on a ride with her friends. She wasn't "special." She wasn't "handicapped." She wasn't "disabled." She just was. This is the future. It's not so terrifying a place for your child to be headed, but there is work to be done. You have a child to be parented, and there are concepts to be taught.

If it's any comfort, remember not only that it is the longest trek but also, indeed, that each day's journey that begins with a single step. And only rarely does it move at the same speed as the Gyrator!

Just before Loretta died, a friend of mine came to visit and made a remark that I'll never forget. She said anyone who had ever rubbed shoulders with Loretta would never be the same. There was a quality, a grace about her. She never tried to talk too much because she seemed conscious of her faulty speech, but she would show people she cared about them. There was a gentle quality about her, and the world is better because she was here.
    —*Florence Schulten*

References

Americans with Disabilities Act (ADA) of 1990, PL 101-336, 42 U.S.C. §§ 12101 *et seq.*

Bogdan, R., & Taylor, S.J. (1994). *The social meaning of mental retardation: Two life stories* (Reissue ed.). New York: Teachers College Press.

Canning, C.D. (1990). Parental view of adolescence. In S.M. Pueschel, *A parent's guide to Down syndrome: Toward a brighter future* (pp. 269–275). Baltimore: Paul H. Brookes Publishing Co.

Champagne, M.P., & Walker-Hirsch, L.W. (1986–1993). *Circles* (Vols. I–III). Santa Barbara, CA: James Stanfield.

Champagne, M.P., & Walker-Hirsch, L.W. (1992). The Circles Concept for use as a counseling strategy: An old dog learns new tricks. *The NADD Newsletter, 9*(5), 2.

Cohen, W. (1994). *Your baby has Down syndrome* [Videotape]. Pittsburgh: MacKenzie Sara Noca Charitable Trust.

Davies, C. (1995). Couple with Down syndrome win fight to stay married. *Down Syndrome News, 19*(9), 121.

Down Syndrome Association of Greater Cincinnati. (n.d.). Information sheet. Cincinnati, OH: Author.

Down Syndrome Association of Los Angeles. (1995). Information sheet. Los Angeles: Author.

Edwards, J., & Dawson, D. (1983). *My friend David: A source book about Down's syndrome and a personal story about friendship.* Portland, OR: Ednick Communications.

Edwards, J. (1988). Sexuality, marriage, and parenting for persons with Down syndrome. In S.M. Pueschel, *The young person with Down syndrome: Transition from adolescence to adulthood* (pp. 187–204). Baltimore: Paul H. Brookes Publishing Co.

Edwards, J.P., & Elkins, T.E. (1988). *Just between us: A social sexual training guide for parents and professionals who have concerns for persons with retardation.* Austin, TX: PRO-ED.

Elkins, T.E. (1995). Medical issues related to sexuality and reproduction. In D.C. Van Dyke, P. Mattheis, S. Eberly, & J. Williams (Eds.), *Medical and surgical care for children with down syndrome: A guide for parents* (pp. 253–266). Bethesda, MD: Woodbine House.

Endicott, O. (1992). Can the law tell us who is not the marrying kind? *entourage, 7*(2), 9.

Eugenics decision "offensive and outrageous," judge says. (1996, January 26). *The Globe and Mail,* 19.

Fensterheim, H., & Baer, J. (1988). *Making life right when it feels all wrong: How to avoid being an emotional victim with lovers, mates, bosses, friends, family.* New York: Rawson Associates.

Flynn, M.C., Reeves, D., Whelan, E., & Speak, B. (1985). The development of a measure for determining the mentally handicapped adult's tolerance of rules and recognition of rights. *Journal of Practical Approaches to Developmental Handicaps, 9,* 18–24.

G. Allan Roeher Institute. (1987). *Issues surrounding the "Eve" case on sterilization.* North York, Ontario, Canada: Author.

Hingsburger, D. (1990). *i to I: Self-concept of people with developmental disabilities.* Mountville, PA: VIDA Publishing.

Hingsburger, D. (1995). *Just say know!: Understanding and reducing the risk of sexual victimization of people with developmental disabilities.* Eastman, Québec, Canada: Diverse City Press.

Horstmeier, D. (1990). Communication. In S.M. Pueschel, *A parent's guide to Down syndrome: Toward a brighter future* (pp. 233–257). Baltimore: Paul H. Brookes Publishing Co.

Kastner, T.A., Nathanson, R.S., & Marchetti, A.G. (1992). Epidemiology of HIV infection in adults. In A.C. Crocker, H.J. Cohen, & T.A. Kastner (Eds.), *HIV infection and developmental disabilities: A resource for service providers* (pp. 127–139). Baltimore: Paul H. Brookes Publishing Co.

Kempton, W., & Stigall-Muccigrosso, L. (1996). *An easy guide to loving carefully: For men and women* (3rd ed.). Haverford, PA: Winifred Kempton Associates; and Los Gatos, CA: Lynne Stigall-Muccigrosso Associates.

Klass, C.S. (1999). *The child care provider: Promoting young children's development.* Baltimore: Paul H. Brookes Publishing Co.

Knutson Brasington, C. (1995). Reproductive issues for individuals with Down syndrome. *Down Syndrome News, 19*(4), 54.

La Roach, L. (n.d.). *The joy of stress: How to prevent hardening of the attitude.* Alexandria, VA: PBS Video.

Ludwig, S., & Hingsburger, D. (1993). *Being sexual: An illustrated series on sexuality and relationships—Teaching Manual* (Number 17). Toronto, Ontario, Canada: SIECCAN.

Maksym, D. (1990a). *Shared feelings: A parent guide to sexuality education for children, adolescents and adults who have a mental handicap.* North York, Ontario, Canada: The Roeher Institute.

Maksym, D. (1990b). *Shared feelings: A parent guide to sexuality education for children, adolescents and adults who have a mental handicap—discussion guide.* North York, Ontario, Canada: The Roeher Institute.

Mayle, P. (1973). *Where did I come from?* [Illustrated booklet]. Secaucus, NJ: Lyle Stuart.

Morris, D. (1997). *Intimate behavior: A zoologist's classic study of human intimacy* (Reprint ed.). New York: Kodansha International.

National Down Syndrome Congress. (1993) *Facts about Down syndrome* [Information sheet]. Atlanta, GA: Author.

National Information Center for Children and Youth with Disabilities. (1992). The importance of developing social skills. *NICHCY News Digest, 1*(3), 6–7

Perske, R. (1988). *Circles of friends: People with disabilities and their friends enrich the lives of one another.* Nashville: Abingdon.

Pierro, C. (1994, June). Getting past the confusion: Talking with your child about disabilities. *Pacesetter.*

Pueschel, S. (1988). *The young person with Down syndrome: Transition from adolescence to adulthood.* Baltimore: Paul H. Brookes Publishing Co.

Pueschel, S.M. (1990). Prenatal diagnosis. In S.M. Pueschel, *A parent's guide to Down syndrome: Toward a brighter future* (pp. 53–64). Baltimore: Paul H. Brookes Publishing Co.

Rodgers, P.T., & Coleman, M. (1992). *Medical care in Down syndrome: A preventive medicine approach.* New York: Marcel Dekker.

Roizen, N.J., Luke, A., Sutton, M., & Schoeller, D.A. (1995). Obesity and nutrition in children with Down syndrome. In L. Nadel & D. Rosenthal (Eds.), *Down syndrome: Living and learning in the community* (pp. 213–215). New York: Wiley-Liss.

Rousseau, A. (1995). *Friends make the difference: A guide to supporting friendships in our homes, schools and communities.* Vancouver, Canada: British Columbia Association for Community Living.

Russell, M. (1994, July–August). The cost of saying I do: How Social Security policies can silence wedding bells for people with disabilities. *New Mobility,* 38.

Schaefer, N. (1978). *Does she know she's there?* Toronto, Ontario, Canada: Fitzhenry & Whiteside.

Schaefer, N. (1982). *Does she know she's there?* (Updated ed.). Toronto, Ontario, Canada: Fitzhenry & Whiteside.

Schaefer, N. (1999). *Does she know she's there?: The courageous and triumphant true story of a woman and her handicapped child.* Toronto, Ontario, Canada: Fitzhenry & Whiteside.

Schwab, W.E. (1992). Sexuality and community living. In I.T. Lott & E.E. McCoy (Eds.),

Down syndrome: Advances in medical care (pp. 157–166). New York: Wiley-Liss.

Schwab, W.E. (1995). Adolescence and young adulthood: Issues in medical care, sexuality and community living. In L. Nadel & D. Rosenthal (Eds.), *Down syndrome: Living and learning in the community* (pp. 230–237). New York: Wiley-Liss.

Schwier, R., & Melberg Schwier, K. (1999, Summer). Virtual communities on the World Wide Web. *Dialect, 13.*

Senn, C. (1988). *Vulnerable: Sexual abuse and people with an intellectual handicap.* North York, Ontario, Canada: The Roeher Institute.

Shaw, L. (1994). *Honor thy son.* Nashville: Abingdon.

Shaw, L. (1994, July). Honor thy son: It started out as an adventure, but turned into a love story. *Exceptional Parent, 24*(7), 50–51.

Shaw, L., & Shaw, M. (Producers). (1996). *Include us!* [Videotape and educator's guide]. Sioux City, IA: TiffHill Productions.

Sheridan, R., Llerena, J., Jr., Natkins, S., & Debenham, P. (1989). Fertility in a male with trisomy 21. *Journal of Medical Genetics, 26,* 294–298.

Sobsey, D. (1994). *Violence and abuse in the lives of people with disabilities: The end of silent acceptance?* Baltimore: Paul H. Brookes Publishing Co.

Sobsey, D. (1997, April–June). Reality Check campaign gathering momentum nationwide. *Dialect,* 18–19.

Stangle, J. (1991). *Family life and sexual health special education: Secondary. A curriculum for grades 7–12 (FLASH).* Seattle: Department of Health.

United Nations General Assembly, *Universal Declaration of Human Rights,* Articles 15–16, U.N. Sales No. GV.97.0.25 (1948).

Unruh, A.M. (1995, Winter). What about grandparents? Having a grandchild with a disability may mean having support and information needs. *abilities,* 41.

Recommended Resources

General Interest Books

Friendships and Community Connections Between
People with and without Developmental Disabilities
Edited by Angela Novak Amado (Paul H. Brookes Publishing Co.,
Baltimore, 1993)

This book is no longer in print, but check your local library.

Letters to Our Children
Edited by Dorothy E. Badry, John R. McDonald, & Jan LeBlond (Alberta
Children's Hospital, Calgary, Canada, 1993)

Friends Make the Difference: A Guide to Supporting
Friendships in Our Homes, Schools and Communities
British Columbia Association for Community Living (Vancouver, Canada, 1995)

My Friend David: A Source Book About Down's
Syndrome and a Personal Story About Friendship
Jean Edwards & David Dawson (Ednick Communications, Portland, OR, 1983)

Safe and Secure: Six Steps to Creating a Personal Future Plan for People with Disabilities
Al Etmanski with Jack Collins & Vickie Cammack (Planned Lifetime Advocacy
Network, Burnaby, British Columbia, Canada, 1997; available from the publish-
er, 101-B 3790 Canada Way, Burnaby, British Columbia V5G 1G4, Canada)

Captain Chaos Lives Here: A Survival Guide for Parents Raising Very Active Children
Carol Johnson (Chaos Consulting and Training, Calgary, Alberta, Canada, 1992)

Retarded Isn't Stupid, Mom! (Rev. ed.)
Sandra Z. Kaufman (Paul H. Brookes Publishing Co., Baltimore, 1999)

Count Us In: Growing Up with Down Syndrome
Jason Kingsley & Mitchell Levitz (Harcourt Brace & Co, Orlando, FL, 1994)

A Family Love Story: The Magnus Family
Magnus Family (Salt Spring Island, British Columbia, Canada, 1994; available from the authors, 420 Rainbow Road, RR3, Ganges, British Columbia V0S 1E0, Canada; 604-537-5708)

Nobody's Perfect: Living and Growing with Children Who Have Special Needs
Nancy B. Miller with "The Moms": Susie Burmester, Diane G. Callahan, Janet Dieterle, & Stephanie Niedermeyer (Paul H. Brookes Publishing Co., Baltimore, 1994)

Circles of Friends: People with Disabilities and
Their Friends Enrich the Lives of One Another
Robert Perske (Abingdon, Nashville, 1988)

Does She Know She's There?: The Courageous and
Triumphant True Story of a Woman and Her Handicapped Child
Nicola Schaefer (Fitzhenry & Whiteside, Toronto, Ontario, Canada, 1999)

General Interest Magazines

Mental Health Aspects of Developmental Disabilities
(formerly the Habilitative Mental Health Care Newsletter)
(Psych-Media, Inc., Post Office Box 57, Bear Creek, NC 27207-0057; e-mail: magz@emji.net)

Mouth: The Voice of the Disability Nation
(Free Hand Press, Topeka, KS; available from the publisher, 4201 SW 30th Street, Topeka, KS 66614-3023; 785-272-7348)

Ragged Edge
(Advocado Press, Louisville, KY; an on-line edition, *Electric Edge,* is located at http://www.ragged-edge-mag.com)

General Interest Videotapes

And Then Came John
Telesis Productions International (1990; available from Filmmakers Library, New York)

Dream Catchers
University of New Hampshire, Institute on Disability (Durham, 1992)

Include Us!
Lou Shaw & Michele Shaw, Producers (TiffHill Productions, Sioux City, IA, 1996)

Just Friends
Metropolitan Toronto Association for Community Living (Toronto, 1994)

Keys of Our Own
Canadian Association for Community Living (North York, Ontario, 1993)

Opportunities to Grow
National Down Syndrome Society (New York, 1993)

"Ready for Love?" 48 Hours
CBS Television (New York, 1993; videotape and/or transcript available from
48 Hours Transcripts, Box 7, Livingston, NJ 07035; 800-338-4847)

The Road You Take Is Yours
James Brodie Productions, Producer (Attainment Co., Verona, WI, 1997;
available from Paul H. Brookes Publishing Co., Baltimore)

Self-Advocate Means Power
Lower Mainland Community-Based Services Society (Burnaby, British
Columbia, 1993)

Your Baby Has Down Syndrome
Mackenzie Sara Noca Charitable Trust (Pittsburgh, 1994)

The Sterilization of Leilani Muir
(National Film Board of Canada/Office national du film Canada, Ottawa,
Ontario, 1996)

Social Skills/Sexuality

Human Sexuality Handbook: Guiding People Toward Positive Expressions of Sexuality
The Association for Community Living (Springfield, MA, 1985)

Features general and specific policies that are respectful, clear, comprehensive,
and caring.

Starter's Kit for Parents of Children and Adults
with Disabilities on Abuse Awareness and Prevention
Nora Baladerian (Culver City, CA, 1994; available by faxing the author, 310-
390-6994)

This guidebook provides all of "the basics" about abuse and children and adults
with developmental disabilities. It covers data on the incidence of abuse,
warning signs and symptoms, resources, and legal recourse for reporting.

Sexuality, Relationships and Adolescents with
Down Syndrome: A Booklet for Parents and Caregivers
Canadian Down Syndrome Society (Calgary, Alberta, Canada, 1996)

A short, straightforward booklet that parents, caregivers, and friends will find refreshing.

Circles I: Intimacy and Relationships (Rev. ed., 1993)
Circles II: Stop Abuse (1986)
Circles III: Safer Ways (1988)
Marilyn P. Champagne & Leslie W. Walker-Hirsch (James Stanfield Publishing, Santa Barbara, CA)

One of the most widely used systems for teaching appropriate social/sexual behavior to people with developmental disabilities. *Circles I* teaches social and sexual distance, appropriate behaviors, relationship-building skills, and understanding choice and different levels of intimacy. *Circles II* talks about safety issues and self-protection. *Circles III* teaches about sexually transmitted infections and HIV/AIDS.

Dealing with Feelings
Elizabeth Crary (Parenting Press, Seattle, 1993)

A series of six illustrated booklets that discuss feelings such as "Excited, Frustrated, Furious, Mad, Proud," and "Scared."

Pick Up Your Socks...and Other Skills Growing Children Need!:
A Practical Guide to Raising Responsible Children
Elizabeth Crary (Parenting Press, Seattle)

An illustrated booklet for parents with ideas on teaching responsibility.

Uniquely Me: A Personal Care Assistance Program
Exploration Series Press (Massillon, OH, 1994)

Binder and pictures to teach personal care and grooming skills.

Sexuality and People with Intellectual Disability (2nd ed.)
Lydia Fegan & Anne Rauch (Paul H. Brookes Publishing Co., Baltimore, 1993)

Whether used as a guide in teaching children or as a resource in working with adults, this is a frank and practical tool. (This book is no longer in print, but check your local library.)

Finger Tips: A Guide for Teaching About Female Masturbation
Dave Hingsburger (Diverse City Press, Eastman, Québec, Canada, 2000)

An explicit, easy-to-understand videotape and print guide on female masturbation with an emphasis on privacy.

Hand Made Love: A Guide for Teaching About Male Masturbation
Dave Hingsburger (Diverse City Press, Eastman, Québec, Canada, 1995)

An explicit, easy-to-understand videotape and print guide to teach about masturbation for men.

Hear Here: Identifying and Supporting People with Disabilities Who Have Been Abused
Dave Hingsburger (Diverse City Press, Eastman, Québec, Canada, 1997)

A videotape featuring behavior therapists and a law enforcer who discuss what police officers and child abuse investigators need to know, including indicators of possible abuse, disclosure, protocol, and the creation of a ring of safety for people who are vulnerable.

I Contact: Sexuality and People with Developmental Disabilities
Dave Hingsburger (VIDA Publishing, Mountville, PA, 1992)

Presents the basic message that all people can love and make human contact with others; it is written for people who have personal contact with people who have developmental disabilities.

I Openers: Parents Ask Questions About
Sexuality and Children with Developmental Disabilities
Dave Hingsburger (Family Support Institute Press, Vancouver, British Columbia, Canada, 1993)

A book packed with critical questions, issues, and suggestions in a forthright and sensitive manner about self-esteem and sexuality.

i to I: Self-Concept of People with Developmental Disabilities
Dave Hingsburger (VIDA Publishing, Mountville, PA, 1990)

An easy-to-read book that will make the reader think not only about the value of people with disabilities but also his or her own beliefs.

"Is It Okay For Me to Love?"
Dave Hingsburger (*Impact, Vol. 9*, No. 3, Summer 1996)

Outlines some of the challenges faced by people with disabilities as they try to form relationships.

Just Say Know!: Understanding and Reducing the Risk of
Sexual Victimization of People with Developmental Disabilities
Dave Hingsburger (Diverse City Press, Eastman, Québec, Canada, 1995)

An easy-to-read book that features real experiences and puts professional practice into thought-provoking context about the ways to reduce the risk of sexual abuse and to help people heal.

Under Cover Dick: A Guide for Teaching About
Condom Use Through Video and Understanding
Dave Hingsburger (Diverse City Press, Eastman, Québec, Canada, 1995)

An explicit, easy-to-understand videotape and print guide on how to teach condom use with an emphasis on privacy and choice.

Be Cool (Coping with Teasing, Coping with Anger, Coping with Criticism)
James Stanfield Publishing (Santa Barbara, CA, 1993)

Teaches ways to respond to conflict in three different kinds of situations.

LifeFacts: AIDS (Rev. ed. 1995)
LifeFacts: Managing Emotions (1990)
LifeFacts: Sexual Abuse Prevention (1990)
LifeFacts: SmartTrust (1990)
James Stanfield Publishing (Santa Barbara, CA)

The first program helps people avoid the risk of AIDS with a five-step program. The second program helps people cope with anger, sadness, and fear and optimize happiness. The third program teaches essential self-protection skills in recognition, prevention, and protection areas. The fourth program teaches when to trust and when it's smart not to.

Mind Your Manners
James Stanfield Publishing (Santa Barbara, CA, 1991)

This six-part videotape program introduces students to proper social behavior necessary for success in everyday situations. The program includes an introduction to why manners are important and explores manners at home, table manners, manners at school, manners in public, and greetings and conversations.

No-Go-Tell! (Rev. ed.)
James Stanfield Publishing (Santa Barbara, CA, 1990)

The first child protection program for children with disabilities ages 3–7.

Sex Education for Persons with Disabilities that Hinder
Learning: A Primary Level Supplement to the Life Horizons Materials
James Stanfield (Santa Barbara, CA, 1988)

This resource examines issues of sexuality and can be used when developing curriculum or planning lessons.

The GYN Exam
James Stanfield Publishing (Santa Barbara, CA, 1995)

Handbook and videotape offers two new ways to teach about the gynecological examination and to reduce fears and apprehension about it. Developed for girls and women ages 12 and older.

TIPS: Teaching Interpersonal Skills to the Mentally Handicapped
James Stanfield Publishing (Santa Barbara, CA, 1991)

This seven-part program gives students 150 tips for successful social interaction, including getting along with others, getting to know others, getting along with adults, having friends, enjoying free time, living in the community, and being on the job.

AIDS: Training People with Disabilities to Better Protect Themselves
Joel Levy (Young Adult Institute, New York, 1993)

A trainer's manual and video on HIV transmission, condom use and advice on ways to resist unwanted social pressure.

Life Horizons I (Junior High+): The Physiological and
Emotional Aspects of Being Male and Female (Rev. ed.)
Life Horizons II (Junior High+): The Moral, Social, and Legal Aspects of Sexuality
Winifred Kempton (James Stanfield Publishing, Santa Barbara, CA, 1990)

Slides and teaching materials on body parts, attitudes, behaviors, relationships, sex, marriage, parenting, contraception, and sexually transmitted infections.

Socialization and Sexuality: A Comprehensive Training Guide
for Professionals Helping People with Disabilities that Hinder Learning
Winifred Kempton, Toni Davies, & Lynne Stigall-Muccigrosso (Winifred Kempton Associates, Haverford, PA, 1993)

A program to prepare professionals in all fields to train staff or parents to better meet individuals' social-sexual needs; includes a 30-page bibliography.

An Easy Guide to Loving Carefully: For Men and Women (3rd ed.)
Winifred Kempton & Lynne Stigall-Muccigrosso (Winifred Kempton Associates, Haverford, PA, and Lynne Stigall-Muccigrosso Associates, Los Gatos, CA, 1996)

This book is about the sexual aspects of women's and men's bodies, sexual health, and sexual feelings. It also tells how to prevent unplanned pregnancies and about sexually transmitted infections and especially AIDS. Distributed by Planned Parenthood of Southeastern Pennsylvania, 1144 Locust Street, Philadelphia, PA 19107-6797, and by the authors: Winifred Kempton Associates, 3300 Darby Road, C-404, Haverford, PA, 19041; and Lynne Stigall-Muccigrosso Associates, 21450 Bear Creek Road, Los Gatos, CA, 95030.

Saying No!: A Video About Sexual Abuse Prevention
Lower Mainland Community Based Services Society (Burnaby, British Columbia, Canada, 1994)

A powerful videotape that can be used by an experienced group facilitator who can provide appropriate support. The main message for people who have been sexually abused is to tell someone who will listen and take action.

Being Sexual: An Illustrated Series on Sexuality and Relationships
Susan Ludwig & Dave Hingsburger (Sex Information and Education Council of Canada, Toronto, 1993)

Includes booklets on relationships, a woman's body, a man's body, adolescence, male masturbation, female masturbation, heterosexual intercourse, human reproduction, birth control, homosexuality, sexuality and physical disabilities, sexually transmitted diseases, HIV/AIDS, sexual self-advocacy, sexual abuse, and sexuality and aging, plus a teaching manual. Text is simple; illustrations and Blissymbols are used.

Shared Feelings: A Parent Guide to Sexuality Education for
Children, Adolescents and Adults Who Have a Mental Handicap
Diane Maksym (The Roeher Institute, North York, Ontario, Canada, 1990)

A parent guide and discussion guide are available.

"Sexuality Education for Children and Youth with
Disabilities": Special Issue of News Digest (Vol. 1, No. 3)
National Information Center for Children and Youth with Disabilities (Washington, DC, 1992)

Deals with various aspects of sexuality that affect young people with disabilities.

I Am a Beautiful Person–Sexuality and Me: A Video for Parents of Teens with Disabilities
PACER Center, Inc. (Minneapolis, MN, 1996)

A videotape that provides parents with an excellent discussion starter for issues related to sexuality. Features parents and people with disabilities talking about their feelings, concerns, and advice.

Liking Myself
Pat Palmer (Impact Publishers, San Luis Obispo, CA, 1992)

An illustrated booklet for children and youth about self-esteem.

No More Victims: A Manual to Guide Families and Friends
in Preventing the Sexual Abuse of People with Mental Handicaps
The Roeher Institute (North York, Ontario, Canada, 1992)

Part of a series of companion manuals available for families and friends, police, social workers and counselors, and people in the legal profession.

The Right to Control What Happens to Your Body:
A Straightforward Guide to Issues of Sexuality and Sexual Abuse
The Roeher Institute (North York, Ontario, Canada, 1991)

A guide in plain language for people with low literacy skills.

Sexuality in Down Syndrome
William E. Schwab (National Down Syndrome Society, New York, 1990)

An information sheet in basic, plain language that deals with common questions regarding sexuality.

Couples with Intellectual Disabilities Talk About Living and Loving
Karin Melberg Schwier (Woodbine House, Bethesda, MD, 1994)

Features a collection of first-person profiles of people with disabilities in various countries who have found meaningful, intimate relationships and who speak candidly about their hopes and desires.

Changes in You for Boys
Changes in You for Girls
Peggy C. Siegal (Family Life Education Association, Richmond, VA, 1991)

Clearly illustrated, simply worded explanations of the changes in puberty. Each comes with a free parent's guide.

What's Really Worth Doing and How to Do It: A Book for
People Who Love Someone Labeled Disabled (Possibly Yourself)
Judith Snow (Inclusion Press, Toronto, Ontario, Canada, 1994)

An inspiring booklet by a noted speaker and inclusion advocate.

FLASH: Family Life and Sexual Health—
Special Education: Secondary. A Curriculum for Grades 7–12
Jane Stangle (Seattle-King County Dept. of Public Health and Seattle Public Schools, 1991; available from Family Planning Publications, Seattle-King County Dept. of Public Health, 110 Prefontaine Place South, Suite 500, Seattle, WA, 98104)

An easy-to-use curriculum designed for adolescents, with particular attention paid to the cognitive needs of students with disabilities.

Teach•A•Bodies
Teach•A•Bodies, Inc. (7 Don's Drive, Mission, TX, 78572-4350; 956-581-9959; FAX 956-585-3089; e-mail: TABDOLL@aol.com)

These dolls come in a wide range of sizes (including life size) and include babies, toddlers, children, adolescents, adults, grandparents in different skin colors. Skin color customizing also is available. Adult males are wearing a condom; females have a vaginal opening and a clitoris; adult females have a baby in utero. All dolls have all body parts, openings, fingers, toes, tongues, and ears, with a variety of clothing; adult dolls have pubic hair.

Medical and Surgical Care for Children with Down Syndrome: A Guide for Parents
Edited by D.C. Van Dyke, Phillip Mattheis, Susan Eberly, & Janet Williams (Woodbine House, Bethesda, MD, 1995)

Although this very positive and comprehensive book is intended for parents of people with Down syndrome, many of the issues are relevant to people with various disabilities.

Janet's Got Her Period: Planning for Self Care for
Girls and Young Women with Severe Developmental Disabilities
Victorian Health Foundation (Carlton, Victoria, Australia, 1990; available from Social Biology Resource Centre, 139–143 Bouverie Street, Carlton, Victoria, Australia)

Videotape and other materials teach menstrual care using a step-by-step approach.

Let's Talk About Health: What Every Woman Should Know
Women's Health Project, The Arc of New Jersey (New Brunswick, 1994)

A 30-minute videotape that explains the gynecological exam and what to expect. Includes an explanation of breast self-examination and mammograms.

For Brothers and Sisters

Big Brother Dustin
Alden R. Carter (Albert Whitman & Co., Morton Grove, IL, 1997)

I'm the Big Sister Now
Michelle Emmert (Albert Whitman & Co., Morton Grove, IL, 1989)

Be Good to Eddie Lee
Virginia Fleming (Philomel Books, New York, 1993)

How Smudge Came
Nan Gregory (Red Deer College Press, Red Deer, Alberta, Canada, 1995)

Somebody Called Me a Retard Today...and My Heart Felt Sad
Ellen O'Shaughnessy (Walker and Co., New York, 1992)

This book is no longer in print, but check your local library.

Show Me No Mercy
Robert Perske (Abingdon, Nashville, 1984)

Veronica's First Year
Jean Sasso Rheingrover (Albert Whitman & Co., Morton Grove, IL, 1996)

Idea Man
Karin Melberg Schwier (Diverse City Press, Eastman, Québec, Canada, 1997)

Keith Edward's Different Day
Karin Melberg Schwier (Impact Publishers, San Luis Obispo, CA, 1992)

Honor Thy Son
Lou Shaw (Abingdon, Nashville, 1994)

Welcome Home, Jellybean
Marla Fanta Shyer (Aladdin Books, New York, 1988)

Andy and His Yellow Frisbee
Mary Thompson (Woodbine House, Bethesda, MD, 1996)

Kids Explore the Gifts of Children with Special Needs
Westridge Young Writers' Workshop (John Muir Publications, Santa Fe, New Mexico, 1994)

Organizations for Parent Support and Sources of Sexuality Materials and Information

United States

American Association on Mental Retardation Special Interest Group on Sexuality
c/o Leslie W. Walker-Hirsch
Moonstone Sexuality Service
935 Hanover Street
Yorktown Heights, New York, 10598
914-245-3384; FAX: 914-962-9841

The American Association on Mental Retardation has initiated a special interest group on social and sexual concerns, which releases an electronic newsletter, *The Pleasure Dome* (http://www.aamr.org/Groups/divsigs.html) as well as the *Bulletin of Social and Sensuality Training for People with Developmental Disabilities.*

The Arc (formerly Association for Retarded Citizens of the United States)
500 E. Border Street, Suite 300
Arlington, TX 76010
817-261-6003; TDD: 817-277-0553

There are state Arc branches nationwide. Programs and projects target a wide range of needs of children, youth, and adults who have intellectual disabilities.

Coalition on Sexuality and Disability
122 East 23rd Street
New York, NY 10010
212-242-3900

This not-for-profit organization is committed to the advancement of full social integration through educational programs and advocacy and is a resource information clearinghouse.

James Stanfield Publishing Co.
2060 Alameda Padre Serra
Post Office Box 41058
Santa Barbara, CA 93140
800-421-6534; 805-897-1185
FAX in United States and Canada: 805-897-1187

Offers one of the most respected libraries of educational materials available for students with intellectual disabilities. Developed by experts in their fields, there are programs designed for individuals with disabilities, their families, teachers, and advocates. This company specializes in audiovisual materials for teaching socialization and sexuality skills to people with intellectual disabilities. A catalog is available.

National Association for the Dually Diagnosed (NADD)
110 Prince Street
Kingston, NY 12401
914-331-4336; FAX: 914-331-5362

Founded in 1983 as a not-for-profit association designed to promote professional and parental development for individuals who have mental illness with intellectual disability. NADD is a leading organization providing conferences, educational services, and training materials, and it influences policy and program development to address mental health needs of persons with intellectual disabilities.

National Down Syndrome Congress (NDSC)
1605 Chantilly Drive, Suite 250
Atlanta, GA 30324
770-604-9500; FAX: 770-604-9898

A national network of parent groups and organizations serving the needs of families in their local communities. NDSC encourages research, serves as a clearinghouse on information, advises parents on a variety of issues, addresses social policy development, and advocates the full spectrum of human and civil rights. *Down Syndrome News* magazine is available; also available is *D.S. Headline News*, a publication of the Citizen's Committee of NDSC written for and by people with Down syndrome.

National Down Syndrome Society
666 Broadway, Suite 810
New York, NY 10012
800-221-4602; 212-460-9330

Gives accurate, up-to-date information in English and Spanish on Down syndrome to parents, professionals, and other interested people. In the United States, a toll-free hotline is available at all times so that people can receive information, referral to resources throughout the country, and answers to questions in a wide variety of issues. Two publications are available: *Update* and *News 'n Views*, a magazine written by and for people with disabilities.

National Information Center for Children and Youth with Disabilities (NICHCY)
Box 1492
Washington, DC 20013
703-893-6061 (in DC area)
800-999-5599 (outside DC area)
TDD: 703-893-8614

Provides free information and referral services in English and Spanish to assist parents, educators, caregivers, advocates, and others in helping children and youth with disabilities become participating members in the school and community. NICHCY publications cover all aspects of disabilities with a particular focus on children and youth from birth to age 22.

PACER Center, Inc. (Parent Advocacy Coalition for Educational Rights)
4826 Chicago Avenue S., Minneapolis, MN 55417
800-848-4912; Voice/TDD: 612-827-2966; FAX: 612-827-3065

Offers workshops and training to help parents understand special education laws and obtain appropriate school programs for their children.

Parents and Friends of Lesbians and Gays (PFLAG)
National Office
1101 14th Street, Suite 1030
Washington, DC 20005

An advocacy and education organization that promotes the health and well-being of gay, lesbian, and bisexual people and their families and friends. PFLAG

offers support to help them cope with an adverse society. Check your telephone book for local chapters.

PEAK Parent Center
6055 Lehman Drive, Suite 101
Colorado Spring, CO 80918
800-284-0251; 719-531-9400; Voice/TDD: 719-531-9403

An agency for parents of children who have disabilities; provides information services, training, referral services, and consultations on current issues to various disability associations.

Sex Information and Education Council of the United States (SIECUS)
130 West 42nd Street, Suite 2500
New York, NY 10036
212-819-9770; FAX: 212-819-9776
http://www.siecus.org

A national network of more than 2,500 professionals who are dedicated to promoting the delivery of comprehensive sexuality education, providing information, and protecting individuals' sexual rights. A free SIECUS publications catalog is available, and it features some Spanish resources.

Special Needs Project
3463 State Street, Suite 282
Santa Barbara, CA 93105
800-333-6867; 805-683-9633; FAX: 805-683-2341
snpbooks@eworld.com

This clearinghouse has a varied collection of materials on disability issues and often offers hard-to-find books and resources.

Young Adult Institute (YAI)
460 West 34th Street
New York, NY 10001
212-563-7474

A human and health services agency for people with developmental disabilities, their families, and professionals. With more than 90 programs in eight countries, YAI is nationally renowned for its publications, conferences, training seminars, and television programs that offer information and support services. The YAI also has a HIV/AIDS Professional Education Program.

Canada

AIDS and Disability Action Project
British Columbia Coalition of People with Disabilities
204-456 West Broadway
Vancouver, British Columbia V5Y 1R3
604-875-0188; TTY: 604-875-8835; FAX: 604-875-9227

The Coalition has developed brochures, booklets, audiotapes and a Braille book about HIV/AIDS and prevention. The materials are available to consumers and service providers in a variety of disability communities and to HIV/AIDS organizations.

Canadian Down Syndrome Society (CDSS)
Société canadienne du syndrome de Down
Head Office
811 14th Street, NW
Calgary, Alberta T2N 2A4
403-270-8500; FAX 403-270-8291

A national support organization offering current information on a wide variety of topics to parents, self-advocates, and various professionals. The Society provides opportunities for people with Down syndrome to express their views and concerns and to participate in the direction of CDSS. *Opening Doors* magazine is available.

Canadian Association for Community Living
The Roeher Institute
Kinsmen Building, York University Campus
4700 Keele Street
North York, Ontario M3J 1P3
416-661-9611; FAX 416-661-5701

A national advocacy organization for people with intellectual disabilities. There is an Association for Community Living in each province and territory, with additional local branches in each. The Roeher Institute is the education and research arm of the Canadian Association for Community Living. It offers information services, consultations, training and research.

Inclusion Press/Centre for Integrated Education and Community
24 Thome Crescent
Toronto, Ontario M6H 2S5
416-658-5363; FAX 416-658-5067
e-mail: includer@idirect.com
http://www.inclusion.com

Inclusion Press is an independent press dedicated to producing user-friendly books and resources about full inclusion in school, work, and community. The Centre offers training, consulting, and education in various inclusive practices, including Making Action Plans, Planning Alternative Tomorrows with Hope, Circles of Friends, and Solution Circles.

Diverse City Press, Inc.
BM 272, 33 des Floralies
Eastman, Québec J0E 1P0
Voice/FAX: 450-297-3080
http://www.diverse-city.com

A small company that produces and distributes inspiring and informative books, audio compact discs, and videotapes dealing with people with developmental disabilities and a range of social issues.

Sex Information and Education Council of Canada (SIECCAN)
850 Coxwell Avenue
East York, Ontario M4C 5R1
416-466-5304; FAX: 416-778-0785

A national nonprofit organization offering public and professional education about human sexuality. It publishes the *Canadian Journal of Human Sexuality* and other resources.

Sexual Health Resource Network
Sunny Hill Health Centre for Children
3644 Slocan Street
Vancouver, British Columbia V5M 3E8
800-331-1533; 604-436-6535; FAX: 604-436-6535
mharber@wimsey.com
Bulletin board system (dial via modem): 604-434-2227

A province-wide network maintaining a resource library on disabilities, sexual abuse, and healthy sexuality. Training and education services are offered, and a directory of service providers is available.

A Note About Internet Resources

The Internet is a large warehouse of information held on interconnected computers all over the world. You get into it with your computer through a modem and a connection with an Internet service provider (called an *ISP* in computer lingo). Electronic mail (e-mail) is a means to send and receive messages with virtually any networked computer user in the world. E-mail messages can be delivered in a matter of minutes, anytime, anywhere.

The Internet features discussion groups to which you can connect and discuss with others almost any topic imaginable. The World Wide Web holds an almost limitless collection of information. You can search journal articles from universities, government databases, and specific information on disabilities. You can "chat" with other people about issues of common interest and get on lists to receive regular e-mails about a certain topic. One drawback of the Internet is the lack of quality control on information you find "out there." Anyone can put almost anything on the World Wide Web, and they do. The best advice is to be skeptical and cautious about anything you learn from—and the people you meet on—the World Wide Web, just as you would be if you were picking up leaflets of information or meeting someone on the street (Schwier & Melberg Schwier, 1999).

World Wide Web Sites

The sites listed here are a sampling of those that offer information on disability, sexuality, spirituality, abuse and violence, community inclusion, and technology. The World Wide Web is a dynamic collection of information and "stuff," to use a less technical term. Addresses and sites come and go, so even some of the following may have moved by the time you read this list. You can always search for a few key words to help you find what you're looking for if you don't have the exact site address.

http://www.geocities.com/HotSprings/7319/discool.htm
The Disability Cool site is excellent as it covers many areas such as parenting, siblings, computer software, and medical issues.

http://www.nas.com/downsyn
One of the many good Internet sources of information on Down syndrome.

http://www.quasar.ualberta.ca/ddc/ICAD/icad.html
The International Coalition on Abuse and Disability is a free e-mail communications network providing information on violence and disability.

http://www.sexualhealth.com
Sexual Health Network has a mission to "provide easy access to sexuality information, education, counseling, therapy, medical attention and other sexuality resources for people with disability, illness or other health related problems." Public health nurse Susan Ludwig, RN, B.Sc., responds to questions that users post on the site, many of which are about sexuality and people with disabilities.

http://www.siecus.org
The Sex Information and Education Council of the United States offers comprehensive information on sexual issues and sexual rights.

Index

Abstinence from sexual intercourse, 177
Abuse of people with disabilities, 6–7, 18, 27–28, 34, 70–74, 131–135; *see also* Protection from exploitation and abuse
Acceptance of children with disabilities, 3–4, 22–25, 147
Acquired immunodeficiency syndrome (AIDS), 35, 130, 185, 194
ADAPT, *see* American Disabled for Attendant Programs Today
Adolescence, changes of, 34, 97, 105, 110
Adolescent launching, 110
Adopting children with disabilities, 14–16, 26
Advocacy organizations, 3, 17, 18, 59, 137
Age-appropriate possessions, 151
Age-appropriate teaching about sexuality, 32
AIDS, *see* Acquired immunodeficiency syndrome
American Disabled for Attendant Programs Today (ADAPT), 185
Americans with Disabilities Act (ADA) of 1990 (PL 101-336), 185
Anatomically realistic dolls, 66–67
Anger management, 107
Announcing birth of your child with a disability, 3
Anxiety, 115, 117
Appearance, self-awareness about, 64, 82–85
Assertiveness training, 70–74, 102, 107, 138–147; *see also* Protection from exploitation and abuse
Autonomy in decision making, 110

Backward chaining, 101
Bathroom use, 65, 68
Behaviors that may indicate abuse, 143, 152–154
Bigotry, 135
Bipolar disorder, 117

Birth announcements for children with disabilities, 3
Birth complications, 2
Birth control, 162–163, 177–180, 185
Blissymbolics, 129
Body image, 65–66
Body parts
  public versus private, 62–70, 100–101
  teaching names for, 38–39, 67, 125–126, 135
Boundary invasion, 27–28, 37–38, 71, 91–100, 136–137, 154, 195
  Circles program for teaching about, 91–94
  "fictive kin" and, 91
  friendship building and, 47–48, 93–96, 103, 136–137
  principles of, 92
  risk reduction, assertiveness and, 70–74, 102, 134–135, 138–147
  victimization and, 102, 125–126, 131–135
Breast self-examination, 120
Bridges from childhood to adulthood, 110–111

Canadian Charter of Rights and Freedoms, 168, 185
Caution with strangers, 27–28
Cerebral palsy, 18, 135
Charter of Rights and Freedoms (Canadian), 168, 185
Childishness, 111
Choices, 72, 105, 144–147, 192–193; *see also* Assertiveness training
Chores, 77–80, 101
Chromosome abnormalities, 2, 176
Churches, 158–159, 169–170, 183–184
Circles program for relationships, 91–94
Clothing, public versus private, 67, 100–101
Communication skills, 17, 29–32, 87, 114–115
  encouraging conversation, 114